NAVIGATING PROSPERITY AND SECURITY IN EAST ASIA

NAVIGATING PROSPERITY AND SECURITY IN EAST ASIA

EDITED BY SHIRO ARMSTRONG,
TOM WESTLAND AND ADAM TRIGGS

Australian
National
University

ANU PRESS

Australian
National
University

ANU PRESS

Published by ANU Press
The Australian National University
Canberra ACT 2600, Australia
Email: anupress@anu.edu.au

Available to download for free at press.anu.edu.au

ISBN (print): 9781760465650
ISBN (online): 9781760465667

WorldCat (print): 1373222262
WorldCat (online): 1373223509

DOI: 10.22459/NPSEA.2023

Cover design and layout by ANU Press

This book is published under the aegis of the Public Policy editorial board of ANU Press.

Contents

List of illustrations

Figures

Tables

Preface

Global uncertainties that complicate policy choices for countries—felt acutely in East Asia, located between the two superpowers of China and the United States—led to the research set out in this volume. Economic, strategic and security considerations have become enmeshed with great power competition, rising protectionism, outdated multilateral rules and climate change. This book was prepared during the COVID-19 pandemic that exacerbated those uncertainties.

Those who analyse the question of how countries balance or navigate economic, social and national security policy choices in a more contested and uncertain global environment often focus on one aspect—usually national security—without due consideration of others. An example is the framing of these issues as 'geoeconomics', which considers the use of economic tools for geopolitical purposes.

The support of the Economic Research Institute for ASEAN and East Asia, or ERIA, to the East Asian Bureau of Economic Research at The Australian National University for this work is recognition that economic analysis has not been prominent in academic or policy thinking as it relates to choices of national security or geopolitics. Economists have largely vacated the field as strategists and policymakers search for a framework to incorporate economic considerations into strategic policy choices.

A distinguished group of economists from East Asia who have been close to (or involved in) the policymaking processes of selected countries convened to discuss and draft contributions that shed light on how various policy communities have managed these new challenges. Southeast Asia, in particular, is organised around the idea that economic integration into the global economy, especially its major economic neighbours, is a source of national security. And their organising grouping of ASEAN helps them preserve policy options to achieve that goal.

For US allies, especially Australia and Japan, the policy choices appear more constrained with their security guarantor locked in strategic competition with China. The US is dealing with domestic problems like entrenched inequality and fraying democratic institutions. Australia and Japan and the region have China—a China that appears to be an insecure rising power that has become more assertive—as their largest economic partner.

The chapters in this volume do not provide answers to all of these challenges but they make an important contribution in understanding how some countries are managing to navigate prosperity and security. Some countries have managed to do better than others in avoiding the narrowing of their policy options: for example, some have better frameworks for bringing economic and security interests together in national interest choices. More work will need to be done to bring these lessons together and we hope this volume makes a contribution to that thinking.

We are grateful to ERIA and its Research Institutes Network (RIN) for the financial support without which this project would not have been possible. RIN participants provided feedback in developing the project. We are particularly grateful to two anonymous reviewers for suggestions as well as Hank Lim, Christopher Findlay and Gary Hawke for their sage advice.

The authors in this volume contributed much beyond writing their own chapters and we thank them for their insights, generosity and patience in completing this book.

We are indebted to Brandon Harrington for his research assistance in guiding the project to completion.

May we extend our sincere thanks to Elouise Ball, Emily Tinker and ANU Press for working so patiently with us through the production process and to Rani Kerin for her excellent copyediting.

We hope that this collection of essays may help, at this critical point in the history of the global economy, in the development of strategies about how to navigate prosperity and security in Asia.

Shiro Armstrong, Tom Westland and Adam Triggs
2023

Contributors

Shiro Armstrong, Director, Australia–Japan Research Centre; Director, East Asian Bureau of Economic Research; Associate Professor, Crawford School of Public Policy, The Australian National University

Yose Rizal Damuri, Executive Director, Centre for Strategic and International Studies, Jakarta

Gordon de Brouwer, Professor of Economics, Crawford School of Public Policy, The Australian National University

Peter Drysdale, Emeritus Professor of Economics; Head of the East Asian Bureau of Economic Research and East Asia Forum, Crawford School of Public Policy, The Australian National University

Rocky Intan, Researcher, Department of International Relations, Centre for Strategic and International Studies, Jakarta

Amy King, Associate Professor, Strategic and Defence Studies Centre, Coral Bell School of Asia Pacific Affairs, The Australian National University

Shankaran Nambiar, Senior Research Fellow, Malaysian Institute of Economic Research

Dionisius Narjoko, Senior Economist, Economic Research Institute for ASEAN and East Asia (ERIA), Jakarta

Duong Anh Nguyen, Director, Department for General Economic Issues and Integration Studies, Central Institute for Economic Management, Hanoi

Dandy Rafitrandi, Researcher, Department of Economics, Centre for Strategic and International Studies, Jakarta

Rebecca St Maria, Executive Director, APEC Secretariat, Singapore

Adam Triggs, Director, Accenture Strategy; Visiting Fellow, Crawford School of Public Policy, The Australian National University; Non-resident Fellow, Brookings Institution, Washington, DC

Thanh Tri Vo, President, Institute for Brand and Competitiveness Strategy, Hanoi

Shujiro Urata, Professor Emeritus, Waseda University

Tom Westland, Economic Historian of Africa and Asia, Wageningen University & Research, Wageningen; Non-resident Research Fellow, East Asian Bureau of Economic Research

Abbreviations

ADB	Asian Development Bank
AEC	ASEAN Economic Community
AI	artificial intelligence
ANZUS	Australia, New Zealand and United States Security Treaty
AOIP	ASEAN Outlook on the Indo-Pacific
APEC	Asia-Pacific Economic Cooperation
ASEAN	Association of Southeast Asian Nations
ASPI	Australian Strategic Policy Institute
BRI	Belt and Road Initiative
CLMV	Cambodia, Laos, Myanmar, Vietnam
CMIM	Chiang Mai Initiative Multilateralization
CoC	code of conduct
COCOM	Coordinating Committee for Multilateral Export Controls
CPTPP	Comprehensive and Progressive Agreement for Trans-Pacific Partnership
DAP	Democratic Action Party
DFFT	data free flow with trust
DOC	Declaration on the Conduct of Parties in the South China Sea
ECRL	East Coast Rail Link
E&E	electrical and electronics
EEE	Expanded Economic Engagement
EPA	Economic Partnership Agreement

EU	European Union
EVFTA	European Union–Vietnam Free Trade Agreement
FDI	foreign direct investment
FEFTA	Foreign Exchange and Foreign Trade Act
FOIP	Free and Open Indo-Pacific
FTA	free trade agreement
GATT	General Agreement on Tariffs and Trade
GDP	gross domestic product
GFC	global financial crisis
GVC	global value chain
IBRD	International Bank for Reconstruction and Development
IMF	International Monetary Fund
LDP	Liberal Democratic Party
LNG	liquefied natural gas
METI	Ministry of Economy, Trade and Industry
MEXT	Ministry of Education, Culture, Sports, Science and Technology
MITI	Ministry of International Trade and Industry
MNC	multinational corporations
MOFA	Ministry of Foreign Affairs
MOU	memorandum of understanding
MPP	Multi-Product Pipeline
NAFTA	North American Free Trade Agreement
NSS	National Security Secretariat
NTB	non-tariff barrier
NTM	non-tariff measure
OECD	Organisation for Economic Co-operation and Development
PAFTAD	Pacific Trade and Development
PECC	Pacific Economic Cooperation Council
POA	Plan of Action
PPE	personal protective equipment

RCEP	Regional Comprehensive Partnership
SME	small and medium-sized enterprise
SOE	state-owned enterprise
TAC	Treaty of Amity and Cooperation
TPP	Trans-Pacific Partnership
TSGP	Trans-Sabah Gas Pipeline
UK	United Kingdom
UN	United Nations
UNCLOS	United Nations Convention on the Law of the Sea
UNSC	United Nations Security Council
US	United States
USMCA	United States–Mexico–Canada Agreement
VER	voluntary export restraint
WHO	World Health Organization
WTO	World Trade Organization
WWI	World War I
WWII	World War II

1

Economic integration and the new strategic environment in East Asia

Shiro Armstrong, Tom Westland and Adam Triggs

Introduction

The Russian invasion of Ukraine in early 2022 shook the foundations of the post–Cold War settlement in Europe and threw a wrench into the recovery from the COVID-19 economic downturn. It also posed larger questions on the intertwined nature of national security and economic policy. A concerted effort by the United States, Europe and other allies like Australia, Japan and Singapore have isolated Russia, cutting off what was the world's eleventh largest economy from much of the world economy. Most significant, perhaps, has been the freezing of Russia's dollar reserves, held in banks around the world. This has prevented Moscow from mounting any serious attempt to defend the rouble, which has essentially lost convertibility. A sustained sanctions regime could throw the Russian economy back to Soviet-era isolation and stagnation.

The leverage that has been exerted against Russia would not have existed in the absence of a deeply integrated global economy. Without economic interdependence, the only way in which a coalition could have intervened to deter military action in Ukraine would have been militarily, a course of action that could easily have led to nuclear exchange. The geopolitical value of global interdependence has been amply demonstrated. For some, however, the calculus may seem different: the ability of the sanctions coalition to impose steep economic costs on Russia may lead them to wonder if they, too, are vulnerable to concerted action. As several of the case studies in this book demonstrate, however, these fears are largely misplaced. What distinguished the international reaction to Russia's war of aggression in Ukraine from other recent attempts to use economic coercion was that it was *coordinated* as well as concerted: multilateral and not unilateral. This is not to say that unilateral economic coercion cannot impose costs on targeted country, only that those costs are usually severely circumscribed by the operations of global markets, which enable the targets of coercion to find alternative suppliers or purchases for most goods and services.

The COVID-19 pandemic shook a world that was already undergoing profound change. The most significant geopolitical shifts have been the rise of China, and, at the same time, an increasingly inward-looking United States. Growing strategic competition between the two powers has drawn attention to the possibility that such competition may spill over into other domains. The concept of 'economic security' has gained new intellectual ground in a number of countries across the region, while shortages throughout the pandemic have led to calls for a rolling back of the internationalisation of economic production that has characterised the global division of labour in the past several decades. This has taken the form not only of internationalisation of *value* chains, in which production processes are split across international borders, often crossing multiple international borders—but also increasingly complex international *supply* chains, which encompass value chains as well as all the procedures required to deliver goods to the final consumer. These have come under major stress during the pandemic, with bottlenecks in production as well as in logistics due to lockdowns and other workforce disruptions. The major disruptions to the world economy stemming from the sanctions regime placed on Russia have only heightened the sense for many that global economic interdependence is a weakness to be managed, not an opportunity to be seized.

The economic logic of deeper integration, though, remains as compelling as ever for the region. China's transition to a high-income economy will drive growth and structural change across the region. The diversity in levels of economic development across the Asian region will ensure that China's economic transition generates opportunities, particularly in labour-intensive manufacturing, for low and middle-income economies in the region, allowing them to climb global value chains centred on China, progressing from supplying only the most basic and generally labour-intensive production inputs at the beginning of their growth trajectory to more complex and capital-intensive components as they develop. For Asian developing economies, these opportunities are too valuable to be squandered by taking sides in the strategic rivalry between China and the United States. The strategic impetus behind the founding of the Association of Southeast Asian Nations (ASEAN) was to provide collective leadership that could keep Southeast Asian nations from aligning too closely to either the communist bloc or the West. A similar logic is likely to appeal to the region even if geopolitical tensions between China and the US continue to rise. The conclusion of two major plurilateral deals, the Comprehensive and Progressive Agreement for Trans-Pacific Partnership and the Regional Comprehensive Economic Partnership, provide new institutional platforms that join existing arrangements like Asia-Pacific Economic Cooperation (APEC) from which an agenda of deeper economic integration can be pursued.

Even before the pandemic and the Russia–Ukraine war, the geopolitical environment in which an integration agenda could be pursued was not as propitious as it has been in recent decades. The election of President Trump signalled a major inward turn in the United States. The protectionist implications of his 'America First' rhetoric were realised in a range of trade-restricting measures that mainly, though by no means exclusively, targeted China in sectors in which China was increasingly out-competing the United States. More broadly, Trump represented an American retreat from US participation in the rules-based global order—one reversed only partially by the Biden administration. Trump withdrew his country from the Paris Climate Accord, blocked progress in cooperative forums like APEC and the G7, and gravely damaged the authority and effectiveness of the lynchpin of global trade: the dispute settlement system of the World Trade Organization (WTO). While President Biden has re-joined the Paris Climate Accord, his administration has largely followed Trump's lead in stonewalling the WTO. Commerce Secretary Gina Raimondo has described the protection of the US steel industry as a question of 'national security', indicating that Trump's rhetorical and practical marrying of protectionism and national security politics is likely to considerably outlive his presidency.

The decay in the multilateral system has opened up space for some countries to attempt to use market power to exert geopolitical influence on smaller economies—though, unlike with the sanctions on Russia, the fact that coercion has been unilateral rather than plurilateral has considerably blunted their impact. China, for example, showed its displeasure at Australian calls for a World Health Organization inquiry into the origins of the COVID-19 pandemic –interpreted in Beijing as a direct insinuation of guilt and a threat to sovereignty—by imposing restrictions on a number of key Australian exports. Though, in most cases, Australian exporters were able to quickly adjust by finding alternative export markets, the case demonstrated China's willingness to deploy economic coercion for strategic ends. In 2019, Japan removed South Korea from a whitelist of countries to which sensitive products, including key inputs into Korean microchips, could be exported without authorisation. This was widely seen as retaliation for a ruling in the South Korean Supreme Court that several Japanese companies, including Nippon Steel and Mitsubishi, must pay compensation for the use of forced Korean labour during World War II, contrary to a 1965 treaty between the two countries. In both cases, the attempts to use and politicise trade controls as a geopolitical lever were not overwhelmingly successful. South Korean firms, with active support from the government, have invested heavily in domestic production capabilities to circumvent the need for Japanese inputs.

America's actions under President Trump weakened the multilateral system upon which East Asia depends. But even prior to the election of President Trump in 2016, that system had been in a state of neglect, with the United States increasingly disregarding its principles and allowing its institutions to decay. The growing gap between the global system and the global reality of changing economic power and issue areas has been a key source of stress and tension. An early manifestation of stress in the system was the patchwork of bilateral, regional and global arrangements that substituted for comprehensive multilateral reform, undermining its efficiency and effectiveness. These arrangements have the benefit that progress can be made on issues that have been neglected within multilateral arrangements, but they come at the cost of attention and diplomatic energy being directed towards more comprehensive solutions at the global level.

In global finance, for example, the rise of emerging economies has not been reflected in the governance of the International Monetary Fund (IMF). IMF quota reforms, most recently in 2015, have helped reduce these gaps but progress has been slow and piecemeal. Combined with inadequate IMF resourcing and a perceived mishandling of financial crises by the IMF, the failure to achieve necessary institutional reform has led to the creation of competing institutions and mechanisms: the Chiang Mai Initiative Multilateralization and numerous development banks at the regional level, and bilateral currency swap lines at the bilateral level. This fragmentation has seen the share of the Bretton Woods institutions in the global financial safety net fall dramatically, from 80 per cent in 1980 to less than 35 per cent in 2020.

Elsewhere in the system, the problem is that the existing framework has not kept up to date with changes in the global economy over the past few decades. A large share of international economic interactions in the twenty-first century, like services trade, foreign investment and digital trade, are more or less unaddressed by existing multilateral disciplines. If they are covered, it is in bilateral, regional and plurilateral agreements that, while they serve a valuable role in deepening economic integration, do not have the same global reach as the WTO.

Economic shocks, like the Great Depression, the global financial crisis (GFC) and the COVID-19 pandemic, commonly result in a turn towards protectionism. But there is often a delay. The Smoot-Hawley tariff increases in the United States came relatively swiftly after the crash of 1929, but the most damaging tit-for-tat protectionism took several years to spread to the rest of the world (Eichengreen and Irwin 2010). After the GFC, it took some years before President Trump's 'America First' agenda became popular enough for him to win a presidential election. It is very likely that the next decade will see more pronounced protectionist sentiment around the world, if the policy reaction to the Spanish flu of 1918 is any guide: after the last major pandemic, countries that had suffered more deaths from the flu raised tariffs faster and higher (Boberg-Fazlic et al. 2021).

The economic foundations of the peace in Asia

In the depths of WWII, a new economic architecture was conceived that would help to provide economic security to the postwar world. The failure of the settlement at Versailles after WWI, and, in particular, the slide towards protectionist imperial blocs in the interwar period, convinced major thinkers in the United States that the country's economic interests would be best served by a formalised and institutionalised version of the mostly non-discriminatory liberal trading order of the late nineteenth century. In exchange for American aid, the Allied powers agreed to commit themselves to what we now know as the multilateral system, overseen and managed by international institutions: the World Bank, the IMF, and what was then the General Agreement on Tariffs and Trade (GATT) and is now the WTO.

The major accomplishment of this system was to disentangle, to a great degree, economic and security considerations. In particular, the new disciplines limited the ability of states to deploy the classic tools of economic statecraft—sanctions, punitive tariffs and quotas, and export controls, for example. Unlike the concurrent 'arms race' between the Soviet Union and the United States, which resulted from a prisoner's dilemma-style pessimistic logic, there was a real and fruitful disarmament when it came to the tools of state economic coercion, at least within that part of the world governed by the multilateral system. By and large, the hegemony of the United States in the security sphere contributed to stability in East Asia without detracting from the positive-sum game of economic integration.

The exceptions, to a large extent, prove the rule: the multilateral system did not end up being as comprehensive as originally intended; the Cold War did see the world splinter into economic blocs, though these were much more lopsided than the interwar imperial blocs; in 1960, total exports from the Soviet-led Comecon trade bloc were less than half those of the European Economic Community alone (Kaser 1996), and very much less than total GATT-covered trade. With the exception of explicitly communist countries, Asia was part of the multilateral order. Australia, New Zealand, India, Sri Lanka, the Republic of China and Pakistan were all founding members of the GATT, while many other major regional economies were quick to join: Indonesia in 1950, Japan in 1955 and Malaysia in 1957. The countries that rejected the multilateral order, particularly North Korea and China (until the rise of Deng Xiaoping) experienced poverty and stagnation.

In Asia, the Cold War became hot in two major theatres: the Korean War and the Vietnam War, both of which pitted combatants within the multilateral order against combatants in the Comecon sphere (both North Vietnam and North Korea were observers). At the end of the period of *konfrontasi* between Malaysia and Indonesia, the formation of ASEAN in 1967 signalled a new spirit of peaceful cooperation in the region. The members of ASEAN wanted to avoid complete alignment to any of the major regional powers, as other organisations, particularly the Southeast Asia Treaty Organisation had been seen as compromised by overtly tying themselves to a superpower. This principle of non-alignment was embedded in the Zone of Peace, Freedom and Neutrality Declaration of 1971, which explicitly declared Southeast Asia to be a region that should be free from interference from other powers. The early years of ASEAN focused more on political rather than economic cooperation, but, in the 1970s, as the failures of national import substitution industrialisation were becoming obvious, the benefits of economic cooperation and liberalisation began to shape ASEAN's direction more directly. Two major reports on the Southeast Asian economy advocated trade liberalisation, albeit with very different motivations. A UNESCAP report, much influenced by Latin American efforts, suggested that trade liberalisation within ASEAN itself would create a regional market for import-substituting industries, making investment in heavy industry more profitable (Shimizu 2004). In contrast, the Asian Development Bank (ADB) report *Southeast Asia's Economy in the 1970s* strongly advocated an outward orientation, with export-sector liberalisation leading the way in broader economic reform (Drysdale 2017). Over time, the wisdom of the ADB's recommendations became obvious, as the diversity in culture, language, economic and political systems and levels of economic development meant that a form of economic regionalism that was open to the rest of Asia, and the rest of the world, would yield faster growth in Southeast Asia than one that, like European efforts at regional integration, emphasised discriminatory liberalisation.

The increasing economic integration in the region has had security payoffs. One is very simply the link between economic development and military capability. There is a strong correlation between GDP and defence spending, with most countries' military budgets remaining fairly constant as a proportion of national income. The rapid growth in the region has therefore led to a substantial increase in defence capabilities. More important, though, is that the increasingly intertwined nature of economic interactions in the region raises the cost of conflict. A study by the Organisation for Economic Co-operation and Development (OECD) suggests that, in the event of a general global retreat from integrated global value chains, Southeast Asia would suffer an immediate 10 per cent decline in income (OECD 2021). This is a lower-bound estimate of the cost of major geopolitical conflict in the region that spilled over into economic disintegration. Importantly, this scenario would inflict costs on *all* players. Economic integration is not, and has never been, a zero-sum game. Because of the imperative of economic growth in the region, none of the countries in ASEAN are likely to willingly choose to align with either the United States or China.

The challenge for the region in the medium and long-term is to preserve the spirit of this open order in a world that is becoming increasingly polarised between major powers, but in which, importantly, the most important and most dynamic parts of the economy are unavoidably international in nature and require strong, clear rules to guide market participants.

Different countries and governments conceive of security differently. The countries of ASEAN view economic integration into the global economy, including, importantly, its large neighbours, as a source of national security. That is the basis for the broader Asian ideas of collective and cooperative security. At the other extreme are some countries, like North Korea, that take the narrow view of military security above a broader conception of security that includes economic security, or prosperity. Japan in the late 1970s developed the idea of comprehensive security that was a broader conception of security, explicitly including economic integration, given its constrained military and self-defence. This book generally takes national security to include defence of the sovereign state but also the defence of economic interests, its citizens and institutions. Economics and security do not need to be trade-offs but can be complementary, and the chapters in this book examine how countries in East Asia, collectively and some individually, are navigating that challenge.

Balancing economics and security in East Asia

This volume examines the new set of circumstances, with economics and security increasingly entangled with US–China strategic rivalry, complicating international policy choices and threatening the multilateral rules-based economic order on which East Asian economic integration and cooperation is built. The first two chapters set out the nature of the problem, develop a conceptual framework that brings prosperity, national security and social cohesion together in the national interest, and examine how international cooperation can help countries preserve their international policy options. The volume then looks at the economic and strategic policy choices and pressures Australia, Japan, Indonesia, Malaysia and Vietnam face, before drawing conclusions for collective regional action and the implications for the global order.

In Chapter 2, Gordon de Brouwer describes an approach to national policymaking that goes beyond the idea of a 'trade-off' between economic growth and national security. De Brouwer suggests that policymaking must focus on three dimensions of the national interest—prosperity, security and social wellbeing—and then identify and mitigate risks to each of these in a practical way. De Brouwer applies this framework to four key policy issues facing the region: infrastructure, foreign investment and the role of foreign firms, the regulation of dual-use technology and the recovery from COVID-19. In each case, he argues, there are ways to mitigate national security risks that do not threaten prosperity or social wellbeing.

In Chapter 3, Shiro Armstrong outlines a conceptual framework for thinking about the interplay between security issues and economics, predicated on the principle that zero-sum logics apply only rarely to the intersection of economics and security. Mixed interests in this area are common. Armstrong cautions against the return of zero-sum framing in the international sphere in the context of increasing strategic rivalry between China and Japan. Armstrong points out the dangers of introducing security logic into economic policy: national security spending tends to be by necessity of the 'command and control' type, with priorities set and resources allocated by bureaucratic fiat. The focus on 'dual-use technologies' and, in the context of the COVID-19 pandemic, on supply chain resilience—and, in particular, on the idea of 'reshoring' or 'friendshoring' production—risks rolling back the primacy of market forces in large swathes of the international economy in favour of a protectionism that is married to national security objectives. Armstrong argues that this would have major deleterious impacts on both global economic prosperity and, in the long-term, national security as negative feedback loops kick in. Finally, and importantly, Armstrong demonstrates that the multilateral system offers protection for national sovereignty for small and middle powers, preserving policy space that would be encroached upon by the major powers in the absence of rules governing international economic interactions. The multilateral sanctions on Russia in response to the invasion of Ukraine help to make the clear distinction between unilateral sanctions that almost always backfire in the medium term, if not immediately, and those that are coordinated, which can bring real costs to countries that egregiously violate global norms.

In Chapter 4, Adam Triggs and Peter Drysdale examine the challenging global environment Australia finds itself in and how this has made its economic and strategic choices difficult. The chapter reflects on Australia's transition from a closed, inward-looking, protectionist economy to a more open economy after WWII. Australia's postwar growth strategy was built on integration with Asia in particular. Triggs and Drysdale make it clear that Australia's economic openness has been a source of strength. They emphasise that the policy choices to open the Australian economy to global capital and people flows have underpinned the country's specialisation and strong comparative advantage in mining and resource goods, agricultural produce, education and professional services. This economic openness has buttressed Australia's economy against economic shocks and lifted its prosperity. They highlight that openness has brought strong productivity gains and lowered the cost of living for Australians. Triggs and Drysdale also point out that Australia's international engagement has been aided and enabled through its active participation in multilateral frameworks, including the G20, Asia-Pacific Economic Cooperation and WTO. The chapter details how tensions between the United States and China have made it difficult for Australia to manage its relationships with both countries, before moving on to consider Australians' attitudes towards openness and how debates over the sources of Australia's security have played out in the country. Triggs and Drysdale scrutinise the argument that Australia should divert its trading relationships away from China and Asia towards the Five Eyes intelligence sharing countries: Canada, New Zealand, the United Kingdom and the United States. They argue that this is based on a misunderstanding of both how markets work and the role that Australia's domestic policies and institutions play in managing economic prosperity, liberty and international integration. The chapter argues that Australia's prosperity and security cannot be traded off in a binary fashion. Australia must not retreat from openness and international engagement, but, rather, attend to national weaknesses that affect the integrity of its government and the resilience of its markets, their regulation and governance.

In Chapter 5, Shiro Armstrong and Shujiro Urata analyse the response of Japan to a new strategic economic environment. Traditionally tightly aligned with Washington on the security plane while integrated in the East Asian economy, Japanese policymakers have had to grapple with a number of new challenges, including Chinese assertiveness and a new US approach of 'managed' rather than free trade with Asia. The machinery of the Japanese Government has changed to reflect this new environment, with economic and national security issues being brought together within the Japanese bureaucracy, and the establishment of an economic team within the National Security Secretariat. The concept of 'economic security' has been further embedded within the policymaking space with the creation of the Economic

Security Division within the Ministry of Economy, Trade and Industry. Economic security policymaking has emphasised managing risks around technology. A number of policy decisions suggest that this new focus on economic security could result in a rolling back of economic liberalisation. Japan has tightened the screening regime for foreign investment, further restricting what was already an unwelcoming environment for foreign direct investment. It has also imposed export controls on what it deems to be sensitive goods, targeting South Korea in particular with controls on chemical inputs to semiconductor manufacturing—a decision that has largely backfired, leading to investment in South Korea to replace the chemicals it can no longer import easily from Japan, with no obvious improvement in the Japanese semiconductor industry. As Armstrong and Urata argue, it is very far from obvious that the large economic costs of a new focus on 'economic security' as an organising concept will be outweighed by any benefits to national security. Re-emphasising Japan's traditional reliance on the open regional order, though, requires proactive efforts on the part of Japanese diplomacy to renew and reinvigorate that order.

Indonesia is the largest economy in ASEAN and one of the fulcrums of geopolitical competition in the region. As Yose Rizal Damuri, Rocky Intan and Dandy Rafitrandi argue in Chapter 6, Indonesia's traditional approach has been characterised by the principle of *bebas aktif*—that is, a 'free and active' nation that proactively defends its sovereignty and avoids conflict with major powers. The authors argue that this approach may come under strain as geopolitical competition between China and the US heats up. Indonesia's interest lies in containing the economic spillover of this competition as much as possible, while pushing ahead with regional economic cooperation—an approach that can be seen in Indonesia's role in forging the ASEAN Outlook on the Indo-Pacific in reaction to the US's attempt to wedge ASEAN with its Free and Open Indo-Pacific statement.

In Chapter 7, Shankaran Nambiar considers the political economy of Malaysia's complicated relationships with major regional powers. He argues that weak national institutions have resulted in unnecessary difficulties in addressing the security–economics nexus, with Malaysia committing to some China-backed infrastructure projects that it does not need and cannot afford, a situation that required untangling, but at a cost to the political relationship with China. This could have been avoided by more stringent public policymaking that made full use of the relevant institutional capacity. Nambiar recommends a fundamental rethinking of the institutional framework of policymaking in this area.

Thanh Tri Vo and Duong Anh Nguyen argue in Chapter 8 that Vietnam's national interest dictates that it maintain neutrality with respect to major powers, and that this militates in favour of a strategy that centres ASEAN as a buffer between it and both China and the United States. Vietnam has enjoyed spectacular economic growth over the past three decades, and this has been predicated on its increasing integration into the regional economy. At the same time, a number of security questions, and, in particular, the South China Sea issue, have complicated relations with the major powers. By participating actively within ASEAN, and strengthening its role as a cooperative body, Vietnam is able to pursue both an ambitious economic growth agenda as well as securing its national strategic interests.

In Chapter 9, Peter Drysdale, Dionisius Narjoko and Rebecca St Maria describe the role of ASEAN in managing asymmetric power relations in the region. The ASEAN model, they argue, is a significant Asian institutional innovation that effectively marshals countries of very different levels of economic development, political systems and cultural backgrounds to achieve cooperation and regional integration. The ASEAN way is sometimes criticised for being slow moving, but this, the authors argue, is one of the reasons for the organisation's historical success. ASEAN will be forced in the coming decades to confront major policy dilemmas, and this will require the grouping to take a more proactive role in shaping the region than it has to date. ASEAN's collective leadership will be necessary to shape and guide the direction of Asian integration against a backdrop of increasing geopolitical competition in the region.

In Chapter 10, Peter Drysdale, Amy King and Adam Triggs provide an analytical history of the origins of the global postwar order. They argue that British and American thinkers devised a framework that was designed to ensure both economic prosperity and security by binding members into a set of rules to govern economic interactions. The global system was contested from the beginning and was forced to evolve to accommodate new economic realities, such as the rise of Japan, which prompted the creation of the ADB. They point to new stresses in the global order, which have led to the construction of new and competing institutions and mechanisms, like bilateral swap lines and plurilateral trade agreements. While the election of President Biden means that the United States might be less hostile to the reform of global economic institutions, Drysdale, King and Triggs argue that the task of renovating the global order will fall to Asian collective leadership.

References

Boberg-Fazlic, N., M. Lampe, M. Uhre Pedersen and P. Sharp. 2021. 'Pandemics and Protectionism: Evidence from the "Spanish" Flu'. *Humanities and Social Sciences Communications* 8 (145): 1–9. doi.org/10.1057/s41599-021-00833-7.

Drysdale, P. 2017. 'ASEAN: The Experiment in Open Regionalism That Succeeded'. In *The ASEAN Economic Community into 2025 and Beyond*, edited by Rebecca Sta Maria, Shukiro Urata and Ponciano S. Intal, 64–86. Jakarta: ERIA.

Eichengreen, B. and D. Irwin. 2010. 'The Slide to Protectionism in the Great Depression: Who Succumbed and Why?' *Journal of Economic History* 70 (4): 871–97. doi.org/10.1017/S0022050710000756.

Kaser, M. 1996. 'Flaws in the Treuhand Model'. *Acta Oeconomica* 48: 1–2.

OECD (Organisation for Economic Co-operation and Development). 2021. 'Global Value Chains: Efficiency and Risks in the Context of COVID-19'. Paris: OECD. read.oecd-ilibrary.org/view/?ref=1060_1060357-mi890957m9&title=Global-value-chains-Efficiency-and-risks-in-the-context-of-COVID-19.

Shimizu, K. 2004. 'The Origin of Intra-ASEAN Economic Cooperation'. *Economic Journal of Hokkaido University* 33: 113–33.

2

Prosperity, security and social wellbeing in a messy world

Gordon de Brouwer

Over the past few years, the economic and security policy domains have become more complex and increasingly connected. To this already volatile mix has been added the COVID-19 pandemic. Not only is the pandemic the most serious social and economic disruption since World War II, with big and long-lived consequences, but also it has deepened existing stresses on the international system, such as US–China strategic competition and economic nationalism, and weakened international institutions that guide interaction between nations. The pandemic has also accelerated some underlying changes, such as the digitisation of economic and social interaction, the changing nature of work, and, perhaps, trust in government and institutions.

There is a lot at stake now in what sort of society we want to be.

It is important to think carefully and comprehensively about what is going on, and to act in ways that are genuinely strategic and deliver on the national interest. After briefly discussing the changes going on in the world and the complex challenges we face, the second part of this chapter outlines two basic principles for dealing with these challenges, and applies them to current topics such as infrastructure, foreign investment (especially in digital-heavy sectors), dual-use technology and strategies for recovery from the COVID-19 recession. To give the story away, the first principle is to assess an issue through three elements of the national interest (prosperity, security and social wellbeing), and the second is to identify risks broadly and to mitigate them in practical and effective ways. The third part of the chapter suggests some institutional changes and strategies at the national and regional level that can support implementing these principles.

Recent events, changes and challenges

At the end of 2019, the world looked a difficult and messy place. Global growth of 3.25 per cent was barely at its long-run average; there were extensive balance sheet and structural weaknesses in most economies; US–China relations had shifted to outright strategic competition; populist nationalists were leading many G20 nations and running down international frameworks; and countries were grappling with deep challenges, such as technological change, climate change and declining trust in institutions. The risks were mostly negative, big and connected to each other.

By the middle of 2020, these risks had been overwhelmed by the COVID-19 pandemic.

The pandemic is a terrible event in its own right.

The human impact of the pandemic is enormous and tragic. As at 5 October 2021, about 236 million people had been infected, a third of them in the United States, and the rate of increase remains positive. Around 4.8 million deaths (Worldometer 2021) had been recorded, with around 1.2 million in Europe, 2.3 million in the Americas (predominantly the US and Brazil), 1.1 million in Asia and 212,000 in Africa. In some countries, the spread has been more or less contained and lockdowns eased; in others, especially those with inadequate health systems and governance, the spread and deaths will continue. Sadly, these numbers will be rapidly out of date, and recurrences are a real prospect. The rise in unemployment is only matched by the Great Depression.

The economic impact of the pandemic is profound. The pandemic is the worst economic event since WWII. In April 2020, the International Monetary Fund (IMF 2020) predicted that the global economy would contract by 3 per cent in 2020 and rebound by 5.8 per cent in 2021 if the pandemic was contained and policy responses were adequate. Just a month later, the IMF stated that it expected the outcome to be even worse. This may look like a V-shaped recovery, but the loss of employment, human capital and structural damage wreaked by the pandemic means that recovery will take much longer.

The pandemic has intensified some of the pre-existing challenges and accelerated some of the changes already underway.

Politics has become hotter. The pandemic has intensified US–China tension, driven in part by limited transparency by the Chinese Government and a US administration on the defensive about relatively high US infections and deaths in an election year. Indeed, President Trump described COVID-19 as an attack worse than the attacks on Pearl Harbor and the World Trade Center (BBC News 2020). The pandemic has seen nationalist responses to a global problem, shown by beggar-thy-neighbour outbursts about protective equipment. It has further weakened international bodies, exemplified by the withdrawal of US funding for the World Health Organization (WHO) and the barely visible responses of the G20 relative to what it did in London in April 2009. It remains to be seen whether the pandemic deepens people's distrust of governments and institutions: the pandemic might increase distrust and division in countries where the death rate is high (e.g. US and UK) but it could have the opposite effect in countries where the death rate, at least so far, is low (e.g. Australia and New Zealand). It remains to be seen whether the pandemic strengthens local communities, whether this extends to foreigners in the community, and whether public trust in domestic and international institutions changes in different circumstances.

The pandemic has sharply accelerated the digitisation of economic and social activity. With person-to-person contact so severely constrained, a lot of activity that involved interaction has shifted to digital means, from shopping and banking to meetings and personal services. Many workplaces have shifted to employees' homes, providing flexibility, supporting creativity and, in some cases, boosting productivity, but at the cost of isolation. A considerable amount of learning has shifted online. An unexpected array of government services, including many justice, health, human and community services, have been successfully delivered online. For those countries with widely accessible broadband and digital infrastructure, lockdown has been an opportunity to improvise and make positive change, with the issue being the extent to which these changes become permanent. Yet for others, the digital divide has deepened; especially for those who work in informal sectors, digital alternatives have been scarce, and economic and social inequalities have been exacerbated, including in the quality of education. The concern remains that accelerated digital transformation opens economies and societies to even greater cyber penetration, disruption and attack by state and non-state actors, further weaponising economic and social interaction. Put into the broader context of deteriorating relations between the major powers, a bigger digital economy is yet another place where intensifying US–China strategic competition plays out.

The economic consequences of the pandemic will deepen existing structural and balance sheet weaknesses. Governments have significantly extended fiscal and monetary support. While this has been essential to put a floor on the economic impacts of lockdown, it will significantly and universally increase government debt at a time when the balance sheets of households, businesses and the financial sector are all weaker. This matters because weak balance sheets create a vulnerability to further shocks. In the words of the doyen of economic crisis economists Rudi Dornbusch (2002, 750) two decades ago: 'good balance sheets, no crisis'. If balance sheets across the board have deteriorated, the world economy is more vulnerable to future shocks and pandemic recurrences, so the need to work together to resolve problems is even more pressing. The policy imperative is to enable sources of economic dynamism and employment, rather than not increasing debt. On top of deteriorating balance sheets, the ever-present problems remain of weak governance and market distortions in terms of market power, poor regulation and barriers to entry across developed and emerging economies alike.

As before the pandemic, security risks are high and rising. The Middle East is unstable, the Korean Peninsula is uncertain, Russia and China are assertive (especially, in China's case, in the South China Sea), the US is volatile and unpredictable, non-state terror risks from extremist movements are continuing, global efforts to contain nuclear and chemical proliferation are weaker, and cyber risks are growing. Trust between nation states is deteriorating.

So, what should countries do in this unhappy world?

This note sets out some principles to frame national responses, applies those principles in practical ways to infrastructure, foreign investment, dual-use technology and economic recovery strategies from COVID, and looks at ways to strengthen domestic, regional and global institutions.

For countries in which the relationship with the US and China both really matter—not just formal security allies of the US such as Australia, Japan, the Philippines, Singapore and South Korea, but others such as India, Indonesia, Malaysia, Thailand and Vietnam—these developments are sometimes stated as forcing a binary choice between economics and security, between China and the US. This framing does not help to provide countries with enduring solutions that are in their individual national interest.

In the first instance, it oversimplifies the problem.

Yes, China is assertive militarily and aggressive in its use of cyber technologies; it also deploys political language and so-called 'wolf-diplomacy' that deeply jars with democracies, undermines long-established, trusted relationships and sits oddly with an expressed commitment to international rules, institutions and cooperation. However, its interests are also served by avoiding conflict. It is politically and socially a lot more complex than some commentators assert. It has committed to core parts of the rules-based global order. Moreover, it is a very big country in the region in which we live: China is here to stay and the rest of Asia cannot just move away. China's prosperity and stability is a bedrock of the prosperity, national power and security of countries in Asia, the Pacific and beyond.

The US is not just the leading global and regional military power but also an economic powerhouse of ideas, technology and innovation. It really matters to other countries. Yet the withdrawal of US leadership from global norms and institutions, trashing of the World Trade Organization (WTO), United Nations Framework Convention on Climate Change and WHO, and rejection of basic principles of openness, predictability and some element of fairness as the basis of international interaction, is shocking and counsels caution in relying on it alone or too much. Many countries would have some sympathy with some elements of US criticism of international institutions, but they generally see reform as a way to get the international system to work better, rather than undermine and weaken it for short-term national gain or because they think that international frameworks necessarily undermine national sovereignty. The election of President Biden marks a big shift in tone at the top, but it remains to be seen what this means for changes in policy: the US's position on climate change will change but it remains to be seen how its approach to international trade, investment and monetary arrangements does. Nationalist populism is not far from the surface: while Biden received a record 81 million votes in the 2020 election, Trump's 74 million votes was also a record for a candidate and showed a deeply divided and unstable nation.

Second, it is a false choice. Binary choice does *not* reduce security risks. Binary choice increases security risks because it puts us all into a corner and reduces compromise and the possibility of finding a balance. In so doing it raises the prospect of conflict. This does not mean being weak on national security. Having a highly agile, well-trained and well-resourced military, as well as offensive and defensive intelligence capabilities, is essential to the national interest.

Two principles to deliver prosperity and security, with four applications

This is not a pretty picture. But it is certainly not a cause for despair and isolation. Two principles can help guide a way through. These principles define the national interest and underline the importance of mitigating risk in light of all elements of the national interest.

Principle 1: The national interest has three components—security, prosperity and social cohesion (or social harmony, inclusion and wellbeing)—and they should always be part of framing the problem and solutions.

All three components matter. More than ever, they reinforce each other. Security underpins prosperity, prosperity pays for power and security, and social cohesion reduces economic and security risks.

It is worth noting the specific reference to three rather than two factors—that is, adding social cohesion to prosperity and security. The debate is typically framed around how to balance economic and security interests. The social dimension is not often discussed but it is essential and too often overlooked. The people-to-people component of international relations really matters (Australian Government n.d.-a.). Broad-based, open and warm people-to-people links create a strong political incentive for governments to find balance in their relations with others.

At a national level, social cohesion and inclusion are important domestic policy objectives. In a country where immigration is so important, such as Australia, ensuring that all people have a sense that they belong to the nation matters. Talk of 'China as a threat' is easily personalised and Chinese Australians—about 1.2 million people or 5 per cent of the population—hear themselves being described as a threat and their loyalty questioned. Where there is concern about foreign influence, alienating key parts of the population makes the problem worse, not better, and undermines a key source of influence back to China about Australian values and priorities.

There is debate, at least in Australia, about the importance of values, rather than just interests, in foreign policy and international relations. In Australia, the values debate is often articulated as follows: free speech, equality and democracy should not be compromised just for the opportunity to export more or to avoid upsetting China's government. The fact that values are raised in this way highlights how important social cohesion and identity are as part of the national interest. However, it also shows just how murky the values debate is. Values are hard to define: how different, for example, are Australian and Chinese values? Chinese values typically relate to the importance of family, respect for parents, the power of education and the value of work—and these are certainly not alien to what many Australians would say is important to them. The real point is that the two countries' political systems are different, and part of the Australian national interest lies is protecting Australia's social and political institutions. Saying that Australian values are notably different from Chinese or, more generally, Asian values does not bear scrutiny—think of how important democracy is to people across so much of Asia—and it certainly alienates a good part of immigrant Australia.

COVID-19 has brought the importance of social wellbeing and cohesion to the fore. The costs of this crisis are deeply social as well as economic and they have exacerbated tension between the major powers. The policy responses to the pandemic were centred on limiting the health impact. The isolation and social damage this has caused, such as domestic violence, racial attacks, self-harm and homelessness, has been a major social challenge and a key part of public and private responses.

Principle 2: Identify the risks to the national interest in its three dimensions and identify practical ways to mitigate them.

Risks can affect security, prosperity and social cohesion. The optimal forms of mitigation can be identified by thinking beyond a single domain. As a general proposition, it is in a country's interest that countries that pose a security risk to it have other strong interests to balance, effectively raising the cost of conflict and creating an incentive to find an enduring solution.

The key to mitigating a security risk might lie in the economic or social domains. For example, strengthening domestic economic governance, market systems and people-to-people connections supports cooperation rather than confrontation. Many of these actions not only help mitigate security risk but also mitigate the economic and social risks outlined above and support prosperity and social wellbeing in their own right. For example, markets that are more competitive and have greater integrity are more likely to innovate in quality goods and services and be more focused on people—which, as Adam Smith pointed out in *The Wealth of Nations*, is the whole purpose of markets—supporting productivity, improving resilience and sharing prosperity across society. Indeed, greater concentration of market power over the past decade may be one reason for slower growth in productivity, investment and wages, and so policies to make it easier for new firms to enter and to limit market power and concentration are likely to have significant economic, social and indeed security benefits (IMF 2019).

Defence and security are public goods, typically provided by governments. Risk mitigation, in contrast, need not be directly provided by governments. Indeed, the actions of other parts of society—especially business and civil society—can help mitigate risk over time and can be more effective in doing so than governments. The responsibility of government is not to manage risk directly itself but to enable and create incentives for others to maximise the three elements of the national interest and mitigate risks. This is typically achieved by strong domestic laws, markets, and regulatory and integrity governance supported by effective monitoring, compliance and systems for dealing with breaches.

But what does this mean in practice? The following section discusses in detail four applied examples with strategies to implement these principles: infrastructure, foreign investment and foreign firms, dual-use technology and the recovery from the pandemic.

Infrastructure

There are huge infrastructure needs across Asia and the Pacific, both within economies and between them. The Asian Development Bank (ADB) estimates that developing Asia needs investment of US$26 trillion in infrastructure to 2030 (ADB 2017), and as much as US$40 trillion by 2040 for the Asia-Pacific Economic Cooperation group (APEC) and India, mostly in roads and energy (Heathcote 2017). The impact of infrastructure on internal and external connectivity and on economic and social development is profound, and everyone is staggered by the size of the need.

Yet there is growing tension between the major powers about the strategic objectives of donors, and there is particularly concern in the security community (China Power Team 2017) that China is using the Belt and Road Initiative as a strategic play to gain leverage over governments and acquire critical infrastructure, especially in cases when countries cannot repay debt (Camba and Jia Yao 2018). It helps to frame this debate from the perspective of the recipient country. Simply refusing foreign investment deprives the recipient of what might be economic and social infrastructure important for its prosperity and social cohesion. It deprives China of the opportunity to support the development of others commensurate with its economic size and power and, as a major trading country, its own deep interest in a stable and prosperous world. Moreover, framing regional infrastructure primarily through the lens of US–China strategic competition risks freezing infrastructure funding and investment from private sources and nobbling cooperation within multilateral development banks—all to the significant detriment of the recipient country.

All donor countries use aid and financial assistance as a tool of foreign policy; therefore, the interests of the recipient country are best served by engaging with a variety of donors and organisations (intermediated through a key multilateral development agency when it is a small country) so that it is not hostage to dependence on a single large donor. Meanwhile, strong governance—including objective economic and social cost-benefit analysis, competitive, open and non-discriminatory bidding, and independent dispute resolution—is essential to secure the benefits of the investment. The standard toolkit of international and development economics can help allay security concerns, as well as help lock in economic and social benefits. Japan's approach of working case by case with China on priority infrastructure investments in Asia and the Pacific provides a practical and effective way to lift governance, manage risks and deliver outcomes.

Foreign investment and the role of foreign firms

There is a huge bank of empirical and analytical work on the benefits of open investment and the importance of foreign investment to domestic innovation, economic growth and jobs. Yet there are also concerns that such investment can be used against a country to gain leverage over a government. As in the debate about the Belt and Road Initiative, much of this is focused on China. The security concern is threefold. First, it is thought that foreign ownership of domestic assets renders them more liable to be used by the foreign power, including by enabling cyber attacks on those assets. Second, it is argued, China is quick to use economic assets as a political tool in its dealings with others, as shown by the fear that China would withhold crucial rare earths from Japan in 2010 and a range of commodity and agricultural imports from Australia in 2020. Third, changes requiring Chinese firms and citizens to cooperate with Chinese intelligence agencies, and to have Communist Party cells in management in private companies, effectively render even private entities instruments of the state.

From this perspective, foreign investment, especially from China, is seen as potentially undermining national sovereignty, particularly as US–China strategic competition rises. Let us look at each element of the argument in light of the principles set out above.

If security risks are changing, it is important to keep front of mind just how important an open investment regime and market-based economic system is to sustaining innovation, growth and development. Closing borders and markets destroys economies and the source of their power. The better approach is to identify risks and workable risk mitigation to minimise security risks and maximise opportunities for prosperity.

The idea that foreign-owned assets can be used against a country is hardly new. The beauty of foreign investment is that both countries have an incentive to make the asset work and be profitable. China has a powerful economic and political incentive not to misuse its assets, including foreign assets. Why would it want to waste its wealth and opportunity for its own broad-based economic development by creating assets that it would lose in a serious confrontation? The physical assets cannot be repatriated to China in such an event; they would be lost and China's commercial reputation destroyed. There is an overriding incentive to make the assets work. A good example in Australia of how foreign participation in a controversial sector has helped stabilise a market is the live cattle export industry. Indonesian participation in ownership of Australian cattle farms used for live exports has reduced Indonesia's incentive to impose lower quotas or import bans when Australia–Indonesia relations have been difficult. Foreign investment has made the sector more stable and both countries benefit directly from the exports and imports.

There is concern that foreign ownership increases cyber risk. Cyber risk is serious and one of the greatest risks in a digital world for business, universities, not-for-profit bodies and governments. Those risks come from both government and non-government actors. The Chinese Government, directly or indirectly, is often mentioned in the media as one of a group of significant state players. In thinking about cyber risk in the context of foreign investment, understanding the risk matters. Ownership is not the fulcrum of cyber risk. Cyber risk matters regardless of ownership and focusing on ownership itself does not resolve cyber risk (Prevelakis and Spinellis 2007). Controlling ownership is not the primary general instrument to deal with this threat.

Cyber risk can be reduced but not eliminated (Tobar 2018). Risk mitigation is varied (Bochman 2018). Risk mitigation includes strong defences in firms, organisations and other sectors against cyber attacks. Strong internal defences against cyber attacks vary between the type of entity and sector (Sterling 2018), and typically include programs or practices that control or limit access to devices, computers and technology. They can also include regulating how technology is used: in the energy sector, for example, there is a focus on segmenting parts of the energy system to limit the spread of failure following an attack (Bochman 2018).

A more subtle consideration is that market structure, too, matters for mitigation of risks to both security and prosperity. The more participants and the more diverse the structure of the market, the lower is the risk associated with any one firm. From this perspective, policies to encourage product innovation and the creation of new firms, along with policies and laws to protect market contestability, can help mitigate security risks and improve economic outcomes. The debate about foreign ownership of 5G networks and digital security risk might be different, for example, if the 5G sector was competitive and diverse, rather than concentrated in a small number of highly integrated firms (Voon and Mitchell 2019). This is a good topic to explore further, including between countries interested in addressing concentration risks in the technology sector.

Effective risk mitigation also requires domestic enforcement of strong laws against cyber attacks, including those aimed at obtaining sensitive data on individuals. These laws include making cyber penetration and attacks illegal and punishable with specific consequences for the firms and individuals involved, defining digital property rights (including data about people) and protecting privacy, and constraining the use of data obtained through a privacy breach. There are concerns that foreign firms, for example, may be particularly susceptible to theft of personal data, including information about a person's health, finances or behaviour that could be used to coerce or embarrass them (Hamilton 2019). Having a clear legal framework on data privacy creates a domestic legal structure in which foreign firms are expected to operate, and penalties and practices that apply in the case of breach. The primary risk mitigation is the cyber defence of the firm, buttressed by laws and penalties for firms that breach confidentiality or use illegally obtained data. Given that risk can only be reduced and not eliminated, risk mitigation includes having enforceable frameworks in place that address breaches and protect the privacy of the people affected, such as limiting the public naming of people and use of data obtained illegally, even when the breach is by others. A good example is not allowing insurance companies and others to use health information made public by an illegal breach of privacy (Australian Government 2020). It might also be appropriate to impose criminal penalties on the senior management, board members or owners of firms that knowingly breach privacy of individuals.

The use of cyber warfare by large state actors is also subject to the kinds of deterrence logic that govern other aspects of interstate conflict. Analogous to the nuclear arms race, the cyber capabilities of the major powers have most probably reached the stage where a cyber attack by one would lead to a cyber attack by the other. Mutually assured digital destruction changes the risk of cyber attacks between the major powers and their allies outside of explicit war. Ensuring countries' own defensive and offensive cyber capabilities are effective may create a deterrent to overt cyber attacks by state actors.

Foreign investment is sometimes seen as a source of security risk for countries, particularly when the investment comes from countries with different political systems, as is the case for China and some of its partners. But trying to leverage foreign investment for foreign policy carries risks for the country that attempts it. Rather than seeking to minimise exposure to risk by limiting trade and investment links, countries can rely to a great degree on both international and domestic institutional and legal frameworks, as well as market forces, to mitigate risk.

For example, China may be quick to use economic dependence as an instrument of foreign policy, as in the case of limiting rare earths exports to Japan in 2010 (Tabeta and Zhou 2019). China's decision was challenged successfully by the US, Japan and the European Union in the WTO (n.d.) and upheld on appeal, with China accepting and implementing the decision. While countries do include economic sanctions in their foreign policy toolkit at some tipping point, the instance offers some useful insight. The initial action by China led buyers of rare earths to diversify supply chains and innovate with technology to reduce their reliance—a classic case of how flexible markets respond to events and can help manage risk. It highlights, too, the importance of the existence and use of international legal frameworks to defend property and market rights. While China's reputation as a stable commercial partner was damaged by the initial action, and rhetoric on all sides was strong, China did apply the rule of law by following the WTO ruling.

A case in which domestic regulatory frameworks should be optimised to manage risk stems from the change in China's Intelligence Law and greater role of the Communist Party in the management of private firms. These changes mark the assertion of central political control in Chinese commercial life and the primacy of the state. Ultimately, their material rather than symbolic impact depends not on the laws or requirements themselves but on how they are used and applied in practice, even if this is, by its nature, a hard thing to judge. In terms of how other countries respond, it is appropriate to be clear about their own legal frameworks: that foreign firms that operate in its jurisdiction do so under domestic law; that domestic law has strong, enforceable and independent commercial and market integrity and privacy provisions; and that significant (even criminal) penalties exist for breaches of these laws. It may be appropriate to consider making it illegal under domestic law for companies to act on behalf of foreign intelligence agencies—as hard as that would be to prove in a court of law, it marks a line in the sand. Again, more fundamentally, the more diverse and competitive the structure of the domestic market, the more difficult it is for any one firm, foreign or otherwise, to exert influence for economic or other purposes.

Dual-use technology

The third example is applying the principles to dual-use technology. It is widely accepted among economists that, to quote Paul Krugman:

Productivity isn't everything, but, in the long run, it is almost everything. A country's ability to improve its standard of living over time depends almost entirely on its ability to raise its output per worker (Colford 2016).

There is less agreement about what lifts productivity, but the largely agreed factors include improvements in technology, know-how and capital, employee skills and learning, and the degree of competition in markets and dynamism of firms. For economists, new, open and experimental use of technology is synonymous with economic growth. In the security world, being at the technology frontier matters enormously to defence and intelligence capability, making it possible to directly manage long-term security risk. Many elements of digital technology have security and commercial applications—so-called dual-use technology. Technology is a primary determinant of both economic and military advance and an active playground for US–China strategic competition (Nouwens and Legarda 2018).

How do countries balance their interests in technology? In terms of the principles outlined above, the first point is that countries have fundamental economic and security interests in technology. A viable and enduring solution is one that finds some balance between them and eschews solutions in either the economics-only corner or the security-only corner. Countries have grappled with dual-use technology for millennia—knives, ships and the jet engine have all had dual security and economic uses, and the balance has been found in enabling both, protecting specific military applications (including tightly protecting defence science and technology organisations) and continually innovating to compete for the lead.

The idea that general access to technology should be limited or closed because it can be used for both commercial and military purposes is an extreme response with potentially enormous economic costs and potentially little impact on mitigating security risks.

Table 2.1: International payments and receipts for technology, US$billion current prices

	2005		2010		2015	
	payments	receipts	payments	receipts	payments	receipts
Australia	**3.4**	2.7	**7.3**	4.6	**8.0**	4.4
Belgium	5.7	**6.9**	10.0	**11.8**	17.5	**17.8**
Denmark	3.3	**4.6**	5.2	**6.4**	6.0	**7.7**
Finland	**4.6**	3.6	7.8	**9.5**	5.0	**10.8**
Germany	29.1	**31.4**	45.2	**58.2**	53.7	**71.8**
Japan	6.4	**18.4**	6.0	**27.8**	5.0	**32.6**
Korea	**4.5**	1.6	**10.2**	3.3	**16.4**	10.4
Netherlands	17.3	**19.4**	29.4*	**40.0***	50.2	**56.3**
Sweden	7.3	**9.8**	9.8	**17.8**	10.1	**28.0**
Switzerland	**13.9**	11.6	**21.2**	20.8	**34.0**	30.3
UK	13.9	**29.0**	18.4	**31.1**	21.3	**41.1**
USA	31.8	**74.8**	69.6	**100.6**	88.9	**130.8**

Bold indicates which of payment and receipt is larger; * 2011.
Source: OECD (2018).

It is worth observing just how essential access to technology and open markets are to prosperity. Australia, for example, is a small producer and a net importer of technology, while Japan is a moderately sized producer and a net exporter (Table 2.1). In a risk-based framework, the economic premium for Australia is on enabling imports of technology and ideas, building networks, and staying open and connected; for Japan, the economic premium is on protecting intellectual property and access to overseas markets. In a risk-based framework, the security strategy for both is to restrict those technologies that have an overt defence application. Intelligent risk management, for example, tightly guards weapons and intelligence applications of quantum computing and machine learning, but not quantum computing and machine learning in general. Other countries, notably the US and China, lead these technologies, and both are important partners in technology transfer to technology importers like Australia. The notion that a technology-small country simply excludes Chinese technology across the board means that it foregoes significant opportunities for growth with no material impact on the technology-big country.

Recovery strategies from the COVID-19 pandemic — reliable supply chains

The pandemic has severely disrupted production and exchange processes across the globe and forced the closure of borders, particularly to the movement of people, and this is likely to be a disruption that lasts for some time. Governments and businesses have been keen to maintain the movement of goods. The core issue is how the public can be confident that supply chains work and necessary goods and services can be brought to market.

In terms of applying the two principles, it is clear that the challenge has economic, security and social dimensions. The starting point is understanding whether supply chains in fact worked, where the breakdowns and bottlenecks occurred, and how they were remedied. It is important to work off fact rather than presumption.

Each country will have examples of adaptability in markets that kept supply chains working. Consider some examples from Australia. Faced with demand exceeding supply of personal protective equipment, like face masks, gowns and sanitisers, domestic producers responded, with paper manufacturers shifting production into masks and gowns and breweries shifting production of beer into ethanol and then into sanitisers. In response to a shortage of ventilators, domestic manufacturers developed alternative devices, including adapting machines initially designed for other purposes or using 3D printers. As panic buying of items like toilet paper occurred, retail stores repackaged big packs into smaller ones, restricted the number of items that could be purchased, and reduced brands. The role of government in these circumstances was not to take over, but to facilitate, the market. There are many examples of where this was done, such as enabling fast customs clearance of key goods at the border, providing international transport for essential items, or easing limitations on the night-time movement of heavy vehicles to speed up restocking of stores.

The issue is how to manage risks to supply chains. The COVID-19 lockdowns have shown that the connections between the different parts of the economy are many and varied, and they cannot be plotted out in detail with accuracy. In a federation, supply chains can cross over state or provincial borders, so restrictions in one state can have unintended consequences for national supply chains. Supply chains become more complex the longer the time profile; while vehicle and road maintenance do not particularly matter in making supply chains work for one day, they matter greatly in making supply chains work for several months or more. As recent events show, it is important to know broadly who produces what and how businesses are connected.

Yet the way to manage the risks of supply disruption is not necessarily to make sure that more production is on shore or that more items are stored. That may help but it might also just increase other vulnerabilities and concentrate risks domestically. A better approach is to have flexible, innovative and adaptable industrial sectors that understand what is going on quickly and have the technical and management skills, attributes and relationships to respond to events in practical and maybe ingenious ways, with government support to ensure legal and policy frameworks work to support adaptability (even when this means temporarily overriding existing creditor or intellectual property rights). These attributes are associated with open and competitive markets rather than closed, insular and protected ones.

Finally, there is an adding-up constraint in supply chains: we cannot all be exporters and none of us importers. If governments end up seeking to reduce reliance on other countries, this will be reciprocated, and the result will be less prosperity without greater security.

Strengthening national and international institutions to support the national interest

Good institutional design does not solve the economic, security and social challenges that countries face but it can provide a structure in which to identify, assess and determine what is in a country's national interest and to advance shared interests with other countries.

There are two components to thinking about strengthening national institutions. The first is ensuring that government has all the perspectives in mind, enables contestability of views, and ultimately brings the economic, security and social dimensions together coherently and effectively in forming its assessment, strategy and actions. The heart of Australian, Japanese and Singaporean government decision-making is the Cabinet, led by the prime minister and supported by specialist Cabinet committees of a subset of ministers and independent and expert advice from the public service led by the prime minister's department. All these elements are important and essential.

It is worthwhile asking whether the habits of thinking and traditional support structures are still fit for purpose. The tradition in these countries has been largely to separate security, economic and social considerations in separate Cabinet committees and administrative and bureaucratic structures, often with their own culture and language, priorities and view of the world.

In Australia, for example, security has been the domain of the National Security Committee, with—rightly—tightly controlled secrecy and membership dominated by the defence, intelligence and foreign relations departments and agencies (noting that the treasurer and the head of the Treasury department are present). It is timely to ask whether the wider national interest, with broader ministerial and administrative membership, is better suited to address issues that require a more integrated strategic approach. This could include a Strategic Oversight Cabinet Committee of senior security, economic and social policy ministers, led by the prime minister, looking, for example, at the issues outlined above on infrastructure, foreign investment, dual-use technology and supply chains. The National Security Committee should retain responsibility for specific military, security and intelligence strategies and decisions. At the very least, submissions to the National Security Committee that have deep economic and social dimensions should be required to properly address these and seek coordination comments from relevant departments of state.

The Cabinet could be better supported by bureaucratic arrangements that focus on bringing views together and exploring integrated solutions to be considered by the government. At the very least, the role of the Department of the Prime Minister and Cabinet could be strengthened by creating an integrated strategy office or unit in that department to authoritatively bring together afresh and on an equal basis the various perspectives and where solutions may lie. It is not enough to just add a security unit in the Department of the Treasury or an economic unit in security or external affairs departments: these units do help their departments understand issues, but they typically reflect the culture and insight of the home department and are not effective in finding integrated solutions. For example, the risk of a security unit in Treasury is that security is just an economic externality for someone else to fix; the risk of an economics unit in foreign and home affairs departments is that economics becomes geonomics, a tool of statecraft and how to use markets as a weapon (which ultimately undermines prosperity). Public servants should be encouraged to move between the security, economic and social policy domains to gain a broader sense of the nation's interests and to have extensive contacts and networks across the bureaucracy and beyond, with business, academia and the not-for-profit sector.

It is worth asking whether the tools of analysis can be improved in informing integrated strategy. Scenario analysis with a wide range of participants is a useful way to frame risk and look for solutions. Singapore stands out an as an example of a country that uses scenario analysis well in informing integrated strategic policy by its Cabinet (Centre for Strategic Futures 2021). These exercises bring insights into the global interplay of forces in the domains of the economy (technological change and the impact of data and digitisation, productivity and economic inclusion), security (the multipolar order, non-conforming nations and proliferation) and society (trust in institutions, belonging and social media). This analytical framework challenges conventional habits of thinking, strengthens connections and relationships between the different domains, and supports integrated strategic thinking.

Consider now how international institutions and frameworks can be strengthened. International cooperation is not an act of national weakness. Speaking from my own experience in G20 and APEC from the Asian financial crisis to the aftermath of the global financial crisis, no country or economy has ever approached those forums with anything but their own national interest and objectives at the heart of everything decided in each forum. What has been apparent in times of international economic and financial stress is that collective action and cooperation is a common interest of countries, and that the individual interest of countries has been served by frameworks, rules and institutions that support well-regulated, transparent and open markets and business. Finding the shared common interest among countries is not an easy exercise.

What does this mean for countries at a time of rising nationalist populism, US–China strategic competition, and the imperative of integrating economic, security and social dimensions of the national interest?

From the outset, it is important for countries that value international rules, frameworks and institutions to structure interaction between countries, and for countries that value open, transparent and competitive markets as the basis of exchange between countries to state and implement their views. There are some great examples of this. Australia (Coorey 2019) has formally reaffirmed the importance of the Bretton Woods institutions. There has been great collective action and leadership by countries across Asia and the Pacific to reform and open up their trade and investment, despite the withdrawal of the US from the Trans-Pacific Partnership in January 2017. These include the Comprehensive and Progressive Agreement for Trans-Pacific Partnership (CPTPP, see Australian Government n.d.-b) signed by 11 countries in December 2018, and the Regional Comprehensive Partnership (RCEP, see Australian Government n.d.-c) agreed by 15 countries in November 2019 for signature into law in 2020. The CPTPP is open to the US (and others), and the RCEP is open to India to join if and when it sees fit. The creation of an interim alternative appellate body (Lordi n.d.) to that of the WTO, with membership from the European Union, China, Indonesia, Canada, Australia (Sampson 2020) and a few others is an important step in supporting rules-based approaches.

These developments are positive and instructive. They show that countries can determine their own destiny, even when circumstances are difficult or change. While the changes in US posture on economic and security relations and the rise in US–China strategic competition really do complicate life, they do not have to stop other countries from doing what they can to strengthen economic rules, open their own markets and broaden their relationship with China. Indonesia, Japan and Australia, among others, are providing leadership in Asia and the Pacific.

These developments provide a good basis to go further and more strategically use regional forums and institutions that include both the US and China. APEC offers some real opportunities.

As mentioned earlier, infrastructure needs across the region are massive, but action is floundering. APEC is a good place for members to set out their individual priority infrastructure needs, commit to (not just note) key guiding principles around transparency and governance, commit to reforming domestic obstacles to infrastructure investment, engage directly with private investors and multilateral lenders, and lift the domestic capacity of developing economies. This agenda addresses a core economic weakness in the region and helps mitigate both economic and security risks.

Think too about the deteriorating global financial safety net, in which financial crisis prevention and mitigation arrangements have not kept pace with rising capital flows and growing economies; liquidity arrangements (such as central bank swaps) have narrowed; and a key supplementary support mechanism, the New Arrangements to Borrow, is set to expire in November 2022 and should be both extended and increased. The key Asian regional mechanism, the ASEAN+3 Chiang Mai Initiative Multilateralization, is too small and difficult to use, and indeed has never been used. A strong safety net is a good idea in its own right, but it also helps ease some of the concerns, whether founded or not, around 'debt trap diplomacy'. With a strong safety net comprising well-governed and representative institutions, countries that have borrowed unsustainably need not fear losing strategic assets. Every irresponsible borrower has an irresponsible lender, and a well-functioning safety net would recognise that giving a haircut to the lender and liquidity support to the borrower allows debt financing to continue sustainably. A well-functioning safety net makes debt trap diplomacy an uneconomical proposition. Historically, APEC finance ministers have not focused on the regional and global safety net, but it is time now to do so, given that the imperative Asia faces is to persuade the US to restore and build the global financial safety net and ensure that regional and global mechanisms work together smoothly. Having a serious conversation in APEC about financial safety nets would be a break from the past and show that Asia is agile and strategic in its use of forums, informed by the past but not bound by the habits of the past.

Drawing on its informal connections with business (APEC Business Advisory Council) and universities (Pacific Economic Cooperation Council, Economic Research Institute for ASEAN and East Asian Bureau of Economic Research) and its own informal style, APEC is a good place for ministers and officials to focus explicitly on ways to deliver prosperity, security and social wellbeing.

Conclusion

The world has changed. The challenge is to think broadly about all the dimensions of the national interest, being explicit about economic, security and social interests, and to identify the range of risks and think creatively, strategically and practically about how to mitigate risk. Silos do not help in thinking about and addressing challenges in a genuinely strategic way. The real art of contemporary public policy is finding ways that deliver the most for prosperity, security and social wellbeing rather than treating them as competing alternatives to be traded off against each other. COVID-19 has only made this approach more compelling and urgent.

In terms of domestic institutional design, it may help to refashion the way executive government approaches the complex problems it faces, with better integrated strategic advice from the administrative parts of government.

In terms of international relations, this is the time for countries to engage rather than withdraw, as the region has done so well in the CPTPP and RCEP trade and investment agreements and in establishing an alternative appellate body for trade disputes. Countries should look for opportunities to work together and with others in the region, and to engage directly and positively with the US and China. The focus here is on practical and mutually beneficial steps to mitigate, rather than exacerbate, US–China strategic competition. There is a lot still to be gained by active bilateral and multilateral engagement.

References

ADB (Asian Development Bank). 2017. *Meeting Asia's Infrastructure Needs*. Philippines: ADB. doi.org/10.22617/FLS168388-2.

Australian Government. 2020. 'Chapter 6: Civil Penalties—Serious or Repeated Interference with Privacy and Other Penalty Provisions'. Office of the Australian Information Commissioner. www.oaic.gov.au/__data/assets/pdf_file/0021/8319/chapter-6-civil-penalties.pdf.

Australian Government. n.d.-a. 'Chapter 9: Deeper and Broader Relationships'. Australia in the Asian Century, White Paper, October 2012. Accessed 6 August 2021. www.eastasiaforum.org/wp-content/uploads/2014/04/chapter-9.pdf.

Australian Government. n.d.-b. 'Comprehensive and Progressive Agreement for Trans-Pacific Partnership (CPTPP)'. Department of Foreign Affairs and Trade. Accessed 8 August 2021. www.dfat.gov.au/trade/agreements/in-force/cptpp/comprehensive-and-progressive-agreement-for-trans-pacific-partnership.

Australian Government. n.d.-c. 'Regional Comprehensive Economic Partnership'. Department of Foreign Affairs and Trade. Accessed 8 August 2021. www.dfat.gov.au/trade/agreements/not-yet-in-force/rcep.

BBC News. 2020. 'Trump Says Coronavirus Worse "Attack" Than Pearl Harbor'. 7 May 2020. www.bbc.com/news/world-us-canada-52568405.

Bochman, A. 2018. 'Internet Insecurity'. *Harvard Business Review*, 15 May 2018. hbr.org/cover-story/2018/05/internet-insecurity.

Camba, A. A. and K. J. Yao. 2018. 'China's Belt and Road Initiative Paved with Risk and Red Herrings'. *East Asia Forum*, 26 June 2018. www.eastasiaforum. org/2018/06/26/chinas-belt-and-road-initiative-paved-with-risk-and-red-herrings/.

Centre for Strategic Futures. 2021. Home Page. Accessed 14 December 2021. www.csf.gov.sg/.

China Power Team. 2017. 'How Will the Belt and Road Initiative Advance China's Interests?' 8 May 2017. chinapower.csis.org/china-belt-and-road-initiative/.

Colford, C. 2016. 'Productivity for Prosperity: "In the Long Run, It Is Almost Everything"'. *World Bank Blogs*, 15 November 2016. blogs.worldbank.org/psd/ productivity-prosperity-long-run-it-almost-everything.

Coorey, P. 2019. 'Unsteady World Must Re-Embrace Bretton-Woods: Frydenberg'. *Australian Financial Review*, 11 November 2019. www.afr.com/politics/federal/ unsteady-world-must-re-embrace-bretton-woods-frydenberg-20191111-p539cn.

Dornbusch, R. 2002. 'A Primer on Emerging-Market Crises'. In *Preventing Currency Crises in Emerging Markets*, edited by Sebastian Edwards and Jeffrey A. Frankel, 743–54. Chicago: University of Chicago Press. doi.org/10.7208/chicago/ 9780226185057.003.0017.

Hamilton, C. 2019. 'China Has a Very Unhealthy Interest in Our Medical Data'. *Australian Financial Review*, 13 January 2019. www.afr.com/opinion/china-has-a-very-unhealthy-interest-in-our-medical-data-20190113-h1a0c7.

Heathcote, C. 2017. 'Forecasting Infrastructure Investment Needs for 50 Countries, 7 Sectors Through 2040'. *World Bank Blogs*, 10 August 2017. blogs.worldbank. org/ppps/forecasting-infrastructure-investment-needs-50-countries-7-sectors-through-2040.

IMF (International Monetary Fund). 2019. *World Economic Outlook, April 2019: Growth Slowdown, Precarious Recovery*. Washington, DC: IMF. doi.org/ 10.5089/9781484397480.081.

IMF (International Monetary Fund). 2020. 'World Economic Outlook. April 2020: The Great Lockdown'. www.imf.org/en/Publications/WEO/Issues/2020/04/14/ weo-april-2020.

Krugman, P. R. 1997. *The Age of Diminished Expectations: US Economic Policy in the 1990s* (3rd edn). Cambridge, MA: MIT Press.

Lordi, J. n.d. 'Appeal by Other Means: The European Union and Other WTO Members Search for Alternatives to the Organization's Paralyzed Appellate Body'. *Michigan Journal of International Law*. Accessed 8 August 2021. www.mjilonline. org/appeal-by-other-means-the-european-union-and-other-wto-members-search-for-alternatives-to-the-organizations-paralyzed-appellate-body/.

Nouwens, M. and H. Legarda. 2018. 'China's Pursuit of Advanced Dual-Use Technologies'. International Institute for Strategic Studies, 18 December 2018. www.iiss.org/blogs/research-paper/2018/12/emerging-technology-dominance.

OECD (Organisation for Economic Co-operation and Development). 2018. 'Main Science and Technology Indicators, Volume 2018 Issue 1'. Accessed 8 August 2021. read.oecd-ilibrary.org/science-and-technology/main-science-and-technology-indicators/volume-2018/issue-1_msti-v2018-1-en#page87.

Prevelakis, V. and D. Spinellis. 2007. 'The Athens Affair: How Some Extremely Smart Hackers Pulled Off the Most Audacious Cell-Network Break-In Ever'. IEEE Spectrum, 29 June 2007. doi.org/10.1109/MSPEC.2007.376605.

Sampson, G. 2020. 'Bypassing Trump's Fake Complaints Paves Way for WTO Renewal'. *Australian Financial Review*, 6 May 2020. www.afr.com/policy/economy/bypassing-trump-s-fake-complaints-paves-way-for-wto-renewal-20200506-p54q6q.

Sterling, B. 2018. 'Estonian Cyber Security'. *Wired*, 1 September 2018. www.wired.com/beyond-the-beyond/2018/01/estonian-cyber-security/.

Tabeta, S. and M. Zhou. 2019. 'China Moves to Shut Spigot on Rare Earths for First Time in 5 Years'. *Nikkei Asia*, 5 June 2019. asia.nikkei.com/Economy/Trade-war/China-moves-to-shut-spigot-on-rare-earths-for-first-time-in-5-years.

Tobar, D. 2018. '7 Considerations for Cyber Risk Management'. Software Engineering Institute, 9 February 2018. insights.sei.cmu.edu/insider-threat/2018/02/7-considerations-for-cyber-risk-management.html.

Voon, T. and A. Mitchell. 2019. 'Australia's Huawei Ban Raises Difficult Questions for the WTO'. *East Asia Forum*, 22 April 2019. www.eastasiaforum.org/2019/04/22/australias-huawei-ban-raises-difficult-questions-for-the-wto/.

Worldometer. 2021. 'COVID-19 Coronavirus Pandemic'. Accessed 8 August 2021. www.worldometers.info/coronavirus/#countries.

WTO (World Trade Organization). n.d. 'DS431: China—Measures Related to the Exportation of Rare Earths, Tungsten and Molybdenum'. Accessed 8 August 2021. www.wto.org/english/tratop_e/dispu_e/cases_e/ds431_e.htm.

3

International rules and strategic policy space

Shiro Armstrong

Background

The United States and China, the world's two largest economies, are locked into strategic competition and rivalry that complicates international policy choices for the rest of the world, but particularly for their partners in Asia. How do smaller countries, middle powers and the rest of the world navigate their economic, political and strategic choices when China and the US are increasingly applying pressure to choose between them? US allies such as Australia, South Korea and Japan need to balance their security interests alongside their economic interests, but are they destined to a prosperity–security trade-off, the parameters of which are fixed independently of their own strategic behaviour?

Economic policy was never separate from considerations of national security. The recipe for a modern, secure country—a strong economy that is globally integrated through trade and investment and cooperation—has not changed. But economics and security are increasingly entangled in a way that may cause damage to both, creating a dangerous trade-off and a negative feedback loop on both economic and security outcomes. There are policy choices that make countries poorer and less secure and there are policy strategies that can help manage risks to prosperity and contribute to national security. This chapter presents a simple framework to think about these policy choices as they relate to international economic exchange and the security policy choices that confront countries in the region. It also explains how multilateral engagement helps manage some of the risks they face by diffusing power and providing forums for collective action by small and middle powers that provide leverage.

Economic exchange always involves risks, including national security risks and the possibility of economic or political coercion. As Deng Xiaoping famously warned, if you open the window for fresh air, you have to expect some flies to blow in. If you want fresh air, the solution is not to close the window but to manage the flies.

Risks from international economic exchange can be managed with strong domestic rules, regulations and institutions. They can also be managed internationally with strong rules, norms and institutions that reduce the number and capabilities of malign actors, including by shifting the risk onto actors with malign intent. That process is strengthened, not weakened, through international cooperation. Risks have been managed and minimised under the US-led, multilateral, rules-based system that allowed decades of deepening economic ties, including for China, with the rest of the world.

The risks of international exchange have come to dominate the calculus of some policymakers as the world becomes more complex and uncertain. There are three main reasons for this trend: the rise of China, the rise in protectionism in the US and new technologies that international rules do not yet encompass. Added to this is the strategic competition between China and the United States and the pandemic-induced recession that complicates policy choices.

The difficulty in managing China's rise as the world's largest trader and its second-largest economy has been further complicated by President Xi's consolidation of power domestically and a more assertive Chinese foreign policy.

The US largely underwrote a rules-based order over the past 75 years that helped manage risks from economic engagement and reduced the costs of national security. President Trump's 'America First' protectionist agenda and the US–China trade war signalled a departure from the US leadership on which the world had long relied. The structural problems that led to the rise of Trump in the US—growth in inequality, the erosion of the social safety net and the social compact, as well as a political psychology triggered by a *relative* decline in US global power—will, in the best of circumstances, take a generation to remedy. The Biden administration is pursuing a foreign policy for the middle class and those problems still drive US policy strategies and its foreign policy posture. The US under Trump became the biggest threat to the multilateral trading system that, for decades, underpinned both prosperity and security around the world, particularly in East Asia. Under Biden it may not be such an active threat to multilateralism. But its diminished relative size and its strategic competition with a rising China—the largest trading partner for most countries in Asia—mean that it is no longer able to play the same leadership role in that system that it once did.

New technologies like AI (artificial intelligence), 5G telecommunications and the growing importance of digital trade raise new economic opportunities and security challenges for which no clear rules exist. Multilateral rules in the World Trade Organization (WTO) may cover trade in goods adequately but are mostly non-existent for a large proportion of international commerce in the twenty-first century, such as services, investment and data flows. The patchwork of rules from smaller agreements that try to cover these issues leave major gaps at best and cause economic fragmentation in the global economy.

If countries do not get the framework right to manage strategic policymaking in these new circumstances, there could be a return to the economic and security policy environment of the interwar period. That was a period of 'beggar-thy-neighbour' policies, unilateralism, trade discrimination and escalating protectionism through the exercise of raw national power. The multilateral system born at Bretton Woods moved the world to cooperative outcomes with rules that avoided these prisoner's dilemma or lose-lose outcomes.

The next section presents a simple framework to understand how the interaction between prosperity and national security—or economics and security for short—can be understood in the international economy. In Chapter 2 of this volume, de Brouwer developed a framework for thinking through domestic policy choices and this chapter explains how multilateralism helps to preserve the external policy space for countries to pursue economic policies that promote both prosperity and security. The starting point is that the pursuit of economic and security objectives is rarely sensibly framed as a zero-sum game in which a nation cannot attain more of one by surrendering certain amounts of the other. It is a multidimensional game in which (not always, but to a significant degree) these objectives are indeed complementary, and in which more of one enhances attainment of the other and mixed interests are common. The chapter concludes by identifying some principles for international cooperation in bilateral, regional and plurilateral arrangements that may contribute to, rather than divert from, the inclusive multilateral rules that underpin economic and political security in the region.

Entanglement of economics and national security

International trade is driven by mutually beneficial trade and investment and its win-win, positive-sum aspects have helped deliver development and prosperity to countries that have participated in opening up their economies. Many of the most successful development stories are in East Asia. International specialisation has allowed higher levels of production and consumption to spread across the region and accelerated growth through production fragmentation in international supply chains.

Regional economies have achieved economic strength through international economic integration; economic strength and the system of multilateral economic ties have also reinforced political independence and security.

The growth of strategic rivalry between the US and China in recent years has encouraged reversion to narrower conceptions of national security or geopolitics characterised by zero-sum, or even negative-sum, thinking (Blackwill and Harris 2016). For one country to gain, it must do so at the expense of another. The Cold War between the US and its allies against the Soviet Union was an earlier example. Strategic rivalry between countries is often framed such that any gain by a strategic competitor registers as a loss for the other. There are also positive-sum elements between countries when one country's stability and security has positive spillovers to others, but usually military security—the contest for territorial control, for example— and great power rivalry is zero-sum.

Under the US-led multilateral economic order, for those countries that had committed to the system even during the Cold War, the conduct of trade policy could, to some extent, be pursued separately from national security considerations (Cooper 1972). Under that system, participants surrendered the right to use trade levers to exercise political coercion, except in special and unusual circumstances. The General Agreement on Tariffs and Trade (GATT) allowed trade between countries under agreed multilateral trade rules that largely quarantined them from geopolitics. There were, of course, economic and political disputes between countries, and some of those disputes led to trade sanctions and political coercion outside the rules, but disputes were generally nested in the multilateral geopolitical order and were the exception, not the rule. Many could be resolved peacefully within the GATT framework. In that way, international economic policy was largely siloed from national security policy. Within its ambit, the US hub-and-spokes security system added to political stability in an environment where multilateral trade rules could manage economic exchange to the benefit of countries that signed up to them.

That was then, while the rules could keep pace with developments in commerce and before the rise of China and other emerging countries meant that the system could no longer be led mostly by one superpower, the US. The system has steadily and fundamentally changed. China joined the GATT's successor, the WTO, in 2001 and grew to become the world's largest trader and the largest trading partner of around 130 countries.

The level of uncertainty about the ability and willingness of the US to lead the multilateral trading system has grown in tandem with these developments. The US withdrew from the 12-member endeavour under the aegis of the Trans-Pacific Partnership (TPP) agreement whose aim was to create new rules, disciplines and market liberalisation in the Asia-Pacific. US non-participation in the TPP evolved as a bipartisan policy position. Under the Trump administration, the US actively undermined the WTO by deploying trade measures and doing deals outside of the established rules (notably, but not only, in its trade war with China), as well as vetoing the appointment of appellate body judges to the dispute settlement system. Many of those policies remain in place under the Biden administration.

In the past half decade, there has also been an eruption of instances of economic coercion. These have led to ideas about the pervasiveness of weaponised interdependence and the mobilisation of the weaponisation of trade—or securitisation of trade—to pursue political goals (Farrell and Newman 2019). US tariffs on imports from China, and sanctions on Chinese companies or US and other companies selling to Chinese companies during the Trump administration, introduced many national security exemptions to multilateral commitments. These measures were outside of established rules and norms and were deployed for political purposes that were responded to tit-for-tat in an array of Chinese measures. Chinese trade sanctions on Australia from 2020 were also deployed for largely political purposes and their legality is yet to be tested in cases brought before the WTO.

The perception of economic exchange between countries as weaponised or giving an adversary leverage turns positive-sum economic exchange into a zero-sum or negative-sum calculus. Economics and national security thinking have thus become entangled in a way that complicates policy choices and that can lead to countries becoming poorer and potentially less secure.

Complementarity of economics and security

The most basic complementarity of economics and security starts with the need for a strong economy to finance a military and defence force. National security includes military security and protecting sovereignty: both are achieved more readily if a nation achieves economic strength. Economic exchange builds national wealth and power and is a source of economic and therefore military strength.

For centuries there has also been a recognition that economic exchange between countries has a peace dividend by increasing the costs of conflict. Montesquieu (1748, Book XX, Chapter 2) argued 'peace is the natural effect of trade' because trade made countries reciprocally dependent. Karl Polanyi famously argued that the 'long peace' in Europe in the nineteenth century was enforced by high finance, which would tolerate no expensive wars that would threaten the fiscal stability of states to which it loaned money and in which it conducted most of its profitable business (Polanyi 1944; Flandreau and Flores 2012). Economic engagement between countries can strengthen national security by reinforcing and habituating adherence to a rules-based order that creates a bigger and broader plurality of interests. Foreign investment creates foreign stakeholders in the health of an economy in which they are invested.

While trade may encourage peace, it can also be a source of conflict. There is 'the possibility of using trade as a means of political pressure ... in the pursuit of power' (Hirschman [1945] 1980, v, xvi). The gains from trade between nations can be unequally distributed within countries as well as between countries, leading to a change in the structure of power within a country and between countries. Economic interdependence can introduce vulnerability in relations with another nation (e.g. through exposure to a dominant resource or strategic goods supplier) and sensitivity to dependence (e.g. through the effect of economic shocks such as inflation or exchange rate volatility in one country on another).[1]

---

1   See Mansfield and Pollins (2001) for a review of this literature on sensitivity and vulnerability.

The multilateral trading system that Hirschman foreshadowed to address these vulnerabilities through trade in 1945 was conceived to help manage these negative externalities from growing trade shares. Its real world manifestation, the GATT, was designed to discourage and constrain the use of trade sanctions for political pressure while the other Bretton Woods institutions were designed to help manage the sensitivity to international economic dependence and manage the change in the structure of power between countries. The multilateral system is protection for small and medium powers: while it reduces the costs of trade coercion to both perpetrator and victim, the reduction is comparatively far greater for the 'victim' nation, which can use the system to find new markets for its imports or exports.

Confidence in the multilateral trading system is fracturing under the pressures unleashed by China, the US and new technologies. Trade and international commerce is once again increasingly seen as a source of vulnerability in relations with other countries. The use of trade as an instrument of political pressure in the way that characterised the interwar period Hirschman described threatens to return (at least in some measure).

Economics and security in a negative feedback loop

Economic policy deployed for national security or geopolitical purposes, sometimes called *geoeconomics*, can make countries weaker, poorer and less secure. Economic exchanges, in this conception of the world, are thought of as tools to achieve zero-sum or negative-sum outcomes instead of creating mutually beneficial economic outcomes. This misdirection can damage both economic and national security outcomes. North Korea is an extreme case in which the pursuit of security objectives through self-sufficiency strategies ignores economic considerations: North Korea has secured itself from vulnerability to economic dependence on other countries, and from sensitivity to economic shocks from other countries, at the cost of prosperity and durable military strength.

Ever since US president Jefferson's *Embargo Act 1807*, which banned trade, sent the newly founded US into a recession with little impact on European powers but threatening its own security, governments have misapplied economic tools in ways that result in self-harm. A recent example is the Trump administration's tariffs on steel, aluminium, washing machines and solar panels, and the tariffs it threatened on automobiles. These measures, justified in the name of national security, would merely make the US poorer and weaker.

China has blatantly deployed economic coercion for geopolitical purposes and its securitisation of trade has also been largely counterproductive. Its restriction of rare earths exports against Japan over territorial disputes was checked by application of the multilateral trade rules and the emergence of alternative suppliers led it to lose market power. Its economic sanctions against South Korea over the Terminal High Altitude Area Defense system, on the other hand, largely lay outside the discipline of multilateral rules. China's economic sanctions against Australian barley, wine and other commodity exports are the most comprehensive and glaring Chinese attempts so far at economic coercion. But these measures have not been without cost to China, as they increased Chinese costs and prices and undermined confidence in Chinese trade because of significant changes in the political risk calculus for businesses. Nor did China's coercive measures lead to political capitulation by South Korea or Australia.

New technologies have also multiplied security concerns about 'weaponised interdependence'. Economic network risks are being exploited by both state and non-state actors with cyber theft and cyber attacks. The US domination of the inter-bank exchange market (SWIFT), for example, meant that Europe had to comply with unilateral US sanctions against Iran. Yet arguments that technology is providing asymmetric leverage ignore the fact that technology is also increasing the supply of alternatives and making markets more contestable. To the extent that nations exploit their current technological advantages, those advantages will not last long if they do not remain open and connected to new ideas.

National security relies on the logic of command and control and applying resources in contests of attrition. That is not how economies work. A focus on security risks without considering forgone economic benefit or mitigation strategies to deal with those risks leads to all-or-nothing outcomes when all-or-nothing outcomes are not the only option—in the language of economics—to corner solutions when the utility-maximising solutions are interior ones. Concern about foreign influence over technology has led the US and some of its allies to decouple from Chinese technologies, such as 5G telecommunications, AI, machine learning and quantum computing. Such disengagement can damage national security, not only in areas where China already has technologies that are more advanced than the rest of the world.

Innovation in the modern economy means working with ideas from wherever they are sourced around the world. There is no other way of staying close to the global technology frontier. An inability to keep up with the technological frontier will make countries poorer and reduce the strategic options available to them.

If trade and investment is not managed with robust domestic regulation and international rules, positive-sum economic exchange may indeed become zero-sum or negative-sum games. If domestic rules and institutions are unable to regulate foreign investment, the risks that come from allowing foreign ownership of economic and strategic assets might outweigh the economic benefit from the investment. Foreign ownership of an asset that includes health and other sensitive data, for example, would need strong laws, credible enforcement and punishment, and capability to police those laws. In the case of data assets, it is often not the ownership of the asset that is the fulcrum of risk, but the cyber security surrounding that asset (see Chapter 2). Without the capacity and effort to identify the risks and regulate appropriately, perceptions of risk may too easily outweigh the potential benefit of trade and investment transactions and the benefit from them will be foregone.

The direct economic benefit from a foreign investment and its positive externalities, including its peace dividend, will be forgone because of the negative externality of risk to national security. With proper domestic rules and regulations, however, the security and other risks can be readily mitigated.

Multilateralism and preserving policy options

Domestic rules and institutions help manage some of the risks from malign actors and actions in international economic exchange. Enforceable international rules and trusted norms in a multilateral trading system that help diffuse economic and political power are an essential complement in the national armoury of smaller powers in managing these risks.

Multilateralism requires that participating nations cede political power and sovereignty and binds them to principles of equal treatment in international transactions. Countries have been prepared to cede this power to avoid more costly beggar-thy-neighbour prisoner's dilemma behaviour and trade outcomes. The GATT was created to avoid these outcomes that were pervasive in the 1930s. Under a well-functioning multilateral trading system, countries inoculate themselves against their own protectionist or nationalist instincts and constrain their own ability to deploy unilateral and discriminatory measures against partners. Trade and international economic policy can be protected from the vagaries of protectionist and politically motivated policies—whether for geopolitical or domestic reasons—if societies are able to maintain domestic support for international economic policies. Trumpism in the US and Brexit have shown that policies and institutions that share the gains from globalisation and the maintenance of a robust social safety net are critical.

The economic principle of most favoured nation treatment has a vital political dimension. Agreement to an economic equality principle in multilateral rules surrenders some of the particular political leverage that might otherwise be available to countries, especially big countries.

An open multilateral trading system is also a source of resilience for countries hit by shocks. Australia managed to cushion the economic damage from Chinese trade sanctions in 2020 and 2021 by expanding trade with other countries. Japan was able to source rare earth imports from countries other than China when security of supply from China was uncertain, as international supplies responded to the increased price. A virtue of an open international trading system is that it allows markets to adjust to supply and demand disruptions whether from deliberate policies, natural disasters or business cycles, because of the geographic contestability that it embeds in the trading system.

The weaknesses in the multilateral trading system—the gaps in rules and the difficulty of reforming the WTO—have opened up grievances and provided the excuse for its abuse by the major powers, especially the US and China. Their Phase One trade deal in 2019 was done outside the established rules and moved the two countries towards managed trade—that is, trade determined by negotiated quotas instead of by market forces.

There are no multilateral rules and there is no WTO for foreign direct investment. The negative security externalities from foreign investment are currently managed by countries unilaterally by domestic law or to some extent in bilateral or regional agreements; consequently, the burden of managing foreign investment falls heavily on domestic regulation.

In countries where governance is weak, there are often insufficient protections from multinational enterprises that avoid tax, exploit weak labour and environmental standards, and pose security risks in ownership of critical infrastructure and sensitive data. Combined with new digital technologies that also lack governance under multilateral rules, there is a lot of pressure on the capacity of governments to manage foreign investment confidently in particular industries or from particular sources.

International rules can prohibit harmful behaviour. A priority is to work towards the creation of international rules in areas of importance to the international economy where no such rules currently exist. Strategic deployment of regional and plurilateral coalitions can help create rules from the bottom up and support multilateral processes. They have a greater chance of being effective and successful if they engage both China and the US. At a time when the multilateral system is under threat, regional and plurilateral initiatives and agreements need to complement, preserve and strengthen multilateralism, not substitute for it. The proliferation of bilateral and regional agreements are creating new rules in areas like the digital economy, but where multilateral principles are lacking, there is the risk of the fragmentation of rules that seriously detract from multilateral outcomes.

Mutually beneficial engagement makes nations more prosperous. If the security risks are managed, the engagement can also make countries safer and more secure. But without rules of engagement, the security risks can easily dominate or be exploited, compromising both economic and political security goals.

It is possible to find ways to mitigate and spread risks by deepening engagement and by strengthening and extending the rules, not avoiding engagement. Economic engagement builds national wealth and power and, when combined with multilateral rules, broadens the range of strategic policy options available to policymakers. This is what ASEAN helps preserve for its Southeast Asian members, as this book describes. There are solutions, mixed interest games and ways to have risks borne in the market rather than by government or society that can avoid binary all-or-nothing security choices.

Conclusion

Economic engagement and integration into markets increases the costs of harmful international behaviour and enhances national security, but inevitably involves some security risk. If security concerns and policies dominate economic choices, the policy space is narrowed significantly. It is the important job of security agencies to look for and mitigate risks, but economic interests also need to be balanced. Risks can be mitigated through a combination of international cooperation, multilateral rules and strong domestic laws. International rules need to be negotiated and agreed to, as imposing rules on countries will not sustain. ASEAN and East Asia's steady success in economic cooperation, which has come from taking time to forge consensus, has shown to be an effective approach compared to other regions where economic openness appears in retreat.

Reducing trade or investment to avoid security risks is not the right answer in a world of integrated markets and economies, unless countries want to be poorer, weaker, and live in a less certain and stable world. These are shared challenges and opportunities for countries navigating a more complex world.

Large powers, like the US and China, naturally prefer to deal with countries bilaterally where the asymmetry of their power offers most leverage. That forces the world into even harder choices. The US and China, left to their own devices, may try to decouple their economies and divide the global economy into two spheres. They are big and influential players in the system but the response of the rest of the world to their behaviour will be important to the outcome.

Small and middle powers need to get the balance of economics and security right in strategic policymaking and work together to avoid a big power dominated, bilateral world of zero-sum outcomes. Acting strategically and not falling into bilateralism is for them the sensible way forward. Agreements that support, and do not detract from, multilateral outcomes will help to preserve and expand policy options for countries in the region and make them better off economically and more secure, instead of poorer, weaker and less secure.

References

Blackwill, R. D. and J. M. Harris. 2016. *War by Other Means: Geoeconomics and Statecraft*. Cambridge, MA: Harvard University Press. doi.org/10.4159/9780674545960.

Cooper, R. N. 1972. 'Trade Policy Is Foreign Policy'. *Foreign Policy*, no. 9 (Winter): 18–36. doi.org/10.2307/1148083.

Farrell, H. L. and A. L. Newman. 2019. 'Weaponized Interdependence: How Global Economic Networks Shape State Coercion'. *International Security* 44 (1): 42–79. doi.org/10.1162/isec_a_00351.

Flandreau, M. and J. H. Flores. 2012. 'The Peaceful Conspiracy: Bond Markets and International Relations during the Pax Britannica'. *International Organization* 66 (2): 211–41. doi.org/10.1017/S0020818312000070.

Hirschman, A. O. (1945) 1980. *National Power and the Structure of Foreign Trade*. Berkeley: University of California Press.

Mansfield, E. D. and B. M. Pollins. 2001. 'The Study of Interdependence and Conflict: Recent Advances, Open Questions, and Directions for Future Research'. *Journal of Conflict Resolution* 45 (6): 834–59. doi.org/10.1177/0022002701045006007.

Montesquieu, C. 1748 [1989]. 'Spirit of the Laws'. In *Cambridge Texts in the History of Political Thought*, edited by A. M. Cohler, B. C. Miller and H. S. Stone, 337–53. Cambridge: Cambridge University Press.

Polanyi, K. 1944. *The Great Transformation*. Boston: Beacon Press.

4

Complex trade-offs: Economic openness and security in Australia

Adam Triggs and Peter Drysdale

Introduction

The challenging global environment has wedged Australia into a difficult position over its economic and strategic choices. Australia's prosperity is underpinned by its openness. More than a fifth of Australia's GDP comes from trade (World Bank 2020), two-thirds of its population growth comes from immigration (Kehoe 2020) and its A$4 trillion stock of foreign investment has underpinned the growth of Australia's living standards (Australian Government 2020c). Australia relies on the multilateral rules-based system for its global influence and its international economic engagement. Its largest trading partner is China, seven of its top 10 trading partners are in Asia (Australian Government 2020b), while its alliance with the United States is accepted on all sides of politics as the cornerstone of Australia's defence strategy.

These features of its external relations have served Australia well. But the COVID-19 pandemic, tensions with China, tensions between the US and China, attacks on multilateral institutions and the growing globalisation backlash are putting it under increased strain. Declines in trade, investment and immigration have weakened the foundations of Australia's prosperity. Attacks on the global rules-based system have weakened Australia's influence and increased global uncertainty. There is growing distrust of China among increasingly influential figures in Australia's political system, media and think tanks, spiked by China's actions in Xinjiang, Hong Kong, Taiwan, the South China Sea and claims by both sides of political interference in domestic affairs, and this distrust has strained the Australia–China relationship. Australia's relationship with the US has been made more problematic by the former Trump administration's undermining of global institutions, its threats of tariffs on Australian steel and aluminium, the diversion of trade away from Australia by the US–China trade deal, threats to break a politically important refugee resettlement deal agreed by President Obama and the Trump administration's escalation of anti-China actions and Cold War rhetoric. While the election of President Biden has moderated some of these pressures, Trump was no accident. The underlying forces that led to the election of President Trump have not gone away and are reflected in the new administration's policy approach. In some areas, particularly following the COVID-19 pandemic, they have worsened.

These tensions have forced Australian policymakers to ask themselves where Australia's security comes from and how it can be strengthened. It is a question that, until recently, had largely been taken for granted. The complex global environment, and Australia's conflicting and evolving interests within it, has produced divergent views between Australia's business community, trade unions, think tanks, media outlets, academics, civil society and general public on how best to respond. These divergent views across Australian society are reflected in Australia's parliament and Australia's government, which are struggling to articulate a consistent approach in this challenging new world.

An increasingly influential narrative is emerging in Australia that economic openness makes the country less secure and that Australia's security can only be bolstered through economic self-reliance, increased military spending and a deepening of Australia's alliance with the US to the exclusion of relations with other nations, notably China. Those advocating this world view argue that Australia should be substantially less open than it is. International economic relationships should be minimised to enhance Australia's security. Any international economic relationships that we do have, the argument runs, should be with trusted allies. Some have advocated a reorientating of Australia's trading relationships away from China and Asia towards the Five Eyes intelligence sharing countries: Canada, New Zealand, the United Kingdom and the United States.

A less open and more self-reliant Australia is not easily distinguishable in outcome from an Australia that is less reliant on China because it is not an ally. China is the world's second-largest economy; it is larger than the US economy in purchasing power parity terms and on a trajectory to be the largest in market exchange rate terms as well. As the world's largest trader, it is Australia's largest trading partner and that of most of the rest of the world through deep integration and complex supply chains. Economic distancing from China is economic distancing from the world.

The argument for self-reliance is not universal in Australia, but is becoming more widespread. It is an argument that does not withstand close scrutiny, but it raises big policy problems that need to be dealt with. This view of Australia's security is not consistent with Australia's lived experience. It is a world view that is based on a fundamental misunderstanding of how Australia's markets work, a misunderstanding of the role of Australia's domestic policies and institutions and, most importantly, the oversimplified proposition that Australia's economic prosperity, liberty and international integration can be traded off for more security. The arguments that underpin this world view are often inconsistent, anecdotal and based on implausible economic counterfactuals.

This chapter explores the global economic and strategic context Australia faces, how international tensions have shaped the public discourse in Australia, the views of different groups in Australia on how these tensions should be managed and their influence on policy decisions, and how the Australian Government is managing a difficult global environment. The chapter proposes a new framework for thinking about Australia's security, recognising the ways in which Australia's openness is a source of security and how the downside risks that can arise from Australia's openness can be managed through carefully designed domestic frameworks, policies and institutions and a new direction in international diplomacy. The key is to manage the risks from Australia's openness, not to avoid them.

Australia in a global context

Australia's story since the end of World War II is one of radical transition. It went from being one of the most closed, inward-looking, protectionist economies in the world to being one of its more open. Australia adopted a new growth model. It threw out the protectionist, inward-looking, import-substituting policies of the past and replaced them with a growth strategy based on economic reform, open regionalism and integration with Asia (Garnaut 2001).

In the last third of the twentieth century, Australia's tariffs were cut and replaced with openness to the trade in goods and services. Financial restrictions were removed, opening the economy to global capital flows. The Australian currency was floated, buttressing the economy from future regional and global crises. Australia's so-called White Australia policy was scrapped and replaced with one of the largest and diverse immigration programs in the world (Garnaut 2001).

Today's Australia bears little resemblance to these features of its past. It is now a substantial trading nation. Trade allowed Australia to specialise. The country now earns more than a fifth of its GDP exporting goods and services to the world, with strong comparative advantage in the export of mining and resource goods, agricultural produce, education and professional services. Australia imports vital goods and services that have dramatically reduced the cost of living for Australians and that often underpin the competitiveness of many of its exports, such as mining equipment and digital technologies. This specialisation brought about by trade underpinned Australia's productivity growth. It saw sharp falls in the cost of living for the poorest Australians (Australian Government 2018) and delivered the longest period of uninterrupted growth in modern history. Much of Australia's trade liberalisation in the postwar period was done unilaterally, not as part of any international agreement (Corden 2017).

Although the reforms that underpinned this transition were implemented by governments, the outcomes were market-led (Garnaut 2001). Australian businesses and households responded to international prices and established a trade profile for Australia that, unsurprisingly to trade economists, concentrated on the region in which Australia was located and the region that contained the countries that needed the things Australia produced: Asia. Seven of Australia's top 10 trading partners are in Asia. Australia's biggest trading partner, China, accounted for 38 per cent of Australia's exports in 2019, and 48.8 per cent in the second quarter of 2020, far more than our second-largest trading partner, Japan, at 16 per cent (Australian Government 2020b).

Australia's openness is not limited to trade. Australia has historically been a capital importing country, running persistent and substantial current account deficits that, at times, have exceeded 7 per cent of GDP—large by international standards (Debelle 2019). Australian households, businesses and governments import savings because they do not save enough to finance the amount of investment needed to sustain Australia's high standards of living and relatively high population growth. On average, Australia comes up short by almost A\$60 billion annually.[1] Australia's openness to global financial markets has allowed its governments, firms and households to borrow the shortfall, allowing them to save less, utilise foreign know-how, consume more and enjoy lower interest rates that, in turn, have spurred investment and higher standards of living. The total stock of foreign investment in Australia is almost A\$4 trillion (Australian Government 2020c). These investments have allowed projects to commence and companies to form that otherwise would not have been able to do so. More than one in four of the biggest employing businesses in Australia have more than 50 per cent foreign ownership. Foreign investment from the European Union, United States and Canada alone contributed to employing around 676,000 Australians in 2015 (Australian Government 2018).

Australia's markets and economy changed dramatically after opening to the world and so too did its people. Almost a third of the people living in Australia in 2019 were born overseas. Those born in the UK make up the largest share at 3.9 per cent of Australia's total population. But the majority of those born from overseas are from Asian countries, predominantly China (2.7 per cent), India (2.6 per cent) and New Zealand (2.2 per cent), but also the Philippines (1.2 per cent), Vietnam (1 per cent), Malaysia (0.7 per cent) and Sri Lanka (0.6 per cent) (Australian Bureau of Statistics 2020).

Many come to Australia for its universities. Australia's openness to international students has seen education become Australia's third-largest export, substantially increasing the resources available to domestic students. International study in Australia provides one route to permanent residency and citizenship. Tourism and business travel have similarly underpinned growth and job creation, particularly in some of Australia's smaller cities and towns, like Cairns, in Far North Queensland, and Alice Springs, near Uluru, in Central Australia.

---

1   Average current account deficit since 2000: IMF World Economic Outlook Database, October 2019.

Discussion of Australia's defence and security arrangements commonly begins with a reference to Australia's historical links to Britain and our defence treaty with the US after WWII. Australia remains part of the British Commonwealth with the Queen as its formal head of state. Despite these constitutional links, Australia's economic and political relationship with the UK is small. Australia's two-way trade with the UK is less than one-tenth that of Australia's two-way trade with China (Australian Government 2020b). The UK remains a significant source of immigration for Australia, but it is the US that is repeatedly referred to as Australia's most important alliance partner.

Australia's security treaty with the US, the ANZUS Treaty (Australia, New Zealand and United States Security Treaty), was signed in 1951. The treaty commits its signatories to 'consult together' and 'act to meet the common danger'. Specifically, Article 4 states:

> Each Party recognizes that an armed attack in the Pacific Area on any of the Parties would be dangerous to its own peace and safety and declares that it would act to meet the common danger in accordance with its constitutional processes (Parliament of Australia. n.d.).

The ANZUS Treaty has been invoked only once: by Australian prime minister John Howard in the aftermath of the September 11 terrorist attacks in the US. The treaty is commonly referred to as the cornerstone of Australia's defence policy. Australia's then foreign minister, Julie Bishop, summarised the treaty by saying that 'at the heart of the treaty is a commitment to come to one another's aid in the worst of times' (ABC News 2014). Most international experts suggest that the commitments contained in the treaty are more ambiguous than that. Hugh White at The Australian National University, a former senior defence department official and adviser to Labor prime minister Bob Hawke, suggests there are many ambiguities about what 'act' means, noting that 'it doesn't necessarily mean military action' (ABC News 2014).

Despite its important bilateral relationships, Australia's international engagement is primarily through multilateral frameworks. Australia is a member of the G20, Asia-Pacific Economic Cooperation (APEC), Pacific Islands Forum and East Asia Summit, and interacts with the Association of Southeast Asian Nations (ASEAN) through the expanded ASEAN+6 grouping. Australia has 14 free trade agreements and is a signatory to the Comprehensive and Progressive Agreement for Trans-Pacific Partnership and Regional Comprehensive Partnership (Australian Government 2020a), but Australia fundamentally relies on the multilateral framework of the World Trade Organization (WTO) to secure its trading interests, including dispute settlement. Australia has bilateral investment treaties and currency swap lines but is fundamentally reliant on the global rules, institutions and systems in the international financial architecture. Further, despite its own domestic military capabilities, Australia relies on coalitions within bilateral, regional and global security arrangements and institutions. 'The exercise of military force in its own right is not beyond [Australia]' noted Allan Gyngell, former head of Australia's peak intelligence body, the Office of National Intelligence. 'Still, in the places where Australia has used military power most effectively in recent decades … we have always had to work in coalition with others' (Gyngell 2019).

Australia in a challenging global environment

This snapshot of Australia's international engagement offers insights into how the new and challenging global environment has created difficulties for Australia in recent times. Growing tensions between the US and China have put Australia in a tough spot. On the one hand, China is Australia's largest trading partner in both imports and exports. Trade with China amounts to 8 per cent of Australian GDP and is an important source of revenue for Australia's federal government and many state governments. China plays a particularly important role in sectors such as mining, agriculture, education and tourism and there are strong links between its peoples: more than 1.2 million Australians have Chinese ancestry (Australian Bureau of Statistics 2020). Australia's future prosperity is in no small part entwined with that of China—a growing challenge as China's changing economy sees a shift in demand away from mining resources towards services and other imports that have more substitutes and for which there is more international competition.

On the other hand, the US is the 'cornerstone of Australia's defence policy', according to Australia's former foreign minister (ABC News 2014). Australia has fought alongside the US in every conflict that the US has been involved in since World War I. There is a longstanding bipartisan understanding in Australian politics that the US is Australia's most important ally (Collinson 2019). Australia houses US military and intelligence bases within its borders, shares intelligence and participates alongside the US in joint military exercises, including some in the South China Sea.

The incentives of Australia and the US became less closely aligned after the election of President Trump in 2016, although these pressures have moderated since the election of President Biden. The US–China Phase One trade deal diverted agricultural trade away from Australia, hurting Australia's farmers and agricultural sector. Former president Trump's attacks on the WTO and its dispute settlement mechanism weakened the global trading system that Australia relies upon for its prosperity. Trump's withdrawal from the World Health Organization and Paris Climate Accord, and his at times unconstructive engagement in the G20, APEC and East Asia Summit have all weakened cooperation in the multilateral forums Australia relies upon for its international engagement and influence. Bilateral tensions have also increased. President Trump threatened tariffs on Australian steel and other Australian exports, and also threatened to break a politically important refugee resettlement deal agreed with Australia under the Obama administration. There are reliable reports suggesting that Australia faced significant pressure from the US in its decisions on Huawei and 5G (Kehoe 2018), the Asian Infrastructure Investment Bank (Australian Institute for International Affairs 2014) and the Belt and Road Initiative (Murray-Atfield 2020). Many of the measures used against China by the Trump administration remain in place under the Biden administration.

The incentives of Australia and China have similarly become less closely aligned as China has become more assertive in global and domestic affairs. The Australian Government has objected strongly to the Chinese Government's human rights abuses of Uighurs in Xinjiang (SBS News 2019); raised concerns over China's actions towards Hong Kong and Taiwan (Tudge and Morrison 2020); opposed China's militarisation of the South China Sea and formally rejected China's legal claims to disputed islands there (Rothwell 2020). The Australian Government has raised concerns around the governance of institutions (Murphy 2015); criticised the Belt and Road Initiative (Towell, Galloway and Fowler 2020); and accused China of meddling in Australian domestic affairs through interference in its domestic politics (see below), cyber warfare and interference with Australian–Chinese citizens. Australia pre-empted other countries in calling for an international investigation into the origins of COVID-19. China has since advised its tourists and students not to travel to Australia out of fear of racial abuse and imposed trade restrictions on Australian barley and beef. Australia has cautioned its citizens travelling to China about arbitrary legal process.

A more closed Australia, whether the result of international or domestic failures, poses significant challenges for the nation. Exports contribute more than a fifth of Australia's GDP and are linked to more than 1.5 million Australian jobs. Some suggest (Hanson 2020) that domestic demand could fill the gap through a national 'Buy Australian' campaign—either through a change in consumer preferences (while 61 per cent of Australians say they would pay more for Australian-made products, the data suggest the number that actually do is much smaller) (MYOB Team 2019), or through government intervention in the form of trade restrictions. The data show this is not realistic. More than 70 per cent of Australia's agricultural production is exported. More than 25 per cent of its tourism industry relies on international tourists and 35 per cent of university income derives from international students—to say nothing of the extremely high export dependence of its mining industry, three-quarters of which goes to overseas markets, importantly China. The only way domestic demand could absorb this enormous excess supply would be through a substantial collapse in prices, sending the vast majority of Australia's farmers, tourism operators, universities and mining companies into bankruptcy.

The 'Buy Australian' argument is unrealistic, given the challenges facing poorer Australians who would be most severely affected by abandoning trade. For these Australians, trade has dramatically reduced the cost of living. Compared to a decade earlier, audiovisual and computing equipment is 72 per cent cheaper, cars are 12 per cent cheaper, toys and games are 18 per cent cheaper and clothes are 14 per cent cheaper (Australian Government 2018). The adverse impact on poorer Australians from a retreat from trade would be significant.

The 'Buy Australian' view is inconsistent with the core economic principles of trade. Trade allows Australia to specialise—a process that has underpinned the reallocation of resources in the Australian economy, boosting productivity and living standards. If Australia ceases to import goods and services from overseas, those goods and services must be produced in Australia. This means diverting labour, capital, energy and materials away from producing the things that earn Australia the most money overseas so that those resources can instead be used to make the things that we previously imported— things that, by definition, cannot be produced efficiently since they were previously imported. The consequence is a substantial reduction in living standards, productivity and GDP growth.

Trade is similarly vital to Australia's innovation and competition. Australian businesses that actively innovate are more than twice as likely to be exporters as businesses that do not (Australian Government 2018). This is not a coincidence: a closed Australia is a less innovative Australia. Competition creates innovation. Trade in education and tourism are just as vital to Australia's commercial links, international image and influence overseas as they are to its economy: Indonesia's former vice-president, trade minister and finance minister all studied in Australia, for example.

Foreign investment is no different. Without direct foreign investment, the A$60 billion Australia normally borrows annually in all forms abroad would need to come from households, firms and governments through reduced consumption, increased savings and higher interest rates that would reduce investment as well as productivity. Similarly, population growth has accounted for most of Australia's economic growth in recent years, two-thirds of which has come from immigration. A continued reduction in immigration after the COVID-19 pandemic would leave a substantial gap to be filled.

Evolving views and attitudes in Australia

These global challenges have seen divergent views emerge between different parts of Australian society in thinking about openness, particularly in the context of China and the US.

Coverage of China in the Australian media has doubled since 2018 (Streem 2020) and has been overwhelmingly negative (Hu 2020), focused on human rights, foreign interference, espionage and the treatment of Uighurs. Google news searches for 'China' in 2020 are triple the stable average from 2015 to 2018 (Google Trends 2020). Influential individuals within the media and think tanks have advocated distancing from China. They have called on the government to take a more assertive approach towards China and to deepen strategic and economic ties with the US. Australia's openness and links with China are seen as a source of risk, resulting in calls for increased self-reliance, reduced trade and reduced investment links with China. There is a view that economic openness, to the extent that it is required, should centre on countries with which Australia has a security alliance.

Chris Uhlmann, political editor for Australia's second highest rating news program, *Nine News*, has been among the most outspoken critics of China. He describes China as 'a paranoid and increasingly aggressive totalitarian regime that reflexively lies, controls all media, persecutes and jails its domestic critics and threatens the few nations that challenge it with retribution' (Uhlmann 2020). Uhlmann is critical of Australia's economic links with China. 'Australia's business captains and university chiefs have shown they can't handle the truth', he said:

> As long as the rivers of gold flowed, they were happy to urge silence in the face of the militarisation of the South China Sea, industrial-scale cyber theft, the arbitrary arrest of our citizens, rampant foreign interference and the imprisonment of a million Uighurs in Xinjiang (Uhlmann 2020).

The Australian Strategic Policy Institute (ASPI) has been described in the Australian media as 'the think tank behind Australia's changing view of China' (Robin 2020). ASPI is a defence and strategic policy think tank founded by the Australian Government and now funded by the Australian Department of Defence and the defence industry, including major international firms such as Lockheed Martin (ASPI 2022, 21). ASPI has been a strong advocate for Australia to take a hawkish approach to China. Its executive director, Peter Jennings, warns that 'Xi Jinping has cemented his country's path toward becoming a more aggressive, highly nationalistic, military power', and that 'China quite explicitly wants to supplant the US as the prime manager of security in the Indo-Pacific'. Jennings notes that 'the biggest challenge for Australian governments is how to manage the huge risk of being overly dependent on a state whose strategic trajectory fundamentally compromises [Australia's] deepest national security interests'. He advocates a decoupling of Australia from China, noting that 'the Communist party demands a style of supine fealty to their political dominance that cannot be squared with Australian democracy and values' (Jennings 2020). ASPI has been singled out by the Chinese Government 'for spearheading anti-China forces and fabricating various anti-China issues' in Australia, a claim that ASPI rejects (*Global Times* 2020).

The Australian business community has been cautious about damaging the relationship with China, given its importance to the Australian economy. At the same time, they are critical of the damage being inflicted on the global trading system (and multilateralism more generally) by the Trump administration. Jennifer Westacott, the head of the Business Council of

Australia, noted that, 'in China, we have our biggest trading partner. The simple reality is we can't afford not to trade with China' (Westacott 2020). Fiona Simpson, president of the National Farmers' Federation, notes that:

> We must remain being a strong global citizen and at the same time grow our international relationships with China and other countries to overcome inevitable differences that occur in the geo-political arena (Simpson 2020).

The academic community holds a range of opinions but has typically been wary of damaging the relationship with China. Universities are beneficiaries of the Australia–China relationship, given the importance of international students, the majority of whom come from China, and there are increasingly strong research links with Chinese universities. The academic community has tended to be a stronger advocate for multilateralism and globalism, and has advocated increased engagement with the Asian region, particularly ASEAN countries, and global and regional forums to better manage growing tensions with, and between, the US and China (ABER 2020).

Civil society, human rights groups and many in the media have expressed significant concern about government actions in both China and the US. On China, their concerns centre on its actions in Hong Kong, Tibet and Taiwan, its treatment of Uighurs in Xinjiang and its growing surveillance and crackdown on dissent. On the US, their concerns centre on the government's response to the COVID-19 pandemic and treatment of African Americans, Muslim and Jewish Americans, refugees and migrants, the LGBT community and women.

Australians remain positive about their country's openness. Seventy per cent of Australians believe globalisation is mostly good for Australia (Lowy Institute 2020b). Seventy-five per cent believe trade is good for their living standards (Lowy Institute 2020c). A majority of Australians think immigration is about right (or if anything too low) and the current number of international students is about right (Lowy Institute 2020e).

Attitudes have shifted, however, when it comes to particular countries (Lowy Institute 2020e). The attitudes of Australians on Australia's openness vary considerably depending on which country Australia is open to. When asked 'how much do you trust the following countries to act responsibly in the world?', the percentage saying 'somewhat' or 'a great deal' in relation to China has fallen from 60 per cent in 2006 to 23 per cent in 2020 (Lowy Institute 2020d). It has also fallen for the US, but by a smaller margin:

from 60 per cent in 2006 to 51 per cent in 2020 (Lowy Institute 2020d). An overwhelming majority of Australians support 'working to find other markets for Australia to reduce our economic dependence on China' (93 per cent) and 'imposing travel and financial sanctions on Chinese officials associated with human rights abuses' (82 per cent). Few Australians support 'allowing Chinese companies to supply technology for critical infrastructure in Australia' (39 per cent) or 'conducting joint military exercises with China' (39 per cent). A majority believe there is too much Chinese investment in Australia (Lowy Institute 2020a). Attitudes towards the US have also hardened. When asked 'how important is our alliance relationship with the United States for Australia's security?', 78 per cent of Australians believed it was 'important' or 'very important', down from an average of 83 per cent during Barack Obama's presidency (Seymour 2019). Around 70 per cent of Australians had either 'none' or 'not very much' confidence that President Trump would do the right thing regarding world affairs. For President Xi, it was 77 per cent (Lowy Institute 2020f).

In a global context, the attitudes of Australians towards trade, foreign investment, immigration, and economic openness more generally are more positive compared to many other developed economies. The attitudes towards economic openness are consistently higher in Australia than in the United States, United Kingdom and Europe. At the same time, there are clearly differing and evolving views among Australia's business community, trade unions, think tanks, media outlets, academics, civil society and in the general public about how to respond to the current challenging global environment. These views are reflected in Australia's parliament and Australia's government.

Several backbenchers[2] within the governing Liberal Party—National Party Coalition publicly advocate a more aggressive stance towards China. The head of the Commonwealth parliament's intelligence committee, Andrew Hastie, compared China's rise to that of Nazi Germany, warning that, 'like the French [in World War II], Australia has failed to see how mobile our authoritarian neighbour has become' (Hastie 2019). Senator James Paterson and Andrew Hastie were both denied visas to China after speaking in this vein about the mass internment of Muslims in western China. A group of parliamentarians, including Liberal Party members of parliament Andrew Hastie and Tim Wilson, Liberal Party Senator James Paterson and Labor

---

2   A 'backbencher' is a member of parliament who is neither a minister in the government nor a shadow minister in the opposition.

Party Senator Kimberley Kitching, have stickers on their office doors depicting wolf claw marks, and brand themselves the 'Wolverines' after an American high school group who fought off a Soviet invasion in the 1984 film *Red Dawn*. Members of this group proclaim they are pushing back against Chinese influence in Australia (Moore 2020).

The response of the Australian Government has been mixed and cautious, certainly more cautious than some of those in Australia's parliament. It is difficult to characterise the Australian Government's response to the challenges in the global environment as being consistent. This is partly due to the tenuousness of Australia's political leadership in recent years— Australia's prime minister has changed six times since 2007 and each has taken a different approach to international issues, on the conservative side hobbled by the extreme right because of a precarious majority in parliament—but it also reflects the growing divergence of views across society, parliament and the government on how best to manage these global challenges, particularly the relationship with China.

Australia initially declined to join the Asian Infrastructure Investment Bank under Prime Minister Abbott in 2013, only to join at the last minute in 2015. Australia's second-largest state, Victoria, signed a memorandum of understanding (MOU) with China as part of its Belt and Road Initiative despite the Australian Government's refusing to do the same.

The Australian Government has stated that it will consider proposed Belt and Road projects on a case by case basis in third countries, but senior government ministers have simultaneously criticised the Victorian Government for its work with China. A senior minister in the federal government, Peter Dutton, described the Belt and Road Initiative as 'a propaganda initiative from China' that brings 'an enormous amount of foreign interference'. Senator James Patterson accused Victoria of undermining the Australian Government's response to China in the COVID-19 crisis (Taylor 2020). The Australian Government introduced legislation to annul Victoria's MOU under Commonwealth foreign affairs powers, asserting its authority over agreements with foreign state entities. The Chinese Government responded by suspending high level economic dialogues with Australia.

Similar contradictions can be seen in trade. The China–Australia Free Trade Agreement entered into force in December 2015. Its impact was positive. Under the agreement there was significant liberalisation of access to the Chinese market for agricultural commodities and a large surge in bilateral trade growth (Australian Government 2019). Since then, Australia has imposed a raft of anti-dumping duties against Chinese steel and China has imposed various trade restrictions against Australian beef, barley, wine and other exports (Armstrong 2020). Nonetheless, the growth of trade under the agreement has lifted the Australia–China trade share sharply, with China accounting for 38 per cent of Australian exports in 2019 and that share jumping to 48 per cent in June 2020 in the middle on the COVID-19 economic crisis (Cranston 2020b). On investment, Australia's then prime minister, Malcolm Turnbull, stated that 'Australia obviously welcomes Chinese investment' while also blocking the involvement of Chinese firms in Australia's energy sector (blocking Chinese investment in Ausgrid) (SBS News 2017). Amid growing evidence of regulatory discouragement of Chinese investment proposals, Australia has recently subjected all Chinese investment proposals to scrutiny by the Foreign Investment Review Board. Significantly, the Turnbull government also blocked the involvement of Chinese telecommunications giants (e.g. Huawei) in developing Australia's 5G network.

There has been elevated anxiety in recent years about foreign interference in the Australian political system, which, in practice, has focused exclusively on China. Government minister Stuart Robert resigned from the ministry in February 2016 when it was revealed that he attended the signing of a mining deal in Beijing where one of the parties was a major donor to his political party and his attendance, unknown to Chinese officials, was alleged to be in his private capacity rather than his capacity as a government minister. In September 2016, opposition senator Sam Dastyari resigned after reports emerged that he had asked a donor with links to the Chinese Communist Party to pay a travel bill. In 2019, media reports linked a government backbencher, Gladys Liu, to the World Trade United Foundation, which is alleged to have ties to the United Front Work Department of the Communist Party of China, representing the interests of the Chinese Government.

Switching between Mandarin and English, Prime Minister Malcolm Turnbull said in December 2017 that:

> Modern China was founded in 1949 with the words: 'The Chinese people have stood up'. It was an assertion of sovereignty, it was an assertion of pride. And we stand up and so we say, the Australian people stand up (Tillet 2018).

The Chinese Government took deep offence at Turnbull's comparison (Tillet 2018). This was the context in which the Foreign Influence Transparency Scheme was created in which people are required to register if they are acting on behalf of a foreign principal. Despite the concern being primarily about China, the number of people listed on the register from Western countries (mainly the US) is almost triple those from China.

Debating the sources of Australia's security

This environment has forced Australian policymakers to ask themselves where Australia's security comes from. It is an issue that, until recently, had largely been taken for granted. Among the divergent views described above, the view in some areas of the popular press, think tanks, the academic community and among some officials and politicians is that Australia's security is directly weakened by its openness, particularly towards China, and is strengthened by its military spending and its alliance with the US. In this perspective, Australia's openness is seen as a liability, if not an outright threat. Australia is said to be too reliant on trade, foreign investment and immigration, and too reliant on China.

This world view sees trade as something that can be easily weaponised. The concern is that foreign governments will impose tariffs, quotas and restrictions against Australia's exporters to punish Australia for failing to comply with the foreign government's geopolitical objectives. Evidence of Chinese coercive use of trade sanctions is cited to support this argument. Foreign investment is similarly characterised as a threat. It is seen as 'an invasion by stealth' where foreign governments (or companies under the control of foreign governments) hoard assets to achieve strategic political or military objectives. It is argued that, at a minimum, foreign investment diverts wealth and vital goods and services away from Australians, or makes those goods and services unaffordable or unattainable. The same is true for Australia's openness to people. Australia's openness to immigrants, tourists, students and diplomats is seen as an opportunity for espionage, a threat to social cohesion and a risk to political stability. In this worldview, Australians who are of foreign heritage have their allegiance to Australia questioned and their motives viewed with suspicion.

Those advocating this world view argue that Australia should be substantially less open than it is. International economic relationships should be minimised to enhance Australia's security. These relationships, it is argued, should be with trusted allies. Indeed, some have advocated a reorientating of Australia's trading relationships away from China and Asia towards the Five Eyes intelligence sharing countries: Canada, New Zealand, the United Kingdom and the United States. This view of the world is not widely shared in Australia, but it has rapidly become more influential.

This view of the world needs careful scrutiny. It is inconsistent with Australia's lived experience. It is a worldview that is based on a misunderstanding of how Australia's markets work, a misunderstanding of the role of Australia's domestic policies and institutions and, most importantly, a simple paradigm in which Australia's economic prosperity, liberty and international integration is to be directly traded off for more security. The arguments that underpin this worldview are inconsistent, usually anecdotal and based on implausible economic counterfactuals.

The role of markets in Australia's security

Consider first the functioning of Australia's markets. The argument that China is without constraint in punishing Australia through the imposition of restrictions on Australia's exports overlooks how markets adapt to economic shocks. Consider an example. If China purchases less of a good from Australia, the price of that good in Australia relative to that good from other countries will fall, attracting increased demand from other countries. Australia's exchange rate will fall, making Australia's exports relatively cheaper than those from other countries, further offsetting the cost impact of the trade restriction. Australia's automatic stabilisers and discretionary monetary and fiscal policy responses also ease the impact of the shock, and Australia's relatively flexible factor and product markets assist in the adjustment that takes place within the economy: shifting resources from declining sectors to booming ones. Internationally, China may purchase more of that good from another country, given they are buying less from Australia, pushing up the price of that good in that other country and shifting global demand for that good from other countries towards Australia. The net effect is that the hole left by China's demand is partially filled by that from other countries— facilitated by changes in relative prices and exchange rates—and by changes in Australian domestic production.

There are two important qualifications to that argument about the adjustment process, however. First, these adjustments are commonly painful. They result in short-term losses in output, employment and investment. While the Asian financial crisis, the global financial crisis and the COVID-19 pandemic have all seen this process play out to some extent, and while relative prices, the exchange rate, automatic fiscal stabilisers, discretionary fiscal and monetary policies, trade flows and factor markets adjust in each instance to manage global economic shocks, there are permanent losses to income and output. Second, there may be some withdrawal from international markets occasioning direct income loss that is not recoverable through trade substitution at all. Some analysis by economists at the Commonwealth Bank of Australia, for example, suggests that a significant portion of Chinese spending could be replaced by increased demand from other countries, should it not recover after COVID-19 (Cranston 2020a). But this is an implausibly optimistic scenario in the event that an economy of China's scale and importance to international markets be lost as an export market.

Trade is also a two-way street. The narrative around the risks of Australia's openness ignores the fact that Australia has some global market power in key markets. Australia supplies 61 per cent of China's iron ore, 53 per cent of its coal and 23 per cent of its thermal coal. These shares have continued to increase (Armstrong and Drysdale 2019). Australia's currency is the fifth most used currency in the world. It is held widely by central banks around the world. Countries often purchase Australian products because there are no close substitutes, at least not at the same quality, scale or geographic convenience that Australia provides.

In reality, any attempt to minimise economic pain by limiting exposure to overseas markets will end up inflicting the pain it is supposed to avoid. If engaging in international markets carries a *risk* of economic upheaval due to geopolitical tensions, then closing off the economy to foreign flows of goods and factors to mitigate that risk carries the *certainty* of economic upheaval. If disruptions to trade and commerce originate from policy choices that divert trade, the adjustment process will likely be much more costly, as the uncertainty around market intervention will increase the cost of doing business with that country. Adjustments to exogenous shocks from normal market fluctuations will not necessarily increase the reputational cost of doing business with a country compared to the increase in political risk from intervention in the market for geopolitical purposes.

People also buy Australia's exports because they prefer them. Trade restrictions hurt the importer more than the exporter. They represent a tax on your own citizens and deprive them of the goods and services for which they have demonstrated a revealed preference. They increase the cost of living, which hurts the poorest people in society the most. IMF analysis shows that almost 100 per cent of the cost of Trump's tariffs on China are being paid for by American consumers (Cerutti, Gopinath and Mohommad 2019). In a world of global value chains where 70 per cent of world trade is in intermediate goods, trade restrictions hurt businesses, too. President Trump's tariffs on steel were a boon for steel producers in the US but costly for industries that use steel (such as US car manufacturers), who faced higher costs and could export less as a result. More than 40 times as many Americans are employed in industries that use steel than are employed in industries that make steel (Triggs 2020).

Shortening supply chains or bringing supply onshore to reduce vulnerability—an increasing focus by many governments during the COVID-19 pandemic—is underpinned by fallacious reasoning. Eliminating reliance on foreign inputs increases reliance on domestic inputs, which are subject to supply problems in a pandemic and under other shocks. Supply chains that are concentrated onshore are more vulnerable because a natural disaster or homegrown crisis could wipe out whole industries. The best insurance against drought or crop failure in one part of the world is openness to supply from producers all around the world. The key is to manage supply chain risk, not avoid it.

China's attempts at trade coercion with its trade restrictions on a wide range of Australian exports to Chinese markets largely failed. The access to other global markets that the rules-based multilateral trading system provides insulates against some of the cost of markets lost in China, although the adjustment in both Australian and Chinese trade was not without cost to producers and consumers in each country—including loss in the value of Australian exports especially in the short-term and more limited and higher priced products, especially coal, in China. But the options in open international markets guaranteed by the multilateral trading system cushioned the costs of these Chinese policy interventions. Damage to global confidence in trade and economic exchange with China and the global trading system more broadly was a more important cost of the episode, aggravating potential for fracture in the global trading system.

There are similar flaws in the arguments against foreign investment. When foreigners have purchased assets in Australia, that asset is subject to Australia's laws and rules. Concerns about how that asset might be used can be managed through changes to domestic legal and regulatory frameworks. It is also up to the recipient country to decide whether a foreign investment is allowed to take place and under what terms. This provides substantial scope for host governments to screen investment proposals properly and predictably, and to regulate the behaviour of those investors. Foreign investment also aligns the incentives of the two countries; both countries have an incentive to ensure that the asset is profitable and the economy healthy.

This has been Australia's experience. Indonesia imposed restrictions on Australia's beef exports for several years. But since Indonesian companies invested in Australia's beef industry, the Indonesian Government's incentive to restrict imports is significantly reduced. Tariffs and quotas that hurt an Australian industry make little sense when a partner country has investments in that same industry. Foreign investment provides a 'peace dividend'. In the extreme event that a country went to war with Australia, the first thing the Australian Government would do is seize its assets in the country. For some countries, this would represent almost A\$1 trillion in lost assets.

The narratives used by those who oppose foreign investment are often based on a false counterfactual. The assumption made is that if a foreigner had not invested in that project, the project would have gone ahead anyway using Australian capital. Australia's experience shows this to be false. If local savings were available to finance a project on comparable terms to those from overseas, there would be no foreign investment. The fact that foreign investment takes place implies that those projects needed foreign investment. There were no Australian substitutes jumping in when Japanese car factories closed in Victoria and South Australia. These counterfactuals are based on a misunderstanding of how markets function.

Recent concerns about foreign investment during COVID-19 are based on the same false counterfactual. The concern among some in Australia is that foreigners will swoop in while the economy is weak to buy cheap, distressed assets. But if the counterfactual is that those businesses would otherwise collapse—destroying jobs and capital in the process—presumably allowing foreign investors to save them is preferable. Indeed, a critical benefit of a floating exchange rate is that it acts as an automatic stabiliser. When the economy is weak, the exchange rate weakens, making exports cheaper and, importantly, making investment in the economy more attractive. Foreign investment can hence play a critical role in the COVID-19 recovery. Restricting it will do nothing but guarantee a slower recovery for Australia.

The role of domestic policies and institutions in Australia's security

Much of the impact of the world on Australia is determined domestically. Australia's history in managing global shocks has underscored the important role of its domestic policies and institutions in managing and mitigating the impact of those shocks. These policies and institutions act as a buffer, shielding the Australian economy from their impacts. They play a critical role in thwarting attempts at economic coercion; something that is often overlooked in discussions about openness and security. The same is true for Australia's political institutions.

Australia's economic policies and institutions have insulated the Australian economy by buffeting the country through many shocks. As discussed above, Australia's floating exchange rate depreciates, stimulating the economy by making our exports relatively cheaper and our assets more attractive when external income falls unexpectedly. Automatic fiscal stabilisers such as unemployment payments and retraining programs support aggregate demand and help redeploy workers. Australia's deep, flexible capital and financial markets reallocate risks and redeploy financial capital as Australia's strong and well-capitalised banking system buffers the impact on households and firms. Fiscal and monetary policy, supported by strong institutions, expands to support aggregate demand and manage the shock. Flexible product markets see supply chains quickly adjust as supply-side substitution maintains production levels, such as the firms that quickly entered the market to produce hand sanitiser and personal protection equipment during COVID-19.

The other major institution that insulates the Australian economy is our legal system. As mentioned earlier, this is also true for the management of foreign investment. When a foreign firm invests in Australia, it is Australia's legal system that decides whether that investment can take place and under what terms. Any asset located in Australia is subject to the laws and regulations of Australia. The same is true of protections against foreign interference in Australia's political system. The criminal and civil laws around corruption are determined by the Australian legal system. If an Australian politician was legally allowed to receive payments from foreign agents in order to influence Australia's policies, then this would suggest that Australia's legal framework is inadequate. The bribing of Australian politicians by foreign agents is as much the responsibility of the Australian politician as the foreign agent. The incentives and thus actions of both can be shaped by Australia's laws and the effective enforcement of those laws.

The critical challenge facing Australia in shaping laws and regulations around foreign interference is to be clear about the line between acceptable foreign influence and unacceptable foreign interference. President Obama gave a speech on climate change in Brisbane in 2014 that directly contradicted and embarrassed Prime Minister Abbott, as Obama sought to generate public support in Australia for action on climate change. Naturally, some in the government saw this as being inappropriate interference. However, most considered it to be within the bounds of acceptable influence on Australia's public policy.

The Australian Government is more accepting of foreign influence or indeed interference when it comes from allies. Foreign influence and interference in Australian politics from the US, for example, has not generated the same level of concern as it has from China. There are many documented examples of where the US has influenced, or has sought to influence, Australia's domestic policies, including over which foreign investment proposals the government approves and through the direct funding by the US Government of think tanks in Australia. The recent Foreign Influence Transparency Scheme revealed that the majority of Australia's classified 'foreign influencers' comes from its Western allies.

The complex trade-off between economics and security

At the core of concerns around Australia's openness is the idea that economics and security are substitutable: that Australia could give up some of its economic prosperity (by reducing trade, foreign investment and immigration) and enjoy more security as a result. Australia's history shows that such a simplistic trade-off is not supported empirically or theoretically. On the contrary, Australia's history shows that there is a complex trade-off between economics and security and that its security and economic prosperity are closely integrated and self-reinforcing.

Australia's prosperity has underpinned its security. Australia's defence spending is made possible by its prosperous economy, which, in turn, has been built on its economic openness. Australia's wealth has meant a healthier and more educated society that is more cohesive and stable as a result.

The importance of social cohesion and stability can be easily overlooked in thinking about security, despite history showing that less cohesive societies are easier to divide, both internally and externally.

None of this is to say that openness does not have its downsides. COVID-19 has highlighted that the downsides of openness are very real. Openness may make financial crises more severe, health crises more systemic and our economy more exposed to the economies and policies of other countries. But these downsides of openness need to be considered in the context of two things.

First, the downsides of openness during periods of stress need to be weighed against the benefits of openness during periods of prosperity. If tensions with China, for example, were to see a complete halt in Australia–China trade, the cost of the readjustment that would flow from this would need to be weighed against the benefits of decades of trade between the two countries. In the last 10 years alone, two-way trade between Australia and China has surpassed US\$1.2 trillion (around A\$1.72 trillion).

Second, the pain that can be caused by openness needs to be understood in the context of the functioning of Australia's markets and domestic policies and institutions discussed above: both allow stable adjustment to external shocks and shield Australian living standards from the full force of the shock. If foreign shocks have a more profound negative impact on Australia than is optimal, it is likely an indication that Australia's domestic frameworks could be improved or strengthened, in which case we need to ask: which political laws and institutions are permeable to political interference?

Australia's history reveals that its economic engagement in Asia and the world has made it more secure, not just because it has made Australia more prosperous, but because its economic engagement with the economies in the region has facilitated political, social and cultural engagement that, in turn, has increased confidence and reduced conflict between countries. Australia's economic engagement with Asia has encouraged more Australians to learn Asian languages, to better understand Asian cultures and, most importantly, to meet and familiarise themselves with Asian people and societies. This increased cross-cultural understanding, necessitated by Australia's economic engagement with Asia, has reduced the probability of conflict and increased Australia's security.

Australia's engagement with Asia shifts the incentives of all parties to favour diplomacy and constructive engagement over conflict and war. Economic engagement makes war expensive. If there was to be active conflict between the US and China, for example, the US and China would both instantly lose their biggest customer, along with three-quarters of a trillion dollars in two-way trade. Countless US and Chinese businesses would collapse. People would lose their livelihoods. Consumers would see their cost of living skyrocket, to say nothing of the human costs of war and the direct financial costs to government budgets. Both countries would lose trillions of dollars in cross-border investments. China alone has about US$3 trillion in financial assets abroad, mostly in the US. For the American Government, businesses and consumers, the cost of borrowing and consumption would rise sharply. If China were carved out of the US-led global financial system, the consequences for both countries would be devastating.

The 'peace dividend' that comes from economic engagement has been revealed many times in modern history. The countries that lack security and have seen their borders violated and territories invaded by foreign forces have, almost without exception, been poor countries with weak economies, weak financial systems and few substantial or sophisticated economic links to the global economy. It is comparatively 'cheaper' to invade these countries than to invade countries that have strong links to the global economy and, through their openness, are prosperous, as such countries can invest more substantially in their military capabilities and soft powers like diplomacy and foreign aid.

An approach to making Australia more secure

An approach to thinking about Australia's security has two elements: 1) the recognition that Australia's openness is a source of security, not just a source of risk; and 2) the recognition that the downside risks that arise from Australia's openness can be managed through carefully designed domestic and international frameworks, policies and institutions. Strengthening Australia's security means identifying practical ways to bolster openness while ensuring domestic and international frameworks manage any risks that may arise.

Increasing Australia's openness

The COVID-19 pandemic has produced a threat to living standards not seen since the Great Depression. History tells us that closed economies will face a slower recovery coming out of the pandemic than open economies. Yet, growing tensions between the US and China, the weakening of the global rules-based system, the growing backlash against globalisation and geopolitical tensions elsewhere in the world make global cooperation difficult. Despite these pressures, there are at least two things Australia can do to ameliorate this environment.

First, Australia can focus more on the region in which it is located. Japan, Korea, Indonesia and many other Asian countries are in a similar situation to Australia in trying to manage US–China tensions and an increasingly complex global environment. Australia would be better able to manage the US and China by working together with like-minded countries. This may be normally easier said than done. It can be hard to find practical areas of common interest on which countries can work together. But COVID-19 has made this easier. The pandemic has provided many issues of common concern: from financial stability, regional travel protocols and the distribution of COVID-19 diagnostic tests and treatments, to food security, coordinated structural reform and advancing Asia's flagship trade agreement—the Regional Comprehensive Economic Partnership.

Second, Australia should identify practical and constructive ways to engage the US in Asia. There are a range of potential areas for cooperation, including strengthening regional action on climate change (if a Democratic president is elected after the 2020 election that may become more feasible), building consensus on principles and rules around infrastructure and investment, strengthening domestic energy systems, promoting regulatory consistency in the digital economy and setting common standards for emerging technologies.

Regardless of the outcome of the 2020 presidential election, it is unlikely the approach of the US to foreign policy will change quickly. Any future president will struggle to deal with the deep, structural challenges that have fuelled America's backlash against globalisation. President Trump was no accident. His political success was the product of growing inequality and fast-moving economic and social changes, including automation and rapid technological change. Trump blamed immigration and trade for America's woes whereas, in reality, these problems are domestic.

The countries that have done the best out of globalisation are those with strong social safety nets that support people out of work and help move workers from declining industries to growing industries. The US does poorly on both counts. The losers from automation, technology and trade are left to fend for themselves, creating pockets of deep disadvantage among communities who then turn to political extremes for comfort.

Future US presidents will struggle to fix these domestic challenges quickly. One reason Trump directed the ire of Americans towards globalisation is because the White House has more power over foreign policy than domestic policy, even though the latter is where America's actual problems lie. Future presidents wishing to fix the deep problems in the US economy will need to implement bold domestic reforms. This will require a president to achieve at least three things: win the House and the Senate, win a margin large enough to defeat potential filibusters and unite their own side of politics around an agreed policy platform—all while the economy continues to struggle in the aftermath of COVID-19. For now, there is a bipartisan approach to both the anti-China rhetoric and the suspicion of trade.

Australia's focus needs to shift to how to buttress multilateral institutions. None of the big challenges facing the world can be solved bilaterally. Responses to multilateral problems conducted via megaphone diplomacy outside the forum will—at best—entrench deadlocks. At worst, they will legitimise solutions that risk permanently damaging the global system. Australia will have to put more energy into the forums that shape Australia's prosperity—the G20, APEC and ASEAN+6—and take a lead in building coalitions on the issues that matter to the region: changing out-of-date trade rules that are fuelling tensions; reforming the WTO and its dispute settlement mechanism; strengthening inadequate global and regional financial safety nets; cooperating on health policies; and capitalising on opportunities arising from the crisis, including the accelerated adoption of digital technologies and more flexible workplaces.

Managing risks through reformed domestic policies and institutions

There are risks in having an open economy, but these can be managed through robust domestic policies and institutions and international rules. The countries that have done the best out of globalisation are those: 1) with strong social safety nets that support people out of work and help move workers from declining to growing industries; and 2) have flexible economies that allow product, labour and capital markets to adjust quickly, effectively and equitably to external shocks.

Australia does well on both factors by international standards. However, COVID-19 has revealed areas for improvement. First, economists have warned for many years that Australia's safety net could be improved. Government payments to the unemployed have been grossly inadequate. The human cost of this neglect has been substantial. This neglect also means that Australia has weaker 'automatic fiscal stabilisers'—that is, programs that routinely kick in to increase government spending when the economy is slow and then ease that spending when the economy strengthens. The decline in the generosity of these payments over many years (because they are indexed to inflation instead of wages) has made the Australian economy less resilient to external shocks and less able to bounce back. The government has hurriedly increased these payments in response to the COVID-19 pandemic but is yet to announce a permanent long-term solution.

Second, Australia's system for retraining and reskilling workers has also been revealed to be inadequate. This system is highly fragmented across Australian Government initiatives and those in state and territory governments that differ widely in their generosity and scope. Similarly, the supports that are available to people between different industries also vary widely. There is a significant lack of transparency and public awareness of what supports are available. A consistent, transparent federal system would do much to improve the system through which workers are retrained, reskilled and redeployed to new industries. This makes Australia more resilient to external shocks and makes the public more willing to accept economic openness.

Third, COVID-19 has revealed the lack of flexibility in Australia's industrial relations system. Working with trade unions, the government was forced to temporarily suspend a variety of industrial regulations to cope with the pandemic. Developing sustainable, long-term reforms will be critical. These need to be integrated into reforms of social safety nets if they are to be effective and politically feasible. COVID-19 has revealed the downsides of Australia's increasingly casualised workforce. More than 2.6 million Australians are in casual employment with no paid leave. This was bad in normal times because it meant increased uncertainty for households, resulting in less spending, less labour mobility and fewer people taking the risk of starting a business or going for a new job. When COVID-19 struck, this casualised workforce became a bigger liability. More people in insecure work meant more people losing their jobs, exacerbating the downturn.

Fourth, COVID-19 has also revealed how deepening distrust in the Australian Government and other institutions over time has made it harder to manage the pandemic. The Edelman's Global Trust survey asked Australians to rank government, business, the media and non-government organisations by how competent and ethical they were. None were found to be both. According to those surveyed, businesses are competent but unethical. NGOs are ethical but not competent. And the government and the media were neither. There is plenty of low-hanging fruit. Establishing a national anti-corruption authority and reforming political donations are starting points. Criminalising wage theft across Australia would boost confidence in labour markets. Closing generous tax loopholes exploited by the rich would boost confidence in the tax system. Harsher criminal penalties for financial wrongdoers would boost confidence in the financial system. Disqualifying company directors who engage in anti-competitive conduct or who persistently mislead consumers—with financial penalties that are more than a mere cost of doing business—would boost confidence in product markets. Reversing cuts to the national broadcaster's budget would boost trust and information flows: the public have more trust in the ABC than our legal system, police, businesses, charities and every parliament and political party in Australia. Independent news and commentary are essential to good policy outcomes. If the old saying 'never waste a crisis' holds true, then there are plenty of problems Australia could use the COVID-19 pandemic to fix.

Conclusion

Australia's economic openness has been a major source of its economic strength as well as a foundation of its political security. The post-WWII international order in Asia had, until recently, afforded the conceptual separation in government policymaking of the interconnected economic and political risks associated with economic openness. That world has been turned upside down.

The United States' withdrawal of support for the multilateral economic regime that underpins confidence and trust in economic openness, the rise and increased assertiveness of China, and the fracture in US–China economic and political relations challenge Australian policymakers to rethink strategies that have long been ordered around Australia's alliance with the US and reliance on US leadership in the rules-based multilateral economic system. Australia has many national assets in dealing with this geopolitical circumstance, revealed in some measure in its recent management of both the health and economic impact of the COVID-19 crisis, its absorption of the shock of Chinese trade coercion and its management of the Asian and global financial crises.

At home, as we have argued, Australia will need to attend to national weaknesses that affect the integrity of its government and the resilience of its markets, their regulation and their governance. The story of Australia's response to the new geopolitical circumstances that confront it suggests that Australia also has a bigger challenge. That challenge is to define a new and more pluralist security strategy in cooperation with its neighbours to whom it is deeply tied economically and politically and a new international economic diplomacy that no longer relies entirely upon the United States to ensure multilateral outcomes.

The work on that huge agenda has not begun. The objective will not be achieved without vastly elevated engagement in the region. The torture of letting go of Australian security paradigms that were, until now, uncontested, embedded as they are in the assumptions of the old US-centric order and the fabric of institutional and operational enmeshment, is palpable. Confusion reigns over how it might best be done, forming a major obstacle to success in navigating the difficult choices that Australia now faces.

References

ABC News. 2014. 'Fact Check: Does ANZUS Commit the US to Come to Australia's Aid, as Foreign Minister Julie Bishop Claims?' 23 July 2014. www.abc.net.au/news/2014-07-08/does-anzus-commit-us-to-come-to-australias-aid-fact-check/5559288?nw=0.

ABER (Asian Bureau of Economic Research). 2020. 'An Asian Strategy for Recovery and Reconstruction after COVID-19'. 3 June 2020. adamtriggs.files.wordpress.com/2020/08/aber_asian-covid-strategy-paper.pdf.

Armstrong, S. 2020. 'Australia's Trade War with China Is Unwinnable for Both Countries'. *East Asia Forum,* 1 December 2020. www.eastasiaforum.org/2020/12/01/australias-trade-war-with-china-is-unwinnable-for-both-countries/.

Armstrong, S. and P. Drysdale. 2019. 'China Coal Trade Too Big for Beijing to Meddle With … or Australia to Get Alarmed About'. *East Asia Forum,* 25 February 2019. www.eastasiaforum.org/2019/02/25/china-coal-trade-too-big-for-beijing-to-meddle-withor-australia-to-get-alarmed-about/.

ASPI (Australian Strategic Policy Institute). 2022. Annual Report 2021–2022. www.aspi.org.au/annual-reports.

Australian Bureau of Statistics. 2020. 'Australia's Population: Over 7.5 Million Born Overseas. Media Release'. 28 April 2020. www.abs.gov.au/articles/australias-population-over-75-million-born-overseas.

Australian Government. 2018. 'Benefits of Trade and Investment'. Department of Foreign Affairs and Trade, 19 September 2018. www.dfat.gov.au/trade/resources/publications/Pages/benefits-of-trade-and-investment (site discontinued).

Australian Government. 2019. 'ChAFTA Outcomes at a Glance'. Department of Foreign Affairs and Trade. www.dfat.gov.au/trade/agreements/in-force/chafta/fact-sheets/Pages/chafta-outcomes-at-a-glance.

Australian Government. 2020a. 'Australia's Free Trade Agreements (FTAs)'. Department of Foreign Affairs and Trade. www.dfat.gov.au/trade/agreements/Pages/trade-agreements.

Australian Government. 2020b. 'Australia's Trade Statistics at a Glance'. Department of Foreign Affairs and Trade. www.dfat.gov.au/trade/resources/trade-at-a-glance/Pages/default (site discontinued).

Australian Government. 2020c. 'Foreign Investment Statistics'. Department of Foreign Affairs and Trade. www.dfat.gov.au/trade/resources/investment-statistics/Pages/foreign-investment-statistics.

Australian Institute of International Affairs. 2014. 'Australia and the Asian Infrastructure Investment Bank'. www.internationalaffairs.org.au/australia-to-finally-join-the-asian-infrastructure-investment-bank/.

Cerutti, E., G. Gopinath and A. Mohommad. 2019. 'The Impact of US–China Trade Tensions'. *IMF Blog*, 23 May 2019. www.imf.org/en/Blogs/Articles/2019/05/23/blog-the-impact-of-us-china-trade-tensions.

Collinson, E. 2019. 'Anthony Albanese and the People's Republic of China: An Overview'. Australia–China Relations Institute, 18 June 2019. www.australiachinarelations.org/content/anthony-albanese-and-people%E2%80%99s-republic-china-overview.

Cordon, M. 2017. *Lucky Boy in the Lucky Country: The Autobiography of Max Corden, Economist*. Cham, Switzerland: Palgrave Macmillan. doi.org/10.1007/978-3-319-65166-8.

Cranston, M. 2020a. 'Australia Has Trade Avenues beyond China, CBA Says'. *Australian Financial Review*, 10 May 2020. www.afr.com/policy/economy/australia-s-alternative-to-china-s-threat-on-trade-20200710-p55avd.

Cranston, M. 2020b. 'China Hits 48.8pc of Australian Exports'. *Australian Financial Review*, 4 August 2020. www.afr.com/policy/economy/china-hits-48-8pc-of-australian-exports-20200804-p55i9d.

Debelle, G. 2019. 'A Balance of Payments'. Reserve Bank of Australia. Speech to the Economic Society of Australia, Canberra, 27 August 2019. www.rba.gov.au/speeches/2019/sp-dg-2019-08-27.html.

Garnaut, R. 2001. *Social Democracy in Australia's Asian Future*. Canberra: Asia Pacific Press, The Australian National University.

Global Times. 2020. 'Australian Institute Slammed for Hyping Up Anti-China Issues'. 10 June 2020. www.globaltimes.cn/content/1191208.shtml.

Google Trends. 2020. 'Search term: China'. Accessed 17 August 2020. trends. google.com/trends/explore?cat=16&date=today%205-y&geo=AU&q=China.

Gyngell, A. 2019. 'What Can Australia Do? AIIA National President Allan Gyngell's Keynote Speech at the 2019 AIIA National Conference'. 17 October 2019. www. internationalaffairs.org.au/australianoutlook/what-can-australia-do/.

Hanson, P. 2020. 'Time to Stand up for Australians and Buy Australian'. Facebook. www.facebook.com/watch/?v=243199613651588.

Hastie, A. 2019. 'We Must See China—the Opportunities and the Threats—with Clear Eyes'. *Sydney Morning Herald*, 8 August 2019. www.smh.com.au/politics/federal/we-must-see-china-the-opportunities-and-the-threats-with-clear-eyes-20190807-p52eon.html.

Hu, D. 2020. 'Is Australian Media Biased against China?' *The Diplomat*, 15 February 2020. thediplomat.com/2020/02/is-australian-media-biased-against-china/.

Jennings, P. 2020. 'We Need to Reduce Our Dependence on China, and Have the Courage to Call It Out When Required'. Australian Strategic Policy Institute, 1 May 2020. www.aspi.org.au/opinion/we-need-reduce-our-dependence-china-and-have-courage-call-it-out-when-required.

Kehoe, J. 2018. 'US Ramps Up Warning to Australia over Huawei, 5G'. *Australian Financial Review*, 4 March 2018. www.afr.com/politics/us-ramps-up-warning-to-australia-over-huawei-5g-20180303-h0wxyn.

Kehoe, J. 2020. 'What an 85pc Fall in Migration Means for the Economy and Housing'. *Australian Financial Review*, 1 May 2020. www.afr.com/policy/economy/later-migration-plunge-to-hurt-economy-and-housing-20200501-p54p2g.

Lowy Institute. 2020a. 'China: Australian Government Policies towards China'. poll.lowyinstitute.org/charts/australian-government-policies-towards-china/.

Lowy Institute. 2020b. 'Economic and Trade Policy: Globalisation'. poll.lowy institute.org/charts/globalisation.

Lowy Institute. 2020c. 'Economic and Trade Policy: Support for Free Trade'. poll. lowyinstitute.org/charts/support-for-free-trade.

Lowy Institute. 2020d. 'Relations with the US and China: Trust in Global Powers'. poll.lowyinstitute.org/charts/trust-in-global-powers/.

Lowy Institute. 2020e. 'Themes: Economic and Trade Policy'. poll.lowyinstitute. org/themes/economic-and-trade-policy.

Lowy Institute. 2020f. 'World Leaders and Countries: Confidence in Political Leaders'. poll.lowyinstitute.org/charts/confidence-in-political-leaders/.

Moore, C. 2020. '"Wolverines" Take On China: How a Group of Australian MPs with Their Own Secret Stickers Are Pushing Back against Chinese Influence—and Beijing Is NOT Happy'. *Daily Mail*, 1 June 2020. www.dailymail.co.uk/news/article-8375447/The-Wolverines-VS-China-Australian-MPs-upset-Beijing.html.

Murphy, K. 2015. 'Australia Confirms It Will Join China's Asian Infrastructure Investment Bank'. *The Guardian*, 29 March 2015. www.theguardian.com/business/2015/mar/29/australia-confirms-it-will-join-chinas-asian-infrastructure-investment-bank.

Murray-Atfield, Y. 2020. 'Ambassador Intervenes after Mike Pompeo Warns US Could "Disconnect" from Australia over Victoria's Belt and Road Deal'. ABC News, 24 May 2020. www.abc.net.au/news/2020-05-24/mike-pompeo-warning-over-victoria-belt-and-road-deal/12280956.

MYOB Team. 2019. 'Survey: Consumers Are Turning to Local, Bricks and Mortar Retail This Christmas'. 10 December 2020. www.myob.com/au/blog/bricks-and-mortar-retail-outlets-preferred-at-christmas/.

Parliament of Australia. n.d. 'Appendix B—the ANZUS Treaty'. Accessed 9 August 2021. www.aph.gov.au/Parliamentary_Business/Committees/Joint/Completed_Inquiries/jfadt/usrelations/appendixb.

Robin, M. 2020. 'The Think Tank behind Australia's Changing View of China'. *Australian Financial Review*, 15 February 2020. www.afr.com/policy/foreign-affairs/the-think-tank-behind-australia-s-changing-view-of-china-20200131-p53wgp.

Rothwell, D. 2020. 'Laying Down the Law in the South China Sea'. *East Asia Forum*, 30 July 2020. www.eastasiaforum.org/2020/07/30/laying-down-the-law-in-the-south-china-sea/.

SBS News. 2017. 'Turnbull Plays Down Belt and Road Fears'. 23 October 2017. www.sbs.com.au/news/turnbull-plays-down-belt-and-road-fears.

SBS News. 2019. '"We've Raised These Abuses": PM Condemns China's Detention of Uighurs'. 1 November 2019. www.sbs.com.au/news/we-ve-raised-these-abuses-pm-condemns-china-s-detention-of-uighurs.

Seymour, H. 2019. 'Australia's Alliance with the US Is Defined by More Than One President'. *The Interpreter*, The Lowy Institute. 17 July 2019. www.lowyinstitute.org/the-interpreter/australia-s-alliance-us-defined-more-one-president.

Simpson, F. 2020. 'Get Australia Growing—Fiona Simson Press Club Address'. National Press Club, 14 July 2020. nff.org.au/media-release/get-australia-growing/.

Streem. 2020. 'China Coverage Soars as Australia Wrestles with Relationship'. 27 September 2020. www.streem.com.au/2019/09/27/china-coverage-soars-as-australia-wrestles-with-relationship.html (site discontinued).

Taylor, J. 2020. 'China's Belt and Road Initiative: What Is It and Why Is Victoria Under Fire for Its Involvement?' *The Guardian,* 25 May 2020. www.theguardian.com/world/2020/may/25/chinas-belt-and-road-initiative-what-is-it-and-why-is-victoria-under-fire-for-its-involvement.

Tillet, A. 2018. 'Malcolm Turnbull Tries to Get Australia out of the Chinese Diplomatic Freezer'. *Australian Financial Review*, 8 August 2018. www.afr.com/politics/malcolm-turnbull-tries-to-get-australia-out-of-the-chinese-diplomatic-freezer-20180808-h13omv.

Towell, N, A. Galloway and M. Fowler. 2020. '"Sinister Intentions": China Ups Stakes in Belt and Road Stoush with Dutton Attack'. *The Age*, 27 March 2020. www.theage.com.au/national/sinister-intentions-china-ups-stakes-in-belt-and-road-stoush-with-dutton-attack-20200527-p54x1d.html.

Triggs, A. 2020. 'The Trouble with Buying Australian'. *Inside Story*, 10 August 2020. insidestory.org.au/the-trouble-with-buying-australian/.

Tudge, A. and S. Morrison. 2020. 'Joint Statement with the Hon Scott Morrison MP, Prime Minister—Hong Kong'. Australian Government, 9 July 2020. minister.homeaffairs.gov.au/alantudge/Pages/hong-kong-visa-arrangement-20200709.aspx.

Uhlmann, C. 2020. 'We Can't Return to Business as Usual with China'. *Sydney Morning Herald*, 29 April 2020. www.smh.com.au/national/we-can-t-return-to-business-as-usual-with-china-20200428-p54nty.html.

Westacott, J. 2020. 'Jennifer Westacott, Michael Schneider and Frank Tudor Interview with David Speers, Sky News'. Business Council of Australia, 9 August 2020. www.bca.com.au/jennifer_westacott_michael_schneider_and_frank_tudor _interview_with_david_speers_sky_news.

World Bank. 2020. 'Australia Trade Statistics'. World Integrated Trade Solution. wits.worldbank.org/CountryProfile/en/AUS.

5

'Japan First'? Economic security in a world of uncertainty

Shiro Armstrong and Shujiro Urata

Introduction

Japan's economic and national security depends on managing its economic, political and security relationships with its security guarantor and ally, the United States, and its largest trading partner, China. The rise of China and protectionism in the US—most prominently but not limited to the 'America First' agenda, involving increased strategic competition and a trade war between China and the US, the world's two largest economies—has meant a much more uncertain international policy environment for countries like Japan, the world's third-largest economy.

In this uncertain external policy environment, Japan has shown international leadership in its initiative to conclude the Comprehensive and Progressive Agreement for Trans-Pacific Partnership (CPTPP) after the US withdrew from the Trans-Pacific Partnership (TPP), conclude the Japan–EU Economic Partnership Agreement (EPA) and host the G20 Summit. Japan has also signed a bilateral trade agreement with the US that is a departure from multilateral rules and norms, and introduced 'economic security' policies that include export controls and the tightening of foreign investment regulations for security reasons.

Some small but potentially significant reforms to the machinery of government have taken place to better integrate economic policy with national security policy, resulting in the establishment of economic security divisions in key agencies and the Cabinet Office. There does not appear to be a clearly articulated or obvious framework of national security that includes welfare-enhancing economic security guiding policy.

The entanglement of economics and security for Japan has led to a series of policies that appear to promote national security interests over economic prosperity. This chapter reviews Japan's response to the increasingly uncertain external environment, including its leadership in multilateral trade, and its dealings with its major economic, political and security partners. The new developments raise questions as to whether Japan's 'economic security' policies are welfare enhancing or put national (or political) security interests ahead of welfare considerations.

The first section sets out Japan's economic circumstances, the trends in its international economic position and its national security priorities. The chapter then examines Japan's response to an increasingly uncertain external environment through active international economic diplomacy. Finally, the chapter details the new set of economic security policies deployed by Japan to manage the complexities in international commerce, and makes a preliminary assessment as to their effects on Japanese prosperity, before concluding.

Japan's foreign economic position and security policy priorities

Japan's national security depends on the US security umbrella, including its extended nuclear deterrence. The Japanese Self-Defence Forces have gradually expanded their role and capabilities, including allowing for collective self-defence, following a reinterpretation of the *Constitution of Japan*, but the pacifist constitution still limits Japan's ability to defend itself. Reliance on the military alliance with the US, which includes US bases in Japan, has increased with the growth in Chinese power and the North Korean threat.

American leadership of the rules-based order, including the US security network that has secured stability in the Asia-Pacific and leadership of the global economic commons like the World Trade Organization (WTO), has allowed Japan and the broader region to prosper. It is within that framework that China made the commitment to open up its economy and develop with a view to overtaking Japan, becoming the world's second-largest economy and largest trading nation. China is the largest trading partner for Japan and most countries globally.

Japan's strategic priorities lie in managing its economic and security relationship with the US amid fears of alliance abandonment or entrapment, and its economic and political relationship with an increasingly assertive China. This challenge, which is not unique to Japan, is putting pressure on Japanese policy strategies.

Japan may be the world's third-largest economy, but its share of global trade has been falling. Though its total trade grew 1.7 times between 2000 and 2018, its share of world trade fell from 7.2 per cent in 2000 to 4.2 per cent in 2018. The US experienced a similar decline, from 16.2 per cent in 2000, to 11.1 per cent in 2018; meanwhile, Chinese trade managed to grow from 4.7 per cent of total world trade, to 12.1 per cent in the same period. As Japan and the US decline in economic importance relative to China— mainly as a function of the natural slowing of growth in rich countries, but also due to China's successful containment of COVID-19—international economic relations will shift as well.

The decline of Japanese and US trade shares globally is partly a consequence of the rise of China. Global GDP or trade league tables and rankings are not important in themselves but simply describe the reality of the change in structure of global economic power and interdependencies that have implications for the management of economic, political and security relations.

China's increasing weight in global trade relative to the US is reflected in bilateral trade with Japan. In 2000, the US accounted for 24.7 per cent of total Japanese trade compared to 10.9 per cent for China. By 2020, the share of the US in Japan's total trade had fallen to 14.7 per cent and China's had risen to 23.9 per cent. The US was both the largest export destination and source of imports for Japan in 2000, and, by 2008, China was the largest. This shift was particularly notable in the case of exports compared to imports. China's share of Japan's total exports accounted for 8.2 per cent on the eve of China's WTO accession in 2000, growing to 22.1 per cent in 2020. The US accounted for 29.1 per cent of total Japanese exports in 2000 and that fell to 18.4 per cent in 2020 (Figure 5.1).

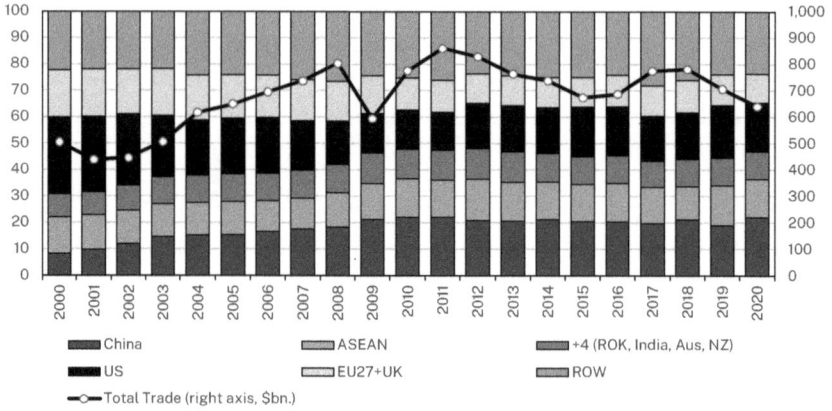

Figure 5.1: Japan's export destination by share and total exports, 2000–20
Source: UN Comtrade online.

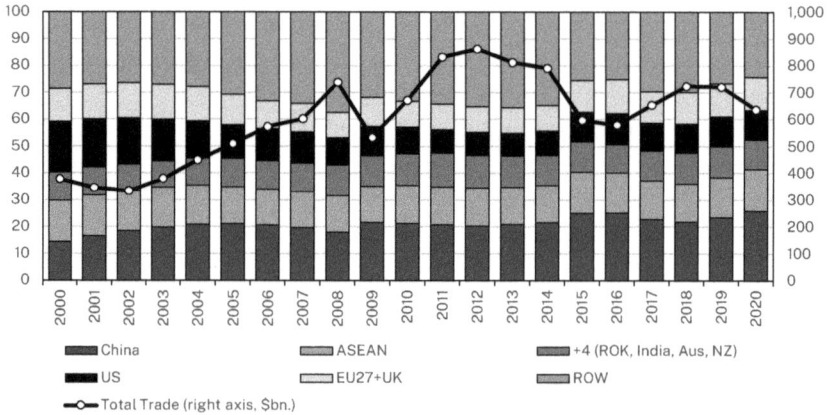

Figure 5.2: Japan's import shares by source and total imports, 2000–20
Source: UN Comtrade online.

Japan's dependence on China for its imports was 25.8 per cent in 2020, growing from 14.5 per cent in 2000, while the US share of Japanese imports fell from 18.8 per cent in 2000 to 11.0 per cent in 2020 (Figure 5.2). In some categories, Japanese reliance on China is heavy: for example, personal protective equipment (PPE) and electronics products. For Japan, China is the source of 75 per cent of imports of face masks, 66 per cent of goggles, 53 per cent of infection protective wear, 99 per cent of laptops and tablet PCs, and 86 per cent of smartphone imports.[1]

---

1   The figures are for 2018 and computed from trade statistics compiled by Japan's Ministry of Finance. These figures will be updated for 2019.

High trade shares with China have become a concern for some policymakers and businesses in Japan in the context of the China–US trade war. Chinese exports to the US that embody Japanese parts and components, or are part of Japanese supply chains that include Japanese value-added, have become exposed to US trade barriers. The high dependence on Chinese manufacturing for Japan's imports of PPE and other electronics has also brought concern about diversification of supply chains, as it has in other countries. There is also the risk of interference in the market, both real and perceived, driven by political differences between Tokyo and Beijing.

Japanese firms have managed the ups and downs of political relations between Tokyo and Beijing, with past boycotts in China of Japanese goods having had little effect on the trade and investment relationship (Armstrong 2012), though there are still issues surrounding intellectual property violations.[2]

Japanese firms have deployed a China plus one strategy with investment diversification in Southeast Asia in addition to China. This has helped expand East Asian production networks and supply chains. The East Asian grouping consisting of China, the Association of Southeast Asian Nations (ASEAN) and the plus four countries (Australia, India, New Zealand and South Korea) are all initial members of the Regional Comprehensive Economic Partnership (RCEP) grouping and account for 44 per cent of Japan's exports and 47.5 per cent of its imports. The share of this group in Japan's trade has stayed relatively consistent through 2000–20 (Figures 5.1 and 5.2). Even this underestimates Japan's impact in deepening trade between East Asian countries, driven by Japanese foreign direct investment, and masks some of the significance of the trade relationships.

Australia accounted for only 2.1 per cent of Japan's trade in 2018 but is the major source of energy imports and strategic raw materials like iron ore. Japan relies on imports for 90 per cent of its energy needs and Australia is the largest supplier, providing over a quarter of Japan's energy needs (Figure 5.3). Australia is the largest supplier of coal and liquefied natural gas (LNG) for Japan accounting for 71.6 per cent of Japan's coal imports and 34.6 per cent of Japan's LNG imports METI 2020a). Australia supplies over half of Japan's iron ore imports.

---

2   According to a survey conducted by the Japan Bank for International Cooperation, 35.5 per cent of the respondents indicated that insufficient protection of intellectual property right is a problem in China. See: www.jbic.go.jp/ja/information/press/press-2019/pdf/1127-012855_4.pdf [in Japanese].

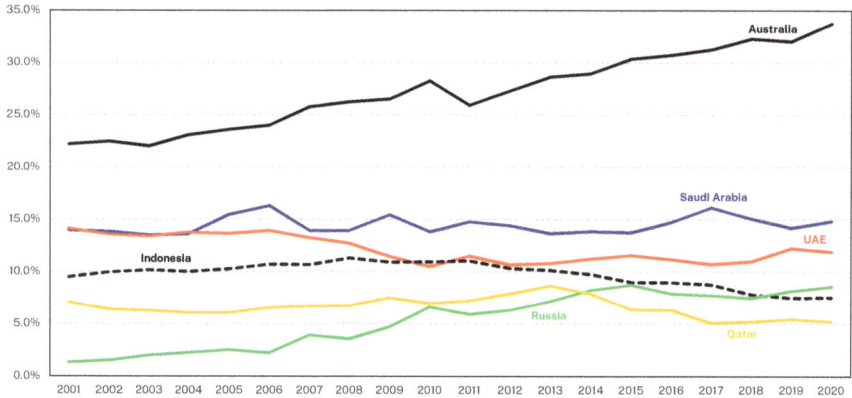

Figure 5.3: Share of Japan's energy imports, 2000–20, gigajoules
Source: Calculated based on Trade Statistics of Japan, MOF, Japan; UN Comtrade, UNSD; BP Statistical Review of World Energy, June 2020, BP.

Japan's energy security depends on reliable energy imports from the international market. Its commitment to the open multilateral trading system helped to secure Japanese energy imports, complemented by bilateral and regional agreements, giving confidence in open markets.

The position of Japanese foreign direct investment (FDI) abroad is in stark contrast to Japan as a host of FDI: Japan has the smallest FDI stock to GDP ratio of any OECD (Organisation for Economic Co-operation and Development) country. Japanese FDI accounted for 5.4 per cent of global FDI stock in 2018, up from 4 per cent in 2000, but Japan only hosted 0.7 per cent of global FDI in 2018—an insignificant share, given the size of the Japanese economy as the world's third largest. Japanese FDI is global. The largest destination is the US, followed by the United Kingdom, the Netherlands and then China, where Japan is the largest source of non-Chinese FDI. Japan's investments in ASEAN economies have also been growing rapidly as wages rise in China and geopolitical tensions encourage geographical diversification in supply chains.

Japan has managed its large trade and investment relationships—including securing energy and strategic raw material imports—under the framework of the multilateral trading system. It has managed its largest economic relationships without bilateral free trade or economic partnership agreements until only very recently. The bilateral agreements that Japan has secured have been complementary to, not substitutes of, the WTO and multilateral rules. It is that multilateral system that is weakening and under threat.

Uncertainty and Japan's international economic diplomacy

Five related major trends are creating unprecedented challenges for countries like Japan:

1. The rapid economic rise of China and accompanying growth in Chinese political and military power.
2. The US's retreat from global leadership of multilateral institutions and economic governance and pursuit of an 'America First' agenda.
3. Strategic competition between China and the US, including a trade war that has only seen a temporary truce in a Phase One trade deal.
4. New technologies centred on cyber and digital that are changing how economies engage and, without agreed multilateral rules, are introducing new vulnerabilities and fault lines between countries.
5. The COVID-19 pandemic, which resulted in a major health crisis and an economic downturn not seen since the Great Depression of the 1930s. While the health and economic fallout from the pandemic has not led to cooperation between the US and China, it has intensified it.

These challenges are particularly acute for Japan given its geographical position between the US and China and economic reliance on both. Japan is also reliant on the US for security. China is its largest trading partner and close neighbour. Japan has relied on the open, rules-based multilateral trading system for its economic development and to secure its economic interests with both China and the US, as well as the rest of the world.

'America First', trade wars and uncertainty

President Donald Trump introduced significant uncertainty for the global economy and dramatically changed the circumstances for countries like Japan. While his brazen and sharp form of leadership cast doubt on Japan's US security umbrella, his approach to trade and multilateralism was a symptom of underlying domestic challenges in the US. The approach to trade with allies and competitors alike caused great uncertainty, with the rise in protectionism in the US largely due to the maldistribution of income and wealth.

Japan's response to these new uncertainties in its external environment was to shift from passive to proactive external policies to protect and shape the multilateral trading system (Urata 2020). Prime Minister Shinzo Abe's active diplomacy and coalition building from the beginning of his return to the prime ministership in 2012 set the groundwork for a leadership role in international economic policy that became seen as necessary with the election of Donald Trump as US president in 2016. One of Trump's first actions was to withdraw the US from the TPP in January 2017, which had been concluded in late 2015 but had not yet entered into force.

The TPP served multiple purposes for its members. In political security terms, Australia, Japan and other US allies and partners saw the TPP as a way to keep the US engaged in the Western Pacific. The US had framed the TPP as the economic arm of its pivot to Asia. In economic terms, the TPP was pushing rule-making and liberalisation. Bilateral agreements were delivering limited and diminished returns in both rule-making and liberalisation; and multilateral rule-making and liberalisation at the WTO had become difficult and stalled.

The TPP was not without its problems and challenges: for example, there were significant gaps in its membership. Just over half of the 21 Asia-Pacific Economic Cooperation (APEC) countries were members, excluding China, Indonesia, South Korea and other major economies. It had the perception of being US led because of the rhetoric and structure of negotiations. It also had a set of liberalisation and rule-making demands from the US that were difficult for negotiating parties to commit to. Many governments expended vast amounts of political capital in agreeing to the high standards of deep liberalisation and new rules, including those demanded by the US. At times, and at worst, it was framed as an agreement that was aimed at containing China's economic rise; at best, it shaped the rules and standards for China to conform to.

For Japan, the TPP was a key pillar of the structural reform arrow of the Abenomics growth strategy, both symbolically and for what it would achieve as a beachhead in liberalising the agriculture sector (Solis 2017; Solis and Urata 2018).

America's withdrawal from the TPP created great uncertainty for the remaining members but also for the global trading system, as it was only one of Trump's pre-election promises. His campaign included threats of high tariffs on Chinese and Mexican imports as well as 'America First' rhetoric that signalled a retreat from multilateralism and global leadership in trade (Productivity Commission 2017). With uncertainty about whether the US Congress and Washington establishment would constrain the Trump administration from its more extreme threats on trade and alliance management, Japan led the conclusion of the CPTPP with the remaining 11 members. Australia, New Zealand and Singapore were key partners in pushing for its conclusion, but it was the economic weight of Japan and its leadership that made the difference (Terada 2019). The CPTPP keeps open the option of eventual US membership in the original TPP (as unlikely as that is in the near future) and maintains almost all of the original TPP commitments but US re-entry would require significant negotiations.

President Trump's election promises were gradually realised throughout 2017 and accelerated in 2018 as it became clear that Congress and other interest groups were unable to reign in the extremes of his administration. Japan was president of the G20 group in 2019. Despite acceleration of the tit-for-tat trade war between China and the US and intensified rivalry, the Osaka G20 Summit resulted in a leaders' statement that delivered several important messages. The APEC Summit in Papua New Guinea in 2018 had failed to produce a leaders' communique for the first time, primarily because of Sino-US tensions. Although a strong missive on multilateralism and avoiding trade protectionism was absent, the Osaka G20 leaders' statement included two issues that were important to Japan: promotion of digital economy under the 'data free flow with trust' (DFFT) initiative and construction of 'high-quality infrastructure'.

The trade war between Japan's two largest trading partners and the world's two largest economies, China and the US, proceeded in fits and starts throughout 2018 and 2019. The Phase One trade deal reached between the two countries brought a truce to the trade war with agreement for China to purchase US$200 billion of agricultural goods and energy from the US over two years. The agreement, which was primarily about the volume of US imports, moved the trading relationship between China and the US towards managed trade, outside of the existing rules and norms of the WTO. The implications for energy and agriculture importers like Japan were significant, as they were for producers and exporters like Australia.

Under pressure from the US, Japan had agreed to purchase corn and other US agricultural products to reduce the bilateral trade imbalance between the two countries. Japan had resisted a bilateral deal with the US, preferring to try to bring the US back to the TPP; however, it eventually acquiesced and agreed to the US–Japan Trade Agreement, largely because the US threatened to impose high tariffs on automobile imports from Japan. Japan was not alone in this. Other countries, such as South Korea, Canada and Mexico, also worked to negotiate deals—including voluntary export restraints and other measures such as the 'poison pill' provision in the United States–Mexico–Canada Agreement (USMCA), which allows the US to hold the deal hostage to Canada or Mexico in negotiations with China—to avoid US tariffs. Those measures were also outside existing multilateral rules, and some, like voluntary export restraints (VERs) had been ended when the Uruguay Round[3] had been completed. Other countries such as Australia negotiated exemptions from US steel and aluminium tariffs, agreeing to VERs.

Repairing the China relationship

The China–Japan relationship has been gradually improving following a low point in 2012, prior to Prime Minister Abe and President Xi coming to power within four months of each other. The large and complementary economic relationship between China and Japan has kept the political relationship from deteriorating too much (Armstrong 2012) and underlying economic interdependence has been a powerful incentive to better manage the political relationship.

Prime Minister Abe's state visit to Beijing in October 2018 was his first bilateral visit (Abe had visited China for APEC in 2014 and the G20 in 2016) since he made the historic 'ice-breaking' visit in 2006 during his first trip abroad as prime minister. In that October 2018 trip, China and Japan agreed to 52 joint infrastructure projects in third-country markets, elevating cooperation in a potentially important area that had been difficult to find common ground on as competitors in infrastructure investment in Asia. The joint infrastructure projects were not agreed upon under the umbrella of China's Belt and Road Initiative (BRI) but will potentially play a significant role in shaping the BRI (Armstrong 2018). Japan had not signed a memorandum of understanding (MOU) with China to join the BRI, and other G7 countries, especially in the Asia-Pacific, found it difficult to engage with China's BRI. Italy was the first G7 country to sign an MOU to cooperate with China on the BRI in 2019. Japanese policy

---

3   The Uruguay Round was the eighth round of multilateral trade negotiations conducted within the framework of the General Agreement on Tariffs and Trade. It led to the creation of the WTO.

initiative had managed to find a way to work with China on a policy priority for both countries and to influence Chinese policy development through engagement. The theatre of infrastructure investment in developing countries and improving connectivity with China was seen as a threat to the existing US-led order by many in the West.[4]

Chinese agreement to joint infrastructure projects with Japan, including state participation in projects, meant that those projects that were largely in Southeast Asia would not proceed without agreement on standards, largely set by Japan. This demonstrates an interest on the part of Chinese authorities, or a faction thereof, to improve standards in their investment projects that had seen some commercial failures and spectacular international political backlash. What is more, China adopted the same language and principles as the Japanese-led Ise-Shima Principles for Promoting Quality Infrastructure Investment in its BRI Summit in 2019. For Japan, this was a positive initiative that would further a common interest with China and help to improve the bilateral relationship without compromising on any interests. The MOU that was signed mirrored the language Japan had used in an MOU on joint infrastructure projects with the US and Australia only months before. The experience of failed projects and geopolitical pushback from its forays into infrastructure investment in Southeast Asia in the 1980s gave Japanese policymakers an understanding of the economic and political challenges currently faced by China.

In managing the relationship with an increasingly unpredictable Trump administration and increasingly assertive Xi Jinping, Japan found itself in an unusual leadership position. As a US ally, Japan had relied on US leadership—as had much of the rest of the world—in regional and global economic initiatives. Even major reforms were largely driven by US pressure, or *gaiatsu*, including the perception of agricultural reform in the TPP negotiations. After successfully leading the conclusion of the CPTPP, the Japan—European Union EPA was concluded and brought into force in February 2019. At the time, it was the largest bilateral economic agreement globally. Japan had also elevated the priority of the RCEP agreement between the 10-member ASEAN, Australia, China, India, Japan, Korea and New Zealand by hosting, in July 2018, the first ministerial meeting outside of ASEAN where the agreement had been conceived. In doing so, Japan had become the de facto leader of multilateralism.

---

4   See, for example, Macaes (2018) for a discussion of these views.

Regional leadership and its challenges

Prime Minister Abe invested political capital in building a strong personal relationship with President Trump and managed the economic and security relationship with the US while gradually improving the bilateral political relationship with China. Japan also strengthened political relations with other countries and regions with active diplomacy. That included Australia, Southeast Asia, Canada, Europe and the Middle East. There was mixed success in some key relationships with efforts to structurally improve relations with Russia by resolving territorial disputes having failed and the bilateral relationship with South Korea gradually deteriorating.

Japan's G20 presidency in 2019 involved navigating the China–US trade tensions at the Osaka G20 Summit while protecting the multilateral system as its top strategic priority. Prime Minister Abe had outlined this approach at the World Economic Forum in Davos earlier that year. The Osaka Summit failed to produce any significant breakthrough, but the leaders' statement did include defence of the multilateral trading system. The expectations for the summit were not high, given the China–US trade war and erratic US president.

On the sidelines of the G20 Summit, Japan launched its DFFT initiative that aimed to set governance standards in digital and cyber—an area devoid of global rules and norms that nevertheless plays an important role in determining the competitiveness of countries and firms.

After the successful conclusion of the Osaka Summit meeting in June 2019, tension between Japan and South Korea resulted in Japan initiating export restrictions on chemicals and other strategic materials. This coincided with a Korean Supreme Court decision to overturn a key agreement that had been the basis for a treaty between the two nations since 1965. The timing of the decision appeared politically driven and both President Moon and Prime Minister Abe used the spat for domestic political gain. As a result, the Japan—South Korea relationship deteriorated to its lowest point since normalisation of diplomatic relations in 1965.

In October 2019, Japan gave into US pressure and signed the US–Japan Trade Agreement, which Japan had resisted signing since President Trump had taken office. Although the agreement fell outside existing multilateral rules and norms, Japan was not alone in signing a defensive agreement with the US. Importantly, given the significance of the relationship between China and Japan, Japan had avoided the 'poison pill' provision that the US had included in the USMCA. In the US–Japan Trade Agreement, the US (more or less) recovered what it had lost in beef and pork market access concessions from Japan when it withdrew from the TPP, but Japan did not achieve the automobile market access concessions it had won from the US in the TPP negotiations. These developments concerning Japan's trade relationship with the US indicate the difficulty Japan faces in protecting the multilateral trading system.

The new economic security posture

There does not appear to be any clear and accepted definition of economic security in Japan. With increased international uncertainty complicating Japan's economic, foreign and security policies, there has been a deliberate effort to break down silos in Japanese policymaking and thinking. Economic security can have different meanings in economic or security agencies.

The election of President Trump and the 'America First' agenda coincided in Japan with a focus on 'economic security', which traditionally meant ensuring national security through economic means and referred to energy, resources and food. A group of ruling Liberal Democratic Party (LDP) legislators led by Akira Amari, a senior LDP member and former minister for economy, trade and industry, proposed the establishment of a council tasked with economic security in March 2019.

The genesis of the 'economic security' concept can be traced back in the early 1980s, right after Japan was hit by global oil shocks. The late Masataka Kosaka of Kyoto University proposed the term 'economic security' (*keizai teki anzen hosho*) as part of 'comprehensive security' (*sogo anzen hosho*), which was a key strategic policy framing of the Ohira government ('Sogo Anzen Hosho Kenkyu Group Hokokusho' [Report of Study Group on Comprehensive Security] 2 July 1980). At that time, Japan's focus on economic security was threefold: 1) preserving the free trade system and solving the North–South problem, 2) ameliorating diplomatic tensions with key trading partners and 3) maintaining energy and food security.

The idea of economic security differs from the idea of economic diplomacy—used by the Ministry of Foreign Affairs (MOFA) since 2006 or so—which was primarily concerned with protecting and developing global economic rules in Japan's national interest. Economic diplomacy was pursued primarily through EPAs.

The term 'economic security' can be found in the *Diplomatic Bluebook*: for instance, in Chapter 3(b) of the 2007 edition (MOFA 2007) or in Chapter 3 Section 3(d) in the 2008 edition (MOFA 2008) referring to energy and food security. The section on 'economic diplomacy' became a full section in the 2011 edition (MOFA 2011). From 2017, MOFA started publishing 'Japan's Economic Diplomacy' (*waga kuni no keizai gaikou*) in addition to its annual *Diplomatic Bluebook*; the former was edited chiefly by the Economic Affairs Bureau. According to MOFA's definition, Japan's economic diplomacy should focus on three aspects: 1) rule-making to bolster free and open global economic systems, 2) supporting the overseas business expansion of Japanese companies through promotion of public–private partnerships and 3) promoting resource diplomacy along with direct investment towards Japan.

Economic security is often understood to overlap with economic statecraft, being 'the use of economic means to pursue foreign policy goals' (Baldwin 1985). Foreign aid, trade and policies governing the international flow of capital can be used as foreign policy tools in pursuit of national security objectives and are considered the most common forms of economic statecraft. Policies governing the international movement of labour could also be deployed to promote foreign policy goals, but such measures are not usually included under the rubric of economic statecraft.

Recognition that China and the US are deploying economic policies and instruments for security purposes has led many countries, including Japan, to try to understand the consequences of this and to develop policy in response. The new entanglement of economics and security has meant that policy silos in economics and security have had to be brought together or integrated in some manner.

Bringing economics and security together in the machinery of government

Since 2019, there have been deliberate efforts to bring economic and national security issues and thinking together in the Japanese bureaucracy, first in METI and then in MOFA. These developments were followed by the establishment of an economic team in the National Security Secretariat (NSS) within the Cabinet Secretariat.

On 2 June 2019, METI set up a new Economic Security Division with 15 officials, led by the director-general of the Trade and Economic Cooperation Bureau. The director of the division also serves as the director of the Security Trade Control Policy Division. METI had also set up a Rule Making Strategy Division, led by the director-general of the Trade Policy Bureau, in July 2014.

In MOFA, the Economic Security Division within the Economic Affairs Bureau has traditionally overseen energy, resources and food security. In October 2019, the National Security Policy Division under the Foreign Policy Bureau reorganised its three sub-divisions: Emerging Security Challenges, Space and Maritime Security Policy, and International Peace and Security Cooperation.

An economic security division was established in the NSS in April 2020.[5] One of the factors that led to the establishment of the economic team was the realisation by METI of the need to take steps to tighten export controls of advanced technology by responding to a similar policy adopted by the US in 2018.[6] METI was sensitive to the US policy on export controls because of its bitter experience in the case of Toshiba's violation of the US Coordinating Committee for Multilateral Export Controls (COCOM) in 1987.[7]

METI tightened the regulation on inward FDI with the *Foreign Exchange and Foreign Trade Act* (FEFTA). The Ministry of Finance that administers the FEFTA could not evaluate technologies from a national security perspective. The expertise and monitoring of different types of technologies falls under the jurisdiction of different ministries. For example, information technology falls under the jurisdiction of the Ministry of Internal Affairs and Communication, while medical and pharmaceutical technologies are the responsibility of the Ministry of Health, Labour and Welfare. The lack of coordination and the compartmentalisation of overlapping responsibilities led to the creation of an economic security division in the NSS that can oversee economic security across government ministries and agencies.

---

5   The National Security Council (NSC) was created in December 2013.
6   Nobukatsu Kanehara, former deputy director for the NSC, quoted in *Yomiuri Shimbun* (20 May 2020).
7   Toshiba and Kongsberg, a state-owned Norwegian enterprise, sold US$17 million worth of computer-controlled machine tools to the Soviet Union between 1981 and 1984 in violation of COCOM, which was established during the Cold War to put an embargo on Western exports to East Bloc countries. The US administration and Congress protested strongly against this case. See, for example, GlobalSecurity.org (n.d.).

The ruling LDP Diet Members' Caucus on Strategic Rule Formulation headed by Akira Amari played an important role in the establishment of the economic team in the NSS. That caucus presented recommendations to the government to set up a National Economic Council modelled after the US's National Economic Council, which would play the role of a conning tower for strategic foreign economic policy.[8] According to Amari, Japan did not recognise the concept of economic security, while China uses economic means strategically to favourably alter the policies of other countries.

The Economic Security Division in NSS is one of seven divisions.[9] It is headed by a former director-general from METI and consists of roughly 20 staff with four councillors from the ministries of Finance, Foreign Affairs, Internal Affairs and Communication, and the National Police Agency, respectively (*Nihon Keizai Shimbun*, 3 June 2020). The Economic Security Division deals with the protection of technology (export control and regulation of inward FDI), cyber security (5G, government–private sector co-ownership of information), international cooperation (Japan–US security cooperation, digitalisation of Japanese yen), coping with the COVID-19 pandemic (quarantine policy, strengthening of supply chains for medical and health equipment) and other matters. One of the goals of Japan's economic security policy is to prevent the outflow of 'critical technology'.[10]

The types of technology that are likely to be targeted for acquisition by non-allied countries include artificial intelligence and 5G communication technology (core technology for the development of a digital economy) as well as robotics and biotechnology (*Nihon Keizai Shimbun*, 4 June 2020). Several methods have been identified to achieve these objectives. One is acquisition of Japanese companies owning technology through FDI. To deal with this possibility, the Japanese Government revised the FEFTA, which is discussed below. Another is cyber theft of technologies from government agencies and private companies. There is also concern about collaborative research with Chinese universities and research institutes. The concern is that advanced technologies would be acquired from Japan by Chinese researchers connected to the Chinese military and used for military

8   Akira Amari, quoted in *Yomiuri Shimbun* (17 May 2020).
9   Others include the coordination team, the strategic planning team, the intelligence team and the three teams handling regional affairs.
10   Minute of a committee under the Industrial Structure Council [Sangyou Kouzou Shingikai], October 2019, www.meti.go.jp/shingikai/sankoshin/tsusho_boeki/anzen_hosho/pdf/20191008001_01.pdf [in Japanese].

purposes. The Japanese Government is planning to enforce the disclosure of sources of funding for joint research projects that are supported by the Japanese Government (*Nihon Keizai Shimbun*, 24 June 2020). The Ministry of Education, Culture, Sports, Science and Technology (MEXT) is the major source of research funding of university and research institutes. It is planning to set up an economic security section to oversee the use of those funds in a manner that ensures 'economic security' (*Yomiuri Shimbun*, 24 August 2020).

China is one of the largest sources of patents globally and a major source of innovation. How Japan and other advanced economies that see joint research as a security threat manage their collaboration with Chinese universities and researchers is an important question for remaining at the technological frontier going forward.

The issues of restricting exports of dual-use technology, theft of sensitive technologies and the protection of other cyber assets are not unique to Japan. US pressure on its allies is increasing to enact extreme measures. Japan has an interest in finding a way to avoid the US tactic of extreme technological decoupling—a middle ground where it can benefit from Chinese innovation and technology while protecting its own sensitive technologies.

The Economic Security Division in the NSS is expected to work with different agencies across the Japanese Government to break up the compartmentalised system and have a consistent strategy. Having a centralised economic security division rather than numerous agencies dealing with economic security issues facilitates cooperation with foreign countries, especially the US (*Yomiuri Shimbun*, 16 May 2020). The Economic Security Division spent its first four months in existence working intensively on the novel coronavirus pandemic. Faced with growing economic frictions, particularly between the US and China, the coronavirus pandemic, rapid advancement in digital technology and other developments, the Economic Security Division is likely to require expansion to undertake its assigned tasks (Tobita 2020).

The machinery of government continues to evolve in Japan, including with the creation of a new ministerial role for economic security in late 2021 as Prime Minister Kishida Fumio took office. There is now better coordination across the bureaucracy and a recognition of the issues, but the policy measures thus far implemented would suggest security considerations dominate economic considerations and a clear framework that balances both, and other factors, has not been articulated. The policy measures adopted thus far are outlined below.

Revision of the *Foreign Exchange and Foreign Trade Act*

As part of its new economic security posture Japan has tightened restrictions on inward FDI to prevent foreign investors from acquiring advanced technology from Japanese companies. The Japanese Government revised FEFTA with the objective of promoting inward foreign investment that would contribute to Japan's economic growth while restricting inward FDI that may undermine or damage national security. One of the reasons for the revision—which passed the National Diet in November 2019 and was enacted in May 2020—was to follow other advanced countries such as the US and the European Union, which adopted new regulation on inward foreign investment to strengthen the screening process from the national security viewpoint (Ministry of Finance 2020). Australia also tightened its regulations around inward FDI in the name of national security in 2020, continuing a trend underway in other Western countries. The revised FEFTA introduced a new exemption scheme regarding the pre-notification by foreign investors to the Japanese Government and also revised the list of industries subject to the exemption (Ministry of Finance 2019). Japan has been relatively closed to foreign investment (see discussion above) and the tightening of FDI for security purposes will likely not help realise more FDI, even with many other advanced economies similarly tightening regulation of FDI.

Prior to this revision, a foreign investor was required to notify the government of its investment if it was acquiring an ownership share of 10 per cent or greater of a listed company in a designated business sector. The designated sectors, which include weapons, aircrafts, nuclear facilities, space, dual-use technologies, cybersecurity and telecommunications, comprise 155 out of 1,465 sectors, using the sector classification of Japan's Standard Industrial Classification.

The exemption scheme of prior notification for stock purchases of companies in designated sectors by a foreign entity was introduced with certain conditions in the revised FEFTA. The threshold for prior notification for purchasing stocks was lowered from 10 per cent to 1 per cent. Foreign financial institutions were given blanket exemptions; foreign sovereign wealth funds, public pensions and other 'general investors' were granted regular exemptions; and investors with a record of sanctions or that were state-owned enterprises were not granted exemptions.[11] For general investors acquiring stock of listed companies in designated sectors, prior notification was exempted in line with following conditions:

a. Investors of their closely related persons will not become board members of the investee company.

b. Investors will not propose to the general shareholders' meeting transfer or disposition of investee company's business activities in the designated business sectors.

c. Investors will not access non-public information about the investee company's technology in relation with business in the designated business sectors (Ministry of Finance 2020, 4).

For general investors acquiring 10 per cent or less of the stock of the listed companies in the core designated business sectors, prior notification was exempted in line with the following conditions in addition to the conditions listed above:

a. Regarding business activities in core sectors, investors will not attend the investee companies' executive board or committees that make important decisions in these activities.

b. Regarding business activities in core sectors, investors will not make proposals, in a written form, to the executive board of the investee companies or board members requiring their responses and/or actions by certain deadlines (Ministry of Finance 2020, 4).

There are 12 core designated business sectors. These are a subset of the designated sectors that include weapons, aircrafts, nuclear facilities and other designated sectors, and parts of cybersecurity, telecommunications and other designated sectors. Investors that use the exemption scheme are required to submit a post-investment report within 45 days of the transaction settlement date.

---

11   The discussions here apply to general investors including sovereign wealth funds and public pension funds. The revised law introduced three different treatments regarding the exemption schemes: a blanket exemption, regular exemption and no exemption—depending on the types of investors. Blanket exemption is applied to foreign financial institutions, while regular exemption is applied to general investors. For investors with a record of sanctions (due to FEFTA violation) and state-owned enterprises (except those who are accredited by the authorities) exemption is not applied. For details, see Ministry of Finance (2020).

The new 1 per cent threshold for prior notification in the revised FEFTA is low compared to other advanced countries, except the US where no threshold is applied (Ministry of Finance n.d.-b). Australia moved to a zero-dollar threshold during the coronavirus pandemic, reduced from a complex and preferential set of thresholds that ranged from zero for some sensitive sectors (all investment proposals screened), to a range of thresholds with higher thresholds of up to AU$1.154 billion for preferential trade or economic partnership agreements (no screening for investments below that threshold). The thresholds applied in the cases of France, Germany and Italy are 33.3 per cent, 10 per cent and 3 per cent, respectively.

The Ministry of Finance released information on the list of companies for which the purchase of stocks by foreign investors is subject to prior notification on 8 May 2020 (Ministry of Finance n.d.-a). The ministry listed 2,102 companies in the designated sectors out of 3,800 listed companies, and 518 companies in the core designated sectors out of 2,102 companies.[12] These data show that 56 per cent of listed companies are subject to prior notification. Criticism has been made about the lack of clarity/transparency in the determination of the companies in the list, and critics have called for a clear explanation of the criteria and/or reasons for the selection (*Nihon Keizai Shimbun*, 5 June 2020). Prior notification was implemented on 7 June 2020.

Several concerns have been raised about the negative impacts of the revised FEFTA (*Nihon Keizai Shimbun*, 23 and 31 May 2020). One is that, for a large number of companies, the purchase of stocks by foreign investors needs prior notification: 56 per cent of the listed companies are classified under the designated sectors. According to *Nihon Keizai Shimbun* (23 May 2020), this kind of wide coverage for prior notification is unusual globally. Although an exemption is possible, the increased coverage of prior notification is likely to discourage foreign investment. Pesek (2019) noted that, with the revised Act, Tokyo would surely lose any chance it had to re-establish itself as a global financial centre. There is also the problem of administering a complex system that requires screening of so many financial transactions. Unlike the US, which has a permanent agency overseeing such transactions (the Committee on Foreign Investment), in the case of Japan, evaluation and screening is undertaken by the Ministry of Finance and other concerned ministries in which the staff in charge are likely to be

---

12   On 5 June 2020, the Ministry of Finance announced that 51 companies were added and 11 companies were removed from the list of companies in the core designated sectors, leaving 558 companies on the list.

rotated every three to four years. As such, consistent and reliable screening may be difficult. Another serious concern is that tighter restrictions on inward FDI may reduce the pressure on companies for necessary reform by discouraging activist investors (*Nihon Keizai Shimbun* 23 May 2020; Pesek 2020). Reducing such pressure would result in increased inefficiency or productivity decline.

Export controls and their politicisation

METI and, more recently, the Economic Security Division of the NSS, oversee export controls of advanced technologies that could end up in a country or with an actor under sanctions from Japan or the US, or be used to undermine Japan's security.[13] The memory of Toshiba being fined for sales to the Soviet Union in the early 1980s for violation of COCOM rules is still fresh for some; but, more importantly, there is the concern that advanced technology will end up in North Korea or in the Chinese military. There are also fears of being caught up in a US–China technological competition and/or technological decoupling.

Japan removed South Korea from its 'whitelist' of preferred export countries for high-tech materials without licensing in August 2019 for fear that the end use of some of those materials are not adequately monitored (METI 2019). This placed a new and additional burden on South Korean firms that rely on imports of those materials. It also introduced significant uncertainty for South Korean multinationals over whether they could secure credit in Japan, and for smaller South Korean firms as to whether they could navigate the new licensing requirements without import disruptions.

The commercial and economic implications are significant. Tightened export controls have been placed on three high-tech materials—fluorinated polyimide, photoresist and hydrogen fluoride—that are key inputs for the South Korean production of memory chips (for which it is the largest producer in the world) and LCD and OLED displays. Japan is the major supplier to South Korea of these materials, accounting for 94 per cent of South Korean imports of fluorinated polyimide, 92 per cent of fluorinated polyimide imports and 44 per cent of hydrogen fluoride imports (Zafar 2019).

---

13   Commercial or industrial espionage and protectionist policies should be differentiated from national security risk, although they are often conflated. The national security label can be liberally applied for protectionist and industrial policy purposes.

The tightening of export controls was heavily politicised. The timing of the export restrictions tied it to the South Korean Supreme Court decision to allow the seizure of Japanese company assets to compensate victims of Japanese occupation of South Korea during World War II. The ruling was contrary to the 1965 treaty between Japan and South Korea. The timing and politicisation of the export controls has resulted in the trade dispute being labelled an economic or trade war that relates to history, economic competition, regional rivalry, disputed territory and existing political tension by some mass media and concerned observers, particularly those from South Korea.[14] The Japanese Government justified its decision with reference to the potential for leakage of material to North Korea.

It is unclear what effect the tightening of Japanese export controls will have on South Korean imports of the materials, the commercial fortunes of Japanese exporters, the international market for those materials, and South Korea's downstream exports of memory chips and displays. There are broader strategic and geopolitical ramifications with Japanese—South Korean political and security cooperation deteriorating, and intelligence sharing agreements with the US at risk of ending.

After several unsuccessful meetings between the two governments, the South Korean Government took the case to the dispute settlement mechanism of the WTO in June 2020. The panel was scheduled to discuss the case in July.

One year after the imposition of export controls by the Japanese Government, several notable developments have been observed in trade and investment concerning the three materials in response to export controls by the Japanese Government.

Several South Korean firms began building facilities to produce these materials with assistance from the South Korean Government. Meanwhile, Japanese firms have been trying to maintain their sales in South Korea, which is a very important market for many Japanese firms, by adopting three main approaches. First, some Japanese firms are trying to maintain exports to South Korea through various channels. For example, some Japanese firms began to export photoresist by using a new policy introduced by METI that allows transactions between specified firms for a maximum of three years without obtaining permission to export for every transaction (*Nikkei Asia*, 20 December 2019). Second, several Japanese firms set up plants in South

---

14 On this view from Japan, see, for example, *Nihon Keizai Shimbun* (1 July 2019). For a Korean view, see Song (2020).

Korea. This type of investment, similar to 'tariff jumping investment' in economic literature, is an expected response from Japanese firms. In this case, exports by Japanese firms are substituted by local production/sales in South Korea by Japanese firms (*Nikkei Sangyo Shimbun*, 24 August 2020). Third, some Japanese firms began exporting the materials to South Korea from their foreign affiliates in other countries. For example, JSR began exporting photoresist from their joint-venture company in Belgium (Kim 2019).

These developments are impacting on the structure and performance of the semiconductor materials industry in Japan and South Korea. Production of these materials in South Korea by South Korean, Japanese and other countries' firms has increased, while production in Japan has declined— or at least has not increased as much as it would have without export control. This type of development will accelerate as production capability/ capacity in South Korea increases, possibly resulting in improvement in the competitiveness of the semiconductor materials industry in South Korea vis-a-vis Japan. This type of consequence, which does not benefit Japan, does not seem to have been expected by the Japanese Government when it implemented the policy.

METI's concern appears to have primarily revolved around South Korea's inability to monitor or control exports of those materials and stop them from reaching North Korea, for example. In hindsight, the Japanese Government would have done better to work closely with the South Korean Government to jointly address these concerns. The politicisation of the issue has increased uncertainty in the trade of those materials between Japan and South Korea, with potential spillovers to other sectors in the bilateral trade and economic relationship.

Supply chains and economic security during the coronavirus pandemic

The COVID-19 pandemic has exposed the vulnerability of supply chains for the Japanese economy. There were initial disruptions to the supply of PPE and electronic equipment as many Chinese factories and suppliers went into lockdown to contain the health crisis. Supply chains have contributed to the rapid expansion of Japanese companies, as they have enabled Japanese companies to achieve fragmented, task-based specialisation under the name of just-in-time production. The outbreak of COVID-19 in Wuhan in China was a reminder of how interconnected economies are, as the adverse economic impacts from China spread rapidly to Japan and many other countries through the disruption of supply chains. Since the initial disruption, supply chains and markets have responded rapidly to shortages.

A case in point is the Japanese automobile industry, a major pillar of the Japanese economy. When Wuhan went into lockdown in late January, factories supplying auto parts also shut down. The shortfall suspended the operations of Japanese automobile assemblers in China, Japan and other parts of the world (Armstrong 2020). Vehicle production in Japan declined by 10 per cent in February from the same month the previous year. While Chinese manufacturing began to recover in March and April thanks to the successful containment of COVID-19 in China, the virus was still spreading in Japan (Kalinova 2020). Factories were shut down in Japan because workers had to stay at home as a state of emergency was declared in April, causing production to drop by approximately 45 per cent compared to the previous year. Production resumed as the state of emergency was lifted in May, but sales of automobiles remained low because of dampened demand, which was mainly due to uncertainty around the continued pandemic and pessimistic future economic prospects.

Disrupted supply chains have caused chaos for consumers and medical staff, especially around the supply of some PPE from China. A shortage of PPE such as facial masks and protective garments, for which Japan is largely reliant on China (50 per cent of its supplies come from China), led to a panic as some consumers paid as much as ¥1,000 (US$9) for a mask, and some hospitals used plastic bags rather than medical garments as PPE.

Faced with supply chain disruption, the immediate response of Japanese firms was to run down inventories and procure products from suppliers in Japan and other parts of the world using existing supply chains. Though supply chains made a rather quick recovery, the pandemic has aroused interest in diversifying supply chains among Japanese companies. Japanese companies are shifting their business strategy from just-in-time to just-in-case. One obvious reason for this is increased concern about the prolonged presence of COVID-19 and the possible emergence of new viruses.

Japanese firms that rely heavily on China for the supply of many goods, including electronics, medical equipment and health products, have other reasons for diversifying supply chains. The intensifying US–China trade war and technology race, as well as concerns over possible forced technology transfers in China, have reduced the attractiveness of conducting business in China. Diversifying supply chains could involve shortening networks by reducing the number of links in the chain, or by redesigning products to make their components less specific. But these changes are costly, which discourages diversification. Government intervention could add further costs to businesses that are better at calculating and mitigating risks, and further onshoring could increase the vulnerability of supply chains to shocks (Armstrong 2020).

Japan's METI is keen to secure sufficiency in domestic supply. It recently introduced a subsidy program to support Japanese companies in their efforts to diversify and strengthen supply chains (METI 2020b). The program has two components. One is to promote domestic investment by relocating overseas production bases to Japan—or reshoring. The other is to construct strong supply chains involving ASEAN member countries to encourage Japanese firms to move or establish their production bases there. These have been widely described as moving Japanese manufacturers out of China and reducing dependence on China as a production base.

The budget allocated to the first and second components are ¥220 billion (US$2 billion) and ¥23.5 billion (US$200 million), respectively. The money can be used to construct buildings, install machinery and conduct feasibility studies. The program covers half to three-quarters of the costs depending on the content of the projects and the size of the firms, with higher subsidy rates for small and medium-sized enterprises (SMEs). For the component to promote reshoring, 57 companies out of 90 applicants were selected in the first tranches in July 2020 and were allocated approximately ¥57.4 billion (METI 2020c; JETRO 2020). For the component to promote diversified supply chains into ASEAN, 30 companies out of 124 applicants were selected in the first tranches in July 2020. Many of the selected companies are producers of medical and health products and auto and electronic parts.

The incentive created by the subsidy for Japanese companies to onshore projects or move them to Southeast Asia appears to have had some effect, but it is not clear whether and how much this program will contribute to the diversification of supply chains of Japanese companies, as it is just one of many factors that will influence a company's decision. Firms will also consider the costs and benefits of diversification, including market size, labour cost, quality of infrastructure, trade and investment policy, and political and social stability in potential investment locations.

Many Japanese multinational corporations (MNCs) have been reorganising their supply chains in Asia regardless of the subsidy. Japanese MNCs and the SMEs that agglomerate around them have been restructuring their supply chains in Asia and investments in China over time due to rising labour costs in China (Japanese Bank for International Cooperation 2020). The China plus one strategy of diversifying investment has been common practice for decades. However, until further analysis of accumulated data is undertaken, it is not possible to know whether it has helped to make supply chains more resilient or turned the subsidies into a form of corporate welfare.

Conclusion

Japan's economic fortunes rely on an open, rules-based multilateral trading system. That commitment to openness and multilateralism has ensured energy and food security for Japan and is the framework within which Japan has managed its large economic relationships with China, Europe and the US. That was the case even before Japan's recent bilateral agreements with Europe, the US and the CPTPP. Except for Japan's trade agreement with the US in 2019, all other trade agreements were pursued to complement the WTO and build on the multilateral global trading system.

The multilateral system upon which Japanese economic prosperity relies is under direct threat from Japan's security guarantor—the US. The US has underpinned Japanese and regional security and has played the primary leadership role in the rules-based order. China's rise, the US's retreat from global leadership to an 'America First' agenda, US–China strategic rivalry and the importance of new areas of commerce that are not subject to multilateral rules have combined to create uncertainty for Japanese policymakers as they navigate an uncertain and dynamic external environment.

Japan has shown leadership in the face of a US retreat from multilateralism by leading the conclusion of the world's largest mega-regional agreement, the CPTPP, and by signing the world's largest 'bilateral' deal with the European Union. Those required political will and proactive diplomacy. Japan is also a key driver of the RCEP agreement that will lock East Asian economies into new rules and new commitments to openness. Japan's economic weight, political stability and proactive diplomacy has meant a more important role for Japan in multilateralism as the US–China relationship has deteriorated.

While managing the political relationship with the US, the Abe administration has pursued a strategy to improve relations with China and actively strengthen security and economic ties globally with a focus on Southeast Asia. The joint Chinese–Japanese infrastructure projects in

Southeast Asia have demonstrated openness by Chinese policymakers to working with Japan and conforming to higher standards and transparency, while Japanese policymakers have managed to influence China's BRI without becoming a formal member.

Japanese initiatives towards China have been undertaken in the context of managing the political and security relationship with the US. The MOU between China and Japan on joint infrastructure projects was modelled on the MOU between Australia, Japan and the US. Japan is not a member of the Chinese-led Asian Infrastructure Investment Bank and only put real political capital behind RCEP once the TPP, and later the CPTPP, was concluded.

The unchartered territory of economic policies with security implications has led to policy choices and strategies that seem to contradict Japan's emphasis and interest on rules, multilateralism and openness, however insignificant the decisions may seem.

The Trump administration forced a trade agreement on Japan that is outside of established rules and moves the Japan–US relationship closer to managed trade. History and politics have become mixed up in the tightening of Japanese restrictions on exports of critical materials to South Korea. These measures have had adverse security and geopolitical implications by further damaging the Japan—South Korea relationship and more explicitly linking economic statecraft to political disputes.

Complex and restrictive measures have been placed on foreign investment in Japan that, at best, reduce the prospects of Japan as a global financial centre and, at worst, inhibit productivity enhancing capital, trade links and technology. Restrictions on FDI by other Western countries is cited as part of the policy rationale.

Institutional changes in government to respond to the new economic security challenges, especially the new Economic Security Division in the NSS, have helped to bring some policy coherence across the Japanese Government, but there is no clearly articulated framework for balancing economic and security interests in the national interest. There also does not appear to be an accepted definition of 'economic security'. Thus far, the tightening of export control regulations and the tightening of FDI regulations are the main outcomes of the new economic security posture. Export controls, which were imposed on South Korea in August 2019, hurt both Japanese and Korean firms. Japanese exporters reduced their export sales, while

Korean users of the controlled materials cut down their production. The ultimate outcome of these actions remains unclear in economic or security terms, but production of those materials has shifted from Japan to South Korea, including Japanese producers setting up subsidiaries in South Korea. It is not clear if the Japanese Government expected such development when it implemented export control. The impacts of tightening FDI regulation cannot be evaluated yet as the policy was only introduced in April 2020. It is also too early to judge the effectiveness of government subsidies for Japanese MNCs to onshore manufacturing or invest in Southeast Asia to make Japanese supply chains more resilient during the COVID-19 pandemic. These are largely interpreted as an economic security measure to become less dependent on China.

The measures that Japan has implemented in the name of economic security, such as export control and revision (more restrictive) of inward FDI policy, incur economic costs and are a retreat from openness. They contribute to a loss of dynamism that is needed to revitalise the Japanese economy with a declining and ageing population.

Considering this point, it is important for Japan to maintain and strengthen the rules-based multilateral trade system, and to have China and the US engaged in the system, to achieve economic prosperity and contribute to political stability in the region. To deal with national security issues involving China, the establishment and management of a mutually beneficial relationship through active dialogue and cooperation, such as joint infrastructure projects with China in Asia, should continue to be pursued. Japan will need to cooperate with like-minded countries such as Australia and New Zealand, as well as with ASEAN and other countries, to keep China and the US engaged in multilateralism.

The entanglement of economics and security for Japan has led to a series of policies that appear to promote national security interests over economic prosperity. Deployed in the name of economic security, they are restricting trade and investment. It is not clear that the policies are consistent with Japan's current external economic position and deep interest in supporting the multilateral system that helps manage that global economic position. Without a clearly defined economic security strategy that has economic prosperity as central to national security, Japan may be forced down a path of restricted or managed trade with non-allies, which will be damaging to Japan's prosperity.

References

Armstrong, S. 2012. 'The Politics of Japan–China Trade and the Role of the World Trade System'. *The World Economy* 35 (9): 1102–20. doi.org/10.1111/j.1467-9701.2012.01473.x.

Armstrong, S. 2018. 'Japan Joins to Shape China's Belt and Road'. *East Asia Forum*, 28 October 2018. www.eastasiaforum.org/2018/10/28/japan-joins-to-shape-chinas-belt-and-road.

Armstrong, S. 2020. 'Economic Distancing from China and the World Would Carry Heavy Costs'. *East Asia Forum*, 7 June 2020. www.eastasiaforum.org/2020/06/07/economic-distancing-from-china-and-the-world-would-carry-heavy-costs/.

Baldwin, D. A. 1985. *Economic Statecraft*. Princeton: Princeton University Press.

GlobalSecurity.org. n.d. 'Toshiba-Kongsberg Incident'. Accessed 29 September 2021. www.globalsecurity.org/intell/world/russia/toshiba.htm.

Japanese Bank for International Cooperation. 2020. *Report on Overseas Business Operations by Japanese Manufacturing Companies*, www.jbic.go.jp/en/information/press/press-2020/0115-014188.html.

JETRO (Japan External Trade Organization). 2020. 'About the Companies Adopted in the First Open Call for Participants (Equipment Introduction Assistance Type (General Frame / Special Frame))'. 17 July 2020. www.jetro.go.jp/services/supplychain/kekka-1.html.

Kalinova, K. 2020. 'Probing Japan's Slow Response to the COVID-19 Crisis'. *East Asia Forum*, 25 April 2020, www.eastasiaforum.org/2020/04/25/probing-japans-slow-response-to-the-covid-19-crisis/.

Kim, J. 2019. 'Samsung Secures Key Chip Supply in Belgium as Tokyo Curbs Exports'. *Nikkei Asia*, 10 August 2019. asia.nikkei.com/Spotlight/Japan-South-Korea-rift/Samsung-secures-key-chip-supply-in-Belgium-as-Tokyo-curbs-exports.

Macaes, B. 2018. *Belt and Road: A Chinese World Order*. London: C. Hurst & Co.

METI (Ministry of Economy, Trade and Industry). 2019. 'Update of METI's Licensing Policies and Procedures on Exports of Controlled Items to the Republic of Korea'. 1 July 2019. www.meti.go.jp/english/press/2019/0701_001.html.

METI (Ministry of Economy, Trade and Industry). 2020a. 'Japan's Energy 2019'. www.enecho.meti.go.jp/en/category/brochures/pdf/japan_energy_2019.pdf.

METI (Ministry of Economy, Trade and Industry). 2020b. 'Outline of the Projects under the FY 2020 Supplementary Budget'. April 2020. www.meti.go.jp/main/yosan/yosan_fy2020/hosei/pdf/hosei_yosan_pr.pdf [in Japanese].

METI (Ministry of Economy, Trade and Industry). 2020c. 'Regarding the Results of the Adoption of Subsidies Related to the "Domestic Investment Promotion Project Cost Subsidy for Supply Chain Measures" (Preliminary Examination) in FY2'. 17 July 2020. www.meti.go.jp/information/publicoffer/saitaku/2020/s200717002.html [in Japanese].

Ministry of Finance. 2019. *Amendment Bill of the Foreign Exchange and Foreign Trade Act*. 21 October 2019. www.mof.go.jp/english/international_policy/fdi/20191021.html.

Ministry of Finance. 2020. 'Rules and Regulations of the Foreign Exchange and Foreign Trade Act'. 24 April 2020. www.mof.go.jp/english/international_policy/fdi/kanrenshiryou01_20200424.pdf.

Ministry of Finance. n.d.-a. 'List of Listed Companies Subject to Prior-Notification under the Foreign Exchange and Foreign Trade Law' [Honpo Jojo Kigyo no Gaitame Ho niokeru Tainai Chokusetsu Toushi-tou Jizen Todokeide Gaitousei List]. Accessed 29 September 2021. www.mof.go.jp/international_policy/gaitame_kawase/fdi/ [in Japanese].

Ministry of Finance. n.d.-b. 'On Proposed Revised Law of a Part of the Foreign Exchange and Foreign Trade Act' [Gaikoku Kawase oyobi Gaikoku Boueki Ho no ichibuwo kaiseisuru Horitsu an ni tsuite]. Accessed 29 September 2021. www.mof.go.jp/international_policy/gaitame_kawase/press_release/kanrenshiryou_191018.pdf [in Japanese].

Ministry of Foreign Affairs. 2007. *Diplomatic Bluebook*. www.mofa.go.jp/policy/other/bluebook/2007/html/index.html.

Ministry of Foreign Affairs. 2008. *Diplomatic Bluebook*. www.mofa.go.jp/policy/other/bluebook/2008/html/index.html.

Ministry of Foreign Affairs. 2011. *Diplomatic Bluebook*. www.mofa.go.jp/policy/other/bluebook/2011/index.html.

Nihon Keizai Shimbun. 1 July 2019. 'Tightening Export Restrictions to South Korea, Government Announcement South Korea Also Takes Countermeasures'. www.nikkei.com/article/DGXMZO46789890R00C19A7EAF000/ [in Japanese].

Nihon Keizai Shimbun. 23 May 2020. 'A Wave of Global Efforts to Block Foreign Takeovers: Japan's Focus on Prior Regulations Has Its Dangers'. www.nikkei.com/article/DGXMZO59427290R20C20A5K14700/ [in Japanese].

Nihon Keizai Shimbun. 31 May 2020. 'June 7: Revised Foreign Exchange Law fully Applied Strengthening Economic Security: Focus on Operation'. www.nikkei. com/article/DGKKZO59798090Q0A530C2EA4000/ [in Japanese].

Nihon Keizai Shimbun. 3 June 2020. 'Economic Team to Develop Cross-Agency Policies to Deal with COVID-19 and Technology Leakage'. www.nikkei.com/ article/DGXMZO59899990S0A600C2EE8000/ [in Japanese].

Nihon Keizai Shimbun. 4 June 2020. 'Advanced Technologies Targeted: Robotics and Biotechnology, Blocking Takeovers'. www.nikkei.com/article/DGXMZO 59944600T00C20A6EE8000/ [in Japanese].

Nihon Keizai Shimbun. 5 June 2020. 'Opinion: The Revised Foreign Exchange and Foreign Trade Law Requires More Transparent Operational Standards'. www. nikkei.com/article/DGXMZO60045650V00C20A6SHF000/ [in Japanese].

Nihon Keizai Shimbun. 24 June 2020. 'Government Subsidies to Prevent Outflow of Advanced Technology Abroad, Subject to Disclosure of Funding Source'. www.nikkei.com/article/DGXMZO60686450T20C20A6MM8000/?n_cid= DSREA001 [in Japanese].

Nikkei Asia. 20 December 2019. 'Japan Partially Reverses Curbs on Tech Materials Exports To South Korea'. asia.nikkei.com/Politics/International-relations/Japan-partially-reverses-curbs-on-tech-materials-exports-to-South-Korea.

Nikkei Sangyo Shimbun. 24 August 2020. 'One Year After Stricter Export Controls, Semiconductor Materials Shifting to Korean Production'. www.nikkei.com/ article/DGXMZO62914600R20C20A8X93000/ [in Japanese].

Pesek, W. 2019. 'Japan's "Idiotic" Investment Restrictions Are Blow to Global Status'. *Nikkei Asian Review*, 19 October 2019.

Pesek, W. 2020. 'Japan Should Encourage Activist Investors, Not Tie Them in Red Tape'. *Nikkei Asian Review*, 27 February 2020. asia.nikkei.com/Opinion/Japan-should-encourage-activist-investors-not-tie-them-in-red-tape.

Productivity Commission. 2017. *Rising Protectionism: Challenges, Threats and Opportunities for Australia*. Canberra: Productivity Commission.

'Sogo Anzen Hosho Kenkyu Group Hokokusho' [Report of Study Group on Comprehensive Security]. 2 July 1980. Accessed 28 November 2020. worldjpn. grips.ac.jp/documents/texts/JPSC/19800702.O1J.html [in Japanese].

Solis, M. 2017. *Dilemmas of a Trading Nation: Japan and the United States in the Evolving Asia-Pacific Order*. Washington, DC: Brookings Institution.

Solis, M. and S. Urata. 2018. 'Abenomics and Japan's Trade Policy in a New Era'. *Asian Economic Policy Review* 13 (1): 106–23. doi.org/10.1111/aepr.12205.

Song, S. 2020. 'After a Year of Restricted Trade with Japan, Korean Materials Industry Has Grown Stronger'. *Korea Herald*, 26 June 2020. www.koreaherald.com/view.php?ud=20200625000809.

Terada, T. 2019. 'Japan and TPP/TPP-11: Opening Black Box of Domestic Political Alignment for Proactive Economic Diplomacy in Face of "Trump Shock"'. *Pacific Review* 32 (6): 1041–69. doi.org/10.1080/09512748.2019.1617771.

Tobita, R. 2020. 'Tokyo Expands National Security Council to Catch Economic Risks'. *Nikkei Asian Review*, 18 March 2020. asia.nikkei.com/Politics/Tokyo-expands-National-Security-Council-to-catch-economic-risks.

Urata, S. 2020. 'A Shift from Passive to Proactive Protector of a Rules-Based Open Trading System'. *AJISS–Commentary* (Special Series: Trajectory of Heisei, way forward to Reiwa), 3 March 2020. www.jiia.or.jp/en/ajiss_commentary/a-shift-from-passive-to-proactive-protector-of-a-rules-based-open-trading-system.html.

Yomiuri Shimbun. 16 May 2020. 'The "Economic Team" to Break Down Vertical Divisions'. www.yomiuri.co.jp/politics/20200516-OYT1T50092/ [in Japanese].

Yomiuri Shimbun, 17 May 2020. 'Grasping Critical Technologies, Hurrying to Prevent Them [Kibigijutsu haaku, bougyo isogu]'. www.yomiuri.co.jp/politics/20200516-OYT1T50267/ [in Japanese].

Yomiuri Shimbun, 20 May 2020. 'A System to Protect and Develop Technology [Gijutsu mamori sodateru taisei wo]'. www.yomiuri.co.jp/politics/20200519-OYT1T50245/ [in Japanese].

Yomiuri Shimbun. 24 August 2020. 'Ministry of Education, Culture, Sports, Science and Technology Reorganized to Promote New Technologies. AI and Quantum Research Next Fall'. www.yomiuri.co.jp/politics/20200824-OYT1T50036/ [in Japanese].

Zafar, R. 2019. 'Semiconductor Raw Material Import Critical for South Korean Industry'. WCCF TECH, 4 July 2019. wccftech.com/semiconductor-import-south-korea-critical/.

6

Strategic interests, regional integration and international economic policy in Indonesia

Yose Rizal Damuri, Rocky Intan and Dandy Rafitrandi

Introduction

The principles that undergird strategic and economic integration policy in Indonesia can be characterised by an emphasis on balance between powers, as well as by an emphasis on both economic and political sovereignty. As tensions between the United States and China intensify, and new opportunities like the Belt and Road Initiative take shape, Indonesian policymakers will increasingly be required to formulate new ways of achieving this balance. Indonesia's role in the formulation of the Regional Comprehensive Economic Partnership (RCEP) provides an indication of what that balance will look like: using established forums like the Association of Southeast Asian Nations (ASEAN) to deepen cooperation in the region in a way that promotes deep economic integration while engaging with and maintaining a balanced approach to all of the region's strategic and economic superpowers. This chapter explores Indonesia's approach to economic integration and security, first elaborating an analytical framework that describes the underlying considerations, and then considering three case studies of policymaking in action.

Indonesia's strategic interests are defined by maintaining balance between superpowers, guided by what is known as the *bebas aktif* (free and active) principles (Anwar 2018). Under these principles, Indonesia's foreign policy refrains from taking part in global and regional rivalry, while at the same time defending its sovereignty and territorial integrity and ensuring stability in Southeast Asia. In addition to its active role in ASEAN, Indonesia also has strategic bilateral partnerships with 13 countries deemed important to its foreign strategic interests, including China and the US (Gindarsah 2016).

Indonesia's balancing attitude can also be observed in trade and economic relations. While China is Indonesia's biggest trade partner, its role in the country's inward foreign investment remains smaller than many other countries, such as Japan and the US. Indonesia also maintains active participation in various economic and trade agreements, promoting inclusive and open cooperation, and finding balance between divergent economic interests. This can be observed in various longstanding multilateral forums such as Asia-Pacific Economic Cooperation, and new ones such as RCEP. Indonesia promoted RCEP in its early stages and played an active role in the conclusion of negotiations (Damuri 2016).

With increasing tensions between the US and China, however, it is increasingly difficult for Indonesia to maintain its balanced position. The return of geopolitical rivalry in East Asia threatens to undermine the strategic autonomy of Indonesia and other countries in Southeast Asia. The US–China trade war continues to exacerbate the slowdown in Indonesian exports due to decreases in its key export commodities. As in the past, Indonesia is actively promoting inclusive and open engagement. Through the ASEAN platform, Indonesia proposed the ASEAN Outlook on the Indo-Pacific as an attempt to balance the rivalry in the region. Still, Indonesia's strategic and economic interests are significantly influenced by geopolitical tensions.

Indonesia's involvement in China's Belt and Road Initiative (BRI) is one example. Despite Indonesia's desire to promote infrastructure financing, the country's involvement in the initiative remains limited. Indonesia only signed a BRI-related memorandum of understanding in 2018 following President Joko 'Jokowi' Widodo's attendance at the 2017 BRI Summit. Much of the concern over the BRI is organically economic, including the fear of an influx of Chinese foreign workers. But domestic politics and geopolitical issues further complicate the matter. China's interests in the South China Sea and rising tensions with some ASEAN members also affect Indonesia's attitude towards the BRI (Damuri et al. 2019).

On the other hand, under President Jokowi, foreign policy prioritises economic diplomacy. In practice, this is defined narrowly as prioritising commercial relations in order to expand Indonesia's exports. Its policies are often implemented in a mercantilist manner. Indonesia strengthens its relations with countries regarded as 'non-traditional' markets, perhaps pursuing bilateral trade agreements. But Indonesia often needs to recalibrate this approach as it does not really support its strategic interests.

This chapter will review the current development of Indonesia's national interests and policy formulation. We argue that two of Indonesia's strategic interests shape its international economic policy: maintaining regional stability and upholding sovereignty. The chapter will attempt describe the interplay between the economic and strategic interests of Indonesia, how they have been affected by the current geopolitical situation and how such interplay often leads to suboptimal policy formulation.

Indonesia's diplomacy, foreign policy and economic integration

How open is Indonesia's economy?

In a globalised world, countries are highly interdependent due to being connected by international trade, investment and migration. This increasing external exposure offers an opportunity to accelerate development but also presents a risk that threatens to destabilise the economy. Indonesia's role in the global economy has also evolved and, at different times, its policy has displayed characteristics of both protection and liberalisation. It is essential to revisit some of the measures of economic openness to show how Indonesia's degree of openness in trade and investment have evolved over time. This section will also explore Indonesia's global value chain participation to measure its involvement in the regional production network. This will be compared to analyses of some other countries' participation.

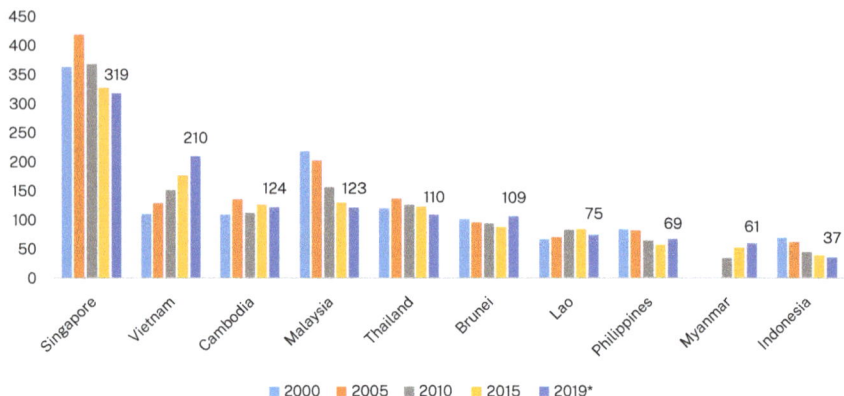

Figure 6.1: Trade (% of GDP)
Source: World Development Indicators.

The first measure is trade openness—or the size of international trade compared to GDP. Figure 6.1 illustrates that Indonesia's openness has been declining since the Asian financial crisis in 1997–98. In 2019, total trade as a percentage of GDP was 37 per cent, like in the early 1970s. A similar trend appears in most ASEAN countries. The only outlier is Vietnam, which successfully doubled its trade openness to 210 per cent over the last 20 years. Brunei, the Philippines and Myanmar have seen an improvement in recent years, although still less significant than that in Vietnam. Figure 6.1 also shows that Indonesia is the most closed country in the region in terms of trade openness; its economy has emerged to be more domestic-oriented over the last 20 years.

Another perspective can be derived from examining the foreign direct investment (FDI) inflow compared to the country's GDP. This reflects the investment climate and opportunity in a country from the perspective of foreign investors. In Indonesia, FDI inflow has been relatively stagnant at 2 per cent for the last 10 years. There was a surge from 2000 to 2014 due to the commodity boom (especially palm oil and coal), but this was shortly followed by a decline. Most of Indonesia's FDI gravitates towards natural resource-oriented sectors, while manufacturing sectors have been shrinking. There was a rise in FDI in the services sector, such as real estate and hotels, as well as in information and technology. But the country's restrictive FDI regime still prevents the realisation of FDI's full potential. Singapore is still the largest investor in Indonesia, while China has climbed into the top three in the last several years. Compared with other ASEAN countries, Indonesia's FDI inflow is relatively moderate.

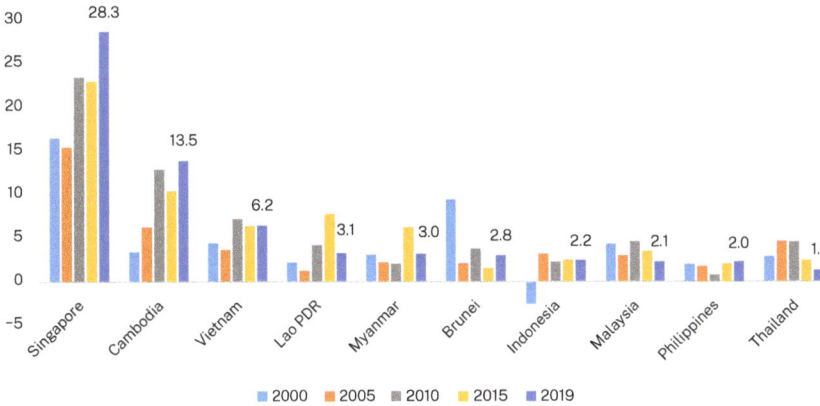

Figure 6.2: Foreign direct investment, net inflows (% of GDP)
Source: World Development Indicators.

Global value chain (GVC) participation is increasingly vital in explaining a country's strategic position in the supply chain. Strong linkages are favourable for multinational firms to conduct business and long-term investment. These capture a country's ability to promote international trade and maintain a hospitable investment climate. The two GVC indicators are backward and forward linkages, which show a country's degree of participation.[1] Among ASEAN countries, Indonesia's forward linkage is quite high while its backward linkage is below average. This shows that Indonesia has limited participation in the GVC due to the low share of foreign value-added in its export products. One explanation is that Indonesia has high non-tariff measures (NTMs) and trade facilitation, especially for import products. From the GVC perspective, the Asian Development Bank (ADB 2019) explains that Indonesia's production is more oriented towards the domestic market, using inputs obtained from the domestic economy and tending towards downstream production.

---

1   Backward linkage refers to the extent of foreign value-added in production and exports, while forward linkage refers to the portion of the country's value-added in other countries' exports.

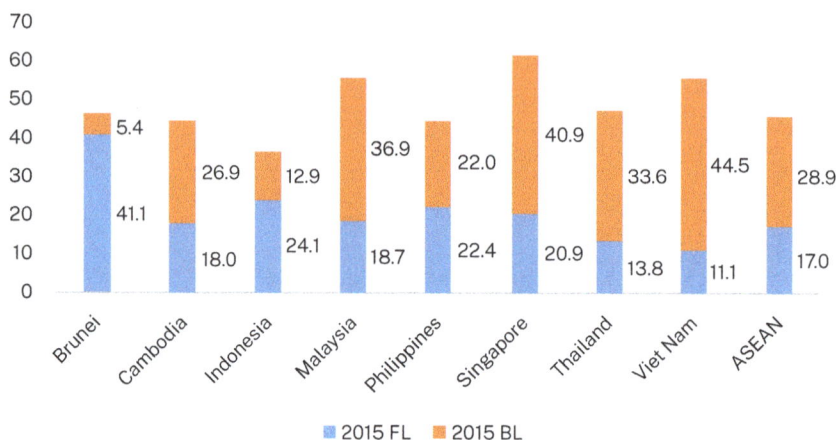

Figure 6.3: Forward and backward linkages in ASEAN countries
Source: OECD TiVA Database (2021).

It is clear that Indonesia has experienced a stagnation, if not a decline, in the measures of economic openness. Several ASEAN countries have performed better in the past 10 years or so. A strong commitment to economic openness is required to optimise the benefits of international trade, investment and the regional supply chain. However, Indonesia does not seem to be well positioned in the supply chain; instead, its economy has become more domestic-oriented in the last decade. The next section will discuss this issue from a foreign policy perspective.

An assessment of Indonesia's foreign policy in trade and investment

One of the drivers of economic openness is unilateral trade and investment policy. Historically, Indonesia's position towards open economic policy has swung like a pendulum. According to Pangestu, Rahardja and Ing (2015), there have been several distinct phases of Indonesia's trade policy. The first major trade and investment policy was the introduction of the open door policy regarding foreign investment in the late 1960s to finance economic activities. The government began to liberate trade regulations quite rapidly, introducing a series of major reforms between 1966 and 1969, while introducing capital account liberalisation and unifying the exchange rate of the rupiah.

By the early 1970s, it became apparent that Indonesia preferred an import substitution policy and a more inward-looking development strategy, supported by the increase in international oil prices, which quadrupled in the mid-1970s. The oil boom that began in 1973 made the country rich enough to afford many government-led economic projects. After the fall of oil prices in the early 1980s, the government began a limited economic policy of deregulation along with tariff reductions and the removal of some non-tariff barriers (NTBs) in manufacturing sectors, especially in labour-intensive industries. By 1992, the average tariff had been reduced to 20 per cent from 26 per cent in 1986, while the incidence of NTBs fell to 5 per cent from 32 per cent. During this period, Indonesia experienced rapid growth, mostly from industrialisation. Foreign investment also surged as many economists referred to Indonesia as the next 'Asian Tiger'.

During the Asian financial crisis in 1997–98, Indonesia pushed its reform agenda with the structural adjustment program attached to the International Monetary Fund's lending package. The package included a gradual reduction of import tariffs, including those on sensitive products of heavy industries; the removal of NTBs and licensing for imports of many agricultural products; and liberalisation in the service sector. However, protectionist measures had returned by the early 2000s in the form of trade regulation and licensing requirements in several products such as textiles, steel, sugar and cloves. This was reflected in the increasing trend of NTMs as both nominal and effective rates increased between 1995 and 2008.

After the global financial crisis in 2007–08, the pendulum in Indonesia swung back towards inward-looking policy. Economic growth was resilient and stable due to the surge of commodity prices such as palm oil and coal. But good economic times had produced bad policies. The government enacted several laws on industry, trade and horticulture that imposed a more restrictive trade and investment regime (Patunru and Rahardja 2015). For example, Law 3/2014 on industry reflects the government's focus on promoting industrial growth by regulation: it allowed the government to restrict the export of raw materials in order to promote domestic processing.

There has been no significant liberalising reform in Indonesia's trade and investment policy in the past five years. Instead, populism and nationalism have been on the rise, not only in Indonesia but also around the world. Ambitions for *swasembada,* or self-sufficiency, translated into more protectionist and anti-import policies, especially in food products. Some examples include import licensing in the agriculture sector and local content requirements in the manufacturing sector. The restrictive investment regime also hampered service sector competitiveness. Recently, the government had a breakthrough in regulatory reform, passing the Omnibus Law, which aims to improve Indonesia's investment climate and create more jobs.

Indonesia and economic integration initiatives

This section examines Indonesia's commitments as a supporter of open regionalism, reflected by its participation in regional integration. Indonesia is active in pursuing economic integration agreements. However, barriers to trade and investment have not been significantly reduced, but rather transformed into burdensome regulatory constraints. This has resulted in the country becoming more inward-looking and having lower participation in the global economy.

In ASEAN, Indonesia's involvement has contributed to economic integration among ASEAN countries. The ASEAN Economic Community (AEC) was established in 2016 as a continuation of the ASEAN Free Trade Area. The AEC reduced most barriers to trade in goods and services as well as investment. Some of the significant milestones achieved by the AEC include the ASEAN Trade in Goods Agreement, the ASEAN Multilateral Agreement on the Full Liberalisation of Air Freight Services, the ASEAN Comprehensive Investment Agreement, the ASEAN Agreement on the Movement of Natural Persons and the ASEAN Framework Agreement on Services, although the level of implementation of each agreement varies. ASEAN also actively engaged with its partners to form ASEAN+1 FTAs. Indonesia also played a pivotal role in formulating the ASEAN Outlook on the Asia-Pacific in response to former president Trump's Free and Open Indo-Pacific Initiative. The former effectively blunted the sharp geopolitical edges on the latter, concentrating instead on economic cooperation rather than strategic competition.

Figure 6.4 shows the development of free trade agreements (FTAs) in effect in East Asia over the last 10 years. Other than a few ASEAN+1 FTAs (and AANZFTA, which includes both Australia and New Zealand), Indonesia is quite passive. Indonesia only has bilateral trade agreements with four countries: Japan, Pakistan, Chile and Australia. The most recent agreement, the Indonesia–Australia Comprehensive Economic Partnership Agreement (IA–CEPA) entered into force in July 2020. Indonesia has pursued few FTAs compared with Vietnam, who has signed FTAs with Japan, South Korea, the

European Union, Chile and the Eurasian Economic Union, as well as the Comprehensive and Progressive Agreement for Trans-Pacific Partnership (CPTPP). However, Indonesia aims to conclude more agreements in 2021, for instance, with the European Union, South Korea and Turkey.

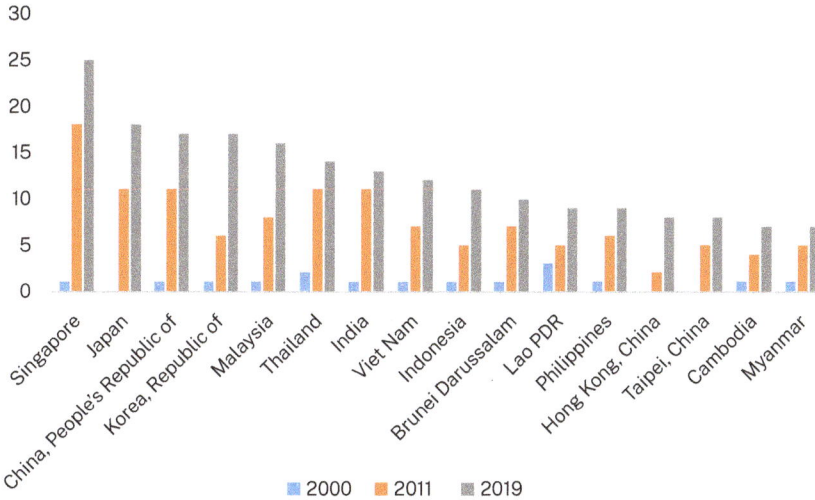

Figure 6.4: Number of FTAs in force
Source: Asia Regional Integration Center (2021).

In recent years, there has been an increasing trend towards deep trade agreements, which refers to a more comprehensive agreement regarding quality and quantity, covering not only trade but also additional policy areas such as investment, labour and environmental protection. This is because some tariffs and other trade barriers were already low. The IA–CEPA, CPTPP and RCEP are a few examples. These agreements include some traditional coverage in goods, services and investment, as well as going beyond WTO commitments in areas such as competition policy, state-owned enterprises (SOEs) and intellectual property rights. The implementation of these agreements requires commitment to further economic reform. The political cost of Indonesia's economy is increasingly high, since all trade agreements require approval based on the Trade Law from the House of Representatives. Negotiating a trade agreement is a lengthy process and requires strong political support and strong coordination among government institutions and other stakeholders.

Security and political interests of economic policy

Conceptual framework

It may be an exaggeration to regard the division between the study of national security and economics as artificial. But it surely has never been as clear-cut as conventional wisdom suggests. Both aspects influence one another in a continuous feedback loop with various paradigms offering different lenses. This section attempts to provide a conceptual framework on how national security considerations influence economic policy, before delving into the case of Indonesia.

Various paradigms within the discipline of international relations offer diverse definitions, classifications and perspectives on national security. Realism stresses that the ultimate purpose of national security is self-preservation and emphasises the role of the nation-state and the threat of aggression from others due to existing in an anarchic international system (Walt 2010). Liberalism highlights the benefits of international cooperation through participation in international organisations, especially on economic cooperation. Constructivism asserts that national security interests are social constructs, emphasising the role of domestic identity, norms and culture in such construction (de Buck and Hosli 2020).

The interplay between the economy and national security is multifaceted and bidirectional. This is especially the case with the link between economic integration and security relationships. In one direction, a closer security relationship can lead to a closer economic relationship between states. Trade improves economic efficiency and allows resources to be utilised for national security purposes, and states are more inclined to trade with states with aligned security interests in order to prevent contributing to the military power of potential adversaries (Gowa and Mansfield 2004). In the other direction, scholars have noted that increased economic integration can lead to closer security relationships. A security alliance commitment can uphold the economic gains from increased trade and safeguard states against internal threats to the trading relationship (Fordham 2010). China's BRI could be understood in this way. It is unlikely that it was economic concerns alone in relieving domestic overcapacity for Beijing that pushed its infrastructure companies to venture abroad.

Another way to think of how national security considerations can work their way into influencing economic policy is through the risk vector model (Retter et al. 2020). Within the paradigm-agnostic model, risk vectors are defined as 'avenues through which national security risks in relation to crucial infrastructure, sectors and processes' can manifest. Examples include ownership, espionage and access to sensitive information, natural resource dependence, supplier dependence, government intervention, corruption and fraud among others. These vectors stem from macroeconomic variables and socioeconomic trends that can be domestic, regional or global in scope. Examples of such variables include domestic investment and consumption, employment and FDI, with trends such as digital transformation, disinformation and political and economic paradigms of foreign states. Due to these variables and trends, and through the risk vectors, a malevolent actor can inflict harm to achieve its objectives. The existence and actions of malevolent actors transform a risk into a threat to national security. A prime example is the China–Australia trade dispute, in which Beijing allegedly banned imports of Australian barley, beef and coal after Canberra called for an international, independent inquiry into the origins of the coronavirus outbreak in Wuhan. This is a clear case of China weaponising its market access through the vector of Australian commodity exports (Laurenceson and Zhou 2022).

Dynamics of Indonesia's interests

This section will attempt to highlight two of Indonesia's national security interests that often influence its economic policy.

Independence and sovereignty

Sovereignty is a core concept that preconditions national security. Without an authority—usually organised as a nation-state—in a given area, considerations of the security of such an area will be rendered moot. There exist diverse historical and legal manifestations of sovereignty, but four key elements must be present: the will and capacity to exercise authority, domestic and international recognition that morphs into legitimacy, a given territory and citizens populating said territory (Biersteker and Weber 1996). Sovereignty can essentially be defined as recognised state authority over a given territory and population.

For Indonesia, there are two dimensions of sovereignty that deserve elaboration. The first is autonomy. To better understand this, it is helpful to review the foundational principles of Indonesia's foreign policy—that is, to be free and active. Born amid the Cold War, popular wisdom dictates that 'free' means constant non-alignment towards any power bloc—that is, eternal neutrality. Yet, Article 3 of Law 37/100 explains that the principle refers to the 'freedom of deciding policy on international issues and no binding itself a priori into any bloc'. This is the essence of autonomy in Indonesia's sovereignty.

The second dimension is territorial integrity. Sovereignty entails the ability to keep the territory under a state's control whole and intact. This was codified into Indonesian law with a clause stating that: 'State defence is organised to defend state sovereignty, the territorial integrity of the Republic of Indonesia, and the safety of citizens from threats towards the unity of nation and state'. This is especially relevant when one considers Jakarta's historical and ongoing challenges with separatism, for instance, with East Timor, Aceh and, presently, West Papua.

While the concept of sovereignty focuses on those two dimensions, it has evolved into various other forms. The notion of sovereignty can be found in various economic-related policies and translated into economic nationalism, economic independence and self-reliance. This preoccupation with sovereignty, especially regarding its economic aspects, can be traced back to the colonial period and the post-independence era.[2] Even after four years of fighting the War of Independence, Indonesian leaders found that they had only achieved political independence, and not economic independence: most production facilities, the banking sector, trade and industry were under the control of Dutch companies (Thee 2011). This gave rise to economic nationalism in the form of acquisitions of many Dutch and foreign enterprises in the 1950s, as well as policies that favoured economic independence and self-reliance. Although the Indonesian economy later became more open, economic nationalism and independence remain key influences on economic policymaking in the country.

Regional stability

Regional stability can be understood as the external dimension of Indonesia's national security interests. The concept can be broadly defined as the lack of conflict among states in Southeast Asia. Dewi Fortuna Anwar (2003) tabulated Indonesia's security concerns and foreign policy outlook in

---

2   Indonesia was governed by the Dutch until 1942, when Japan came and took over the area until 1945. Indonesia declared its independence on 17 August 1945, but was subsequently involved in a war of independence with the Netherlands until 1949.

a framework known as the concentric circles formula. The formula first and foremost rates the importance of countries within Indonesia's foreign policy based on their geographical proximity. Each concentric circle represents importance in hierarchy. The first concentric circle is Southeast Asia. As the premier multilateral grouping in the region, ASEAN is consequently seen as Indonesia's most important foreign policy relationship—or, to use Anwar's term, 'the cornerstone of Indonesia's foreign policy'.

The main component of the definition of regional stability requires the absence of armed, interstate conflict and the management of great power relations in the region. In practice, this means lowering tensions between countries, not necessarily eliminating conflicts of interest, and providing a platform for great powers to remain competitively engaged for them to balance one another's influence. Enmeshing great powers in the regional architecture centred upon ASEAN ensures that they balance one another and also allows ASEAN to preserve its autonomy (Goh 2008). The idea is for ASEAN to engage great powers in economic and defence cooperation while at the same time preserving its own strategic autonomy. Regional mechanisms and initiatives centred around ASEAN—both strategic (the East Asia Summit, the ASEAN Defence Ministers Meeting-Plus and the ASEAN Regional Forum) and economic (the ASEAN Free Trade Area, the ASEAN Plus Agreements and the RCEP)—should be understood through this lens.

Indonesia's strong interest in maintaining regional stability comes from the realisation that the country's economic development depends on its positive relationships with other countries in the region. While it seems quite obvious, the situation was not always like that. From the late 1950s to the mid-1960s, Indonesia's foreign policy had two focuses: its closeness to the Soviet Union and China, and its confrontation with the Federation of Malaya. These policy stances were closely related to the anti-colonialist and independence narratives that the first president of Indonesia, Sukarno, tried to instil in his domestic constituent. However, when Suharto took over as president in 1966, Indonesian foreign policy underwent significant changes. Instead of maintaining a confrontational stance, Suharto's New Order Regime pursued regional stability and cooperation, which were deemed necessary to support economic development. The founding of ASEAN itself in 1967 indicates the country's eagerness for achieving regional stability. Foreign Minister Adam Malik referred to ASEAN as the 'cornerstone' of Indonesian foreign policy.

The underlying factors

With this conceptual framework in mind, it is useful to briefly describe the underlying external and domestic factors that weigh over Indonesian policymaking. There are two chief external factors of note. The first is the rise of China, a monumental phenomenon that has become the backdrop for many new global developments. Deng Xiaoping's reforms in the 1980s laid the groundwork for China's economic rise. The country's growth and development further accelerated with China's integration into global trade networks, starting with its accession to the World Trade Organization in 2001. China is now forecasted to overtake the US as the largest national economy in nominal GDP terms within the next few decades. In terms of Indonesia's economic and security considerations, this presents a complication. China's economic rise has major implications for Indonesia's own geopolitical rise and ambitions, most notably for Jakarta in its assertiveness in the South China Sea. China has become an important trade and investment partner for Indonesia, especially in commodity exports. As the China–Australia trade dispute demonstrates, differing geopolitical interests between states with deeply interconnected economies presents an opportunity for such states to wield economic policy as an instrument of defending national security.

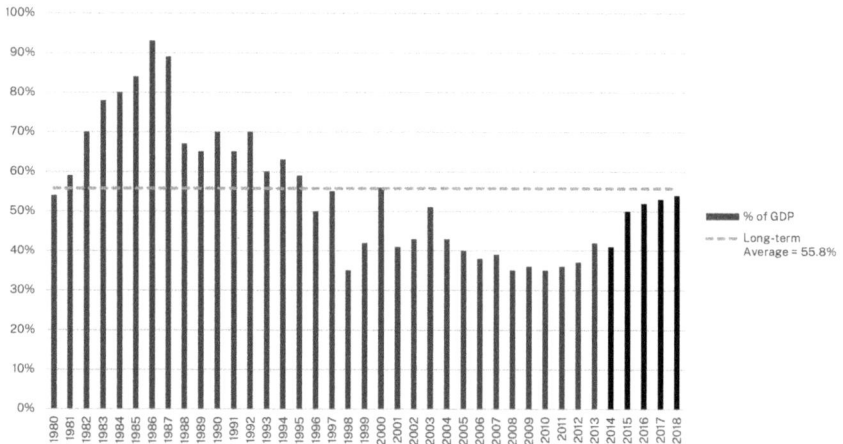

Figure 6.5: Assets of Indonesian SOEs, 1980–2018
Source: Kim (2019).

The second significant external factor is the onset of the coronavirus pandemic. Today's global trade system relies on seamless cross-border flows of raw materials, intermediate goods and finished goods. The COVID-19 outbreak led to the implementation of quarantine measures and border closures to control its spread. This exogenous shock severely disrupted global value chains, particularly during the early stages of the pandemic (Seric et al. 2020). As countries started to feel the impact of supply disruptions due to border closures, national governments resorted to enacting protectionist measures. Calls to rethink the international outsourcing of critical goods and plans to restore production gained momentum. Such ideas would surely be welcome in Indonesia—a country with a history of justifying agricultural import bans by conflating food security with food self-sufficiency.

One notable domestic factor is the return of the prominence of SOEs in Indonesia's economy. Indonesia's dirigiste impulse has always been strong, especially in the early 1980s, which was a high point for the role of SOEs. Prior to the Jokowi era, the average cumulative assets of SOEs in Indonesia as a percentage of the country's GDP was well below the historical average, and the Jokowi era can be seen as the return to the norm. The infrastructure push by President Jokowi has been mostly in the form of capital injections to state infrastructure companies, and it will likely continue to be this way. In addition to its emphasis on deregulation, other scholars have underlined the nationalist features of this trend, which Eve Warburton (2017) coined as 'new developmentalism'. We can expect that 'sovereignty' and 'independence' will be used to justify further protectionist policies advocated by SOEs to insulate themselves from competition and to push for local champions.

How geopolitical and security interests affect foreign economic policy: Cases and analysis

Case 1: Indonesia, ASEAN and regional integration

The interplay of economics and geopolitics has emerged as one of the top risks in recent years. Trade tensions, Brexit, technology rivalry and the WTO deadlock are some examples. Most importantly, the US–China relationship has turned Asia into a battleground for competing influence. When elephants fight, it is the grass that suffers.

Indonesia and other ASEAN countries are affected by this turmoil and have raised this concern as a regional security issue. This is one of the reasons why ASEAN needs more mechanisms to keep great powers in check. Indonesia's foreign policy has evolved to respond to the world's new security circumstances. After becoming a democracy in 1998, Indonesia focused on pursuing a free and active foreign policy and pushing for ASEAN centrality by trying to establish an inclusive regional architecture centred on ASEAN. During Susilo Bambang Yudhoyono's administration (2004–14), Indonesia actively used economic diplomacy and foreign economic policy to convey this message. Although it is less aggressive under President Jokowi, the use of economic initiatives to maintain Indonesia's geopolitical interests—sovereignty and regional stability—remains in place.

The negotiation of RCEP demonstrates Indonesia's role in, and intention to shape, regional integration in East Asia. A region-wide arrangement was in line with the economic and political interests of countries in East Asia in the late 2000s. The existing arrangement of trade in the region—the abundance of bilateral and plurilateral deals, or the 'noodle bowl' effect—posed challenges to the coherence of global trade agreements. There was an increasing need for deeper integration among economies in the region. Politically, deeper and wider regional cooperation is also expected to ease political tension among countries in the region and, in particular, reconcile past differences among the Northeast Asian nations (China, Japan and South Korea). Countries in the region—especially large ones like China and Japan—view FTAs as important instruments of commercial diplomacy to realise their vision of the geopolitical landscape and global strategy (Damuri 2016).

There were two regional proposals under serious discussion in the mid-2000s: the China-promoted East Asia Free Trade Area, which included ASEAN+3 (ASEAN plus China, Japan and South Korea), and the Japan-initiated Comprehensive Economic Partnership of East Asia, which included three other ASEAN partners. Competition ensued between China and Japan for taking the lead in establishing a region-wide agreement, while other countries in the region were divided between the two proposals. The rivalry continued and delayed the process of integration until 2011, when Indonesia—as the chair of ASEAN—proposed a new initiative for regional cooperation as a middle path. ASEAN and its partners adopted the proposal, known as RCEP, during the twenty-first ASEAN Summit on 20 November 2012.

By proposing RCEP, Indonesia wanted to maintain ASEAN's centrality as a primary driving force for a regional integration process in the Asia-Pacific. It became more important in the wake of another integration process in the region: the Trans-Pacific Partnership (TPP), which began with the P4 agreement but expanded and eventually centred on US participation. Four ASEAN countries had participated in TPP negotiations and had the power to divide ASEAN's attention in the economic integration process.

Amid the uncertainty during a global pandemic, ASEAN countries successfully concluded RCEP negotiations, but without India. The agreement is not only economically significant, but also strategic in shaping ASEAN's approach to the new multipolar global order and leveraging the region's dynamism. Asia has been a major beneficiary of the global trade system in the past several decades, and RCEP signals to the world that Asian countries are still open for business.

Using economic integration to support regional stability is not new to Indonesia. After the Cold War era ended in early 1990, Indonesia was worried about the relevance of ASEAN as it was primarily founded as a response to the conflicts and tensions among Southeast Asian countries in the 1960s. ASEAN needed to renew its sense of purpose and find new motives to maintain stability in the region. After the introduction of some unilateral economic liberalisation policies in the late 1980s, along with the possible deadlock of multilateral efforts, Indonesia supported Thailand and Singapore's suggestion to form a free trade agreement among ASEAN member countries (Stubbs 2000).

The use of ASEAN as a platform for economic integration to pursue Indonesia's vision of regional stability continued after the Asian financial crisis. Troubled by its incapacity to deal with the crisis, ASEAN decided to deepen integration processes and institutions. Launched during Indonesia's chairmanship in 2011, ASEAN envisioned an ASEAN Community to be formed in 2020, later brought forward to 2015. One of the pillars was the AEC, which was better prepared and more extensive than the political security and sociocultural pillars. Indonesia's then foreign minister, Hassan Wirajuda (2001–2009), affirmed that Indonesia had always provided intellectual leadership for ASEAN's institutional evolution to better cope with extra- and intra-regional challenges (Weatherbee 2013).

One important feature of Indonesia's initiative of regional economic integration is inclusiveness and open regionalism. The 'Guiding Principles and Objectives for Negotiating' the RCEP, for instance, reflects this position strongly, as has been upheld in many other economic integration agendas that Indonesia supports, such as Asia-Pacific Economic Cooperation.

Case 2: Sovereignty in Indonesia's trade and investment policy

Although Indonesia is very active in pursuing economic diplomacy and promoting regional integration, its trade and investment policy tends to diverge from its foreign policy. As discussed in the previous section, Indonesia's trade and investment policy tends to be more inward-looking and protectionist. While tariff rates continue to decline, other barriers to trade are still increasing. Marks (2017) shows that the nominal rate of protection and effective rate of protection increased between 2008 and 2015, notably for food and agriculture products. In 2018, 48.3 per cent of 10,826 tariff lines were subject to import restrictions and prohibitions (Ministry of Finance of Republic of Indonesia 2018). Since then, the government has tried to reduce the number of restrictions by shifting around half of them to undergo post-border inspection measures.

One explanation is that trade policy is the result of interest group actions to maximise rent-seeking opportunities from trade regulations. Through a complex bargaining process, small but concentrated and organised groups are able to lobby for greater protection for their sectors that often generate excessive profits. As mentioned by Soesastro and Basri (2005), there is evidence that the major beneficiaries of Indonesia's protectionist measures are the capital-intensive and highly concentrated sectors. These sectors are more likely to mobilise resources to lobby for higher protection.

But this overlooks the increasing influence of democratic processes in Indonesia's policymaking, especially in trade and investment. Trade policy instruments are the easiest and most visible action to meet the perceived needs of constituents. Damuri and Pangestu (2018) conducted a survey examining public perception on international economic policy in Indonesia and found that more restrictive and inward-looking policy may be in line with the general public's interests. Politicians and policymakers would gain additional political support by listening to general public opinion on trade and investment policy.

The concern of maintaining sovereignty is an important factor that gives rise to inward-looking sentiment among the general public. Sovereignty is always the top security consideration, either in a narrow sense of territorial sovereignty or in a broader sense of political sovereignty. It is also reflected in international economic policy. As Reid (2018) explains, concerns over sovereignty and nationalism have deep roots in Indonesia's history, especially during the first few years of its independence. Fear over foreign intervention and neo-colonialism remains prevalent among Indonesians, and has been used by politicians to justify further protectionist measures.

This fear is reinforced by the setbacks in Indonesia's production sector and its inability to compete with imported products after the Asian financial crisis. The manufacturing sector grew slower than GDP and lost its competitiveness and global market share, and it was also unable to participate in the global value chains (Aswicahyono, Narjoko and Hill 2008). The agriculture sector could not produce enough to satisfy domestic demand. This, along with an import ban, resulted in increasing prices. While the problems can be traced back to the failure of economic and industrial policies, it still fuels the narrative of sovereignty and economic nationalism. Some territorial disputes with neighbouring countries lend further credence to this narrative, holding back economic relations with some partners. This can be observed in the Indonesia–China economic relationship.

Case 3: Indonesia–China economic relations and the Belt and Road Initiative

Indonesia and China resumed diplomatic ties in 1990 after suspending their diplomatic relationship for more than 23 years. The restoration improved economic relations not only between Indonesia and China but also between ASEAN and China. After the resumption of diplomatic relations, trade between Indonesia and China, which was previously virtually non-existent, grew gradually. The pace picked up after 2000 due to two major developments: the emergence of China as a manufacturing power and its accession to the WTO; and, more importantly, the establishment of the ASEAN–China Free Trade Agreement.

But many Indonesians perceive this trade agreement to be a bad deal since Indonesia has suffered increasing trade deficits. China's exports to Indonesia have been dominated by manufactured mechanical products, such as electrical machinery, other machinery and mechanical appliances, and vehicles and parts, while Indonesia's exports comprise mostly minerals and commodities, giving the impression that China is only interested in securing a supply of raw materials from Indonesia. Negative perceptions of China only grew stronger as Chinese FDI started arriving in Indonesia. Chinese investors are perceived as bringing low-quality investments with dirty technology and environmentally damaging operations. Along with the capital investments came foreign workers from China, generating negative sentiment and increasing social tension in regions where the investments were concentrated.

These negative sentiments have held Indonesia back from formally participating in China's BRI. From an Indonesian perspective, the BRI arrived at a critical juncture to boost its badly needed infrastructure development. In 2018, Indonesia formally signed a memorandum of understanding on promoting cooperation on the development of Regional Comprehensive Economic Corridors. The Indonesian Government proposed 30 other projects with a total value of US$91 billion. These other projects only take part in four designated provinces. Most of them are related to the development of industrial and tourism facilities, with only a few related to connectivity infrastructure.

In addition to negative domestic sentiments about China, Indonesia is also concerned with some unresolved issues in the region that may generate direct and indirect negative impacts on regional stability and potentially also on the implementation of the BRI. One of these issues is the polemic against China's behaviour in the South China Sea. Increasing tensions between the US and China have also contributed to Indonesia's lack of enthusiasm in commencing its formal agreement under the BRI.

Conclusion

Indonesia's strategic diplomacy mantra of *bebas aktif* can be clearly observed in its policy on economic integration. Indonesia is an active participant in, and even initiator of, regional economic integration. Indonesia started several regional integration initiatives, in particular using ASEAN as the vehicle of change, such as the AEC and the RCEP. This behaviour is rooted in the country's strategic interest in pursuing regional stability. Economic integration has been used to pursue that strategic objective with some success. Indonesia's proposals on strengthening strategic cooperation in the region often include an economic agenda. For instance, the ASEAN Outlook on the

Indo-Pacific, which was initiated and promoted by Indonesia, emphasises stronger economic cooperation to support the maintenance of peace and security in the region.

Indonesia's interest in regional stability cannot be separated from its other priority of maintaining independence and sovereignty. Until 1967, upholding sovereignty was done through enacting anti-colonialist narratives that often led to conflict with Western countries and neighbouring countries in the region. The rise of the New Order regime in 1966 under President Suharto placed economic development as the top priority. This required Indonesia to revive its relations with Western powers and cooperate with neighbouring countries. It shifted the attention to reginal stability to support the country's sovereignty and independence, which led to the formation of ASEAN in 1967 and subsequent activities to facilitate stronger regional integration.

While foreign economic policy and diplomacy have been used successfully to achieve these two strategic interests, sovereignty and regional stability sometimes lead to conflicting economic policy. Indonesia is active in conducting trade agreements with various countries, including those under ASEAN initiatives, but the country's trade and investment policy remains relatively restrictive. Various NTMs, which are not normally discussed in FTAs, are being implemented to control exports and imports, and also protect domestic industries. This inward-looking attitude often delays Indonesia's involvement in some major economic cooperation initiatives, such as CPTPP or BRI, or the implementation of trade agreements already in force.

Indonesia should find a balance between these two strategic interests in order to effectively implement international economic policy for both foreign diplomacy and domestic economic development. This can be achieved if Indonesian policymakers and the general public can change their perceptions and interpretations of sovereignty and independence, particularly relating to economic issues. The narrative of economic independence and self-reliance is not compatible with the interdependent nature of the global economy. Further perpetuating this narrative would significantly hinder Indonesia's economic performance and compromise its strategic position in the region.

References

ADB (Asian Development Bank). 2019. *Policies to Support the Development of Indonesia's Manufacturing Sector during 2020–2024: A Joint ADB–BAPPENAS Report*. Manila: Asian Development Bank.

Anwar, D. F. 2003. 'Megawati's Search for an Effective Foreign Policy'. In *Governance in Indonesia, Challenges Facing the Megawati Presidency*, edited by Hadi Soesastro, Anthony L. Smith and Mui Ling Han, 70–90. Singapore: Institute of Southeast Asian Studies.

Anwar, D. F. 2018. 'Indonesia's Vision of Regional Order in East Asia amid US–China Rivalry: Continuity and Change.' *Asia Policy* 13 (2): 57–63.

Asia Regional Integration Center. 2021. 'Free Trade Agreements Database'. aric.adb.org/database/fta.

Aswicahyono, H., D. Narjoko and H. Hill. 2008. 'Industrialization after a Deep Economic Crisis: Indonesia'. *Working Papers in Trade and Development*, The Australian National University. econpapers.repec.org/repec:pas:papers:2008-18.

Biersteker, T. J. and C. Weber, eds. 1996. *State Sovereignty as Social Construct*. Cambridge: Cambridge University Press. doi.org/10.1017/CBO9780511598685.

Damuri, Y. R. 2016. 'RCEP Prospect and Challenges: Political Economy of East Asian Integration'. In *Trade Regionalism in the Asia-Pacific*, edited by B. Sanchita and M. Kawai, 105–21. Singapore: ISEAS–Yusof Ishak Institute. doi.org/10.1355/9789814695459-010.

Damuri, Y. R. and M. Pangestu. 2018. 'Who Is Afraid of Economic Openness? People's Perception of Globalization in Indonesia'. In *Indonesia in the New World: Globalization, Nationalism and Sovereignty*, edited by A. A. Patunru, M. Pangestu and M. C. Basri, 109–25. Singapore: Institute of Southeast Asian Studies.

Damuri, Y. R., V. Perkasa, R. Atje and F. Hirawan. 2019. 'Perceptions and Readiness of Indonesia towards the Belt and Road Initiative'. CSIS Report, Jakarta: Centre for Strategic and International Studies.

de Buck, D. and M. O. Hosli. 2020. 'Traditional Theories of International Relations'. In *The Changing Global Order*, edited by Madeleine O. Hosli and Joren Selleslaghs, 3–21. Cham: Springer. doi.org/10.1007/978-3-030-21603-0_1.

Fordham, B. O. 2010. 'Trade and Asymmetric Alliances'. *Journal of Peace Research* 47 (6): 685–96. doi.org/10.1177/0022343310381689.

Gindarsah, I. 2016. 'Strategic Hedging in Indonesia's Defense Diplomacy'. *Defense & Security Analysis* 32 (4): 336–53. doi.org/10.1080/14751798.2016.1233695.

Goh, E. 2008. 'Great Powers and Hierarchical Order in Southeast Asia: Analyzing Regional Security Strategies'. *International Security* 32 (3): 113–57. doi.org/10.1162/isec.2008.32.3.113.

Gowa, J. and E. Mansfield. 2004. 'Alliances, Imperfect Markets, and Major-Power Trade'. *International Organization* 58 (4): 775–805. doi.org/10.1017/S002081 830404024X.

Kim, K. 2019. 'Indonesia's Restrained State Capitalism: Development and Policy Challenges'. *Journal of Contemporary Asia* 51 (3): 419–46. doi.org/10.1080/00472336.2019.1675084.

Laurenceson, J. and Weihuan Z. 2022. 'Demystifying Australia–China Trade Tensions'. *Journal of World Trade* 56 (1): 51–86. doi.org/10.54648/TRAD 2022003.

Marks, S. V. 2017. 'Non-Tariff Trade Regulations in Indonesia: Nominal and Effective Rates of Protection'. *Bulletin of Indonesian Economic Studies* 53 (3): 333–57. doi.org/10.1080/00074918.2017.1298721.

Pangestu, M., S. Rahardja and L. Y. Ing. 2015. 'Fifty Years of Trade Policy in Indonesia: New World Trade, Old Treatments'. *Bulletin of Indonesian Economic Studies* 51 (2): 239–61. doi.org/10.1080/00074918.2015.1061915.

Patunru, A. A. and S. Rahardja. 2015. *Trade Protectionism in Indonesia: Bad Times and Bad Policy*. Sydney, NSW: Lowy Institute for International Policy.

Reid. A. 2018. 'Challenging Geography: Asserting Economic Sovereignty in a Porous Archipelago'. In *Indonesia in the New World: Globalization, Nationalism and Sovereignty*, edited by A. A. Patunru, M. Pangestu and M. C. Basri, 17–34. Singapore: Institute of Southeast Asian Studies. doi.org/10.1355/9789814 818230-007.

Retter, L., E. J. Frinking, S. Hoorens, A. Lynch, F. Nederveen and W. D. Phillips. 2020. *Relationships between the Economy and National Security: Analysis and Considerations for Economic Security Policy in the Netherlands*. Santa Monica: RAND Corporation. www.rand.org/pubs/research_reports/RR4287.html. doi.org/10.7249/RR4287.

Seric, A., H. Gorg, S. Mosle and M. Windisch. 2020. 'How the Pandemic Disrupts Global Value Chains'. Industrial Analytics Platform, UNIDO. iap.unido.org/articles/how-pandemic-disrupts-global-value-chains.

Soesastro, H. and M. C. Basri. 2005. 'The Political Economy of Trade Policy in Indonesia'. *ASEAN Economic Bulletin* 22 (1): 3–18.

Stubbs, R. 2000. 'Signing on to Liberalization: AFTA and the Politics of Regional Economic Cooperation'. *Pacific Review* 13 (2): 297–318. doi.org/10.1080/095127400363604.

Thee K. W. 2011. *The Introduction, Evolution, and End of Colonial Extractive Institutions in the Netherlands Indies and Its Long-Term Consequences in Independent Indonesia, 1830–2000.* www.yumpu.com/en/document/view/28274655/ch2thee-kian-wieintroduction-indonesiapdf.

Walt, S. 2010. 'Realism and Security'. *Oxford Research Encyclopedia of International Studies.* Wiley-Blackwell.

Warburton, E. 2017. 'Jokowi and the New Developmentalism'. *Bulletin of Indonesian Economic Studies* 52 (3): 297–320. doi.org/10.1080/00074918.2016.1249262.

Weatherbee, D. E. 2013. *Indonesia in ASEAN: Vision and Reality.* Singapore: Institute of Southeast Asian Studies. doi.org/10.1355/9789814519236.

7

Malaysia's economic engagement with China: A consideration of the economics and security nexus

Shankaran Nambiar

Introduction

Malaysia's economic relations with China have been evolving since Malaysia's independence and this economic engagement has been coterminous with China's development and political ambitions. China has progressed from a nation that was drawn into the global economy through President of the United States Richard Nixon's administration and Secretary of State Henry Kissinger to a country that wants to chart its own destiny, independent of any foreign power. Malaysia, for its part, has shifted from a country that viewed China with suspicion to one that has cautiously cultivated economic ties with China. It has more recently identified China as an agent that can drive its own economic development.

China may indeed be a country that seeks to pursue peace, prosperity and progress among developing countries, but the argument is complicated by the perceptions of other countries in the Association of Southeast Asian Nations (ASEAN) and of Western powers. The South China Sea issue has been festering and is yet to be resolved. Malaysia has been dragged into US–China trade tensions, which could well deteriorate into something of broader dimensions. While Malaysia might profit from trade diversion and benefit from investment that might otherwise have flowed to China, the reality may be more difficult to navigate.

The US may prefer that Malaysia make a binary choice between that kind of opportunistic gain from the diversion of trade and investment, or greater economic engagement with China to the exclusion of the US. Malaysia need not and should not take this path. That said, the realities of China's ambitions must be recognised. China's investment projects in Malaysia, as part of its Belt and Road Initiative (BRI), do involve security considerations. But foreign investment is to Malaysia's economic benefit. How can Malaysia navigate its way through these difficult waters, preserving both economic development and national security? This chapter offers an analysis of this question.

It proceeds as follows. The first section provides a backdrop to Malaysia's economic relations with China. The following two sections discuss Malaysia's participation in the BRI and the disagreements that have been voiced on the BRI. Some political parties in Malaysia have not had a consistent stance on the BRI and have changed their position on assuming power. The US and other countries, particularly Western nations, have their own thoughts on how China should conduct itself in the global arena. China is carving out its own role and does not seem inclined to work within a liberal, democratic mindset; it also has ambitious plans to link the world through infrastructure. China's investments in developing countries are thought to involve an element of security risk. The penultimate section deals with perceptions regarding the economic–security nexus and how they can be managed. Finally, some concluding remarks are offered.

Tracing Malaysia's economic relations with China

Malaysia's relations with China have evolved cautiously over the years, influenced by China's position in the global arena as well as international perceptions of the country (for accounts on the political economy of Malaysia's relations with China, see Wong 1984; Xia-Ming 1990; Shee 2004). During the administration of Malaysia's first prime minister, Tunku Abdul Rahman, China was not diplomatically recognised. Nonetheless, there was some trade between the two countries, albeit through Singapore and Hong Kong rather than directly. Tunku, for his part, did not recognise China for two reasons: because of the Cold War between the Soviet Union and the US, and also because of the prevailing US economic embargo against China. The underlying factor that would have influenced Tunku was probably his disinterest in offending the US and being seen as within the communist axis of strategically aligned countries.

Malaysia's relationship with China took a sharply positive turn when Tun Abdul Razak, Tunku's successor, assumed the position of prime minister. Razak established firmer links with China, ushering in direct trade between both countries, ultimately leading to Razak visiting China. Razak's visit was preceded by unofficial visits between officials of both countries, the most significant perhaps being an international trade delegation from China to Malaysia in 1971, resulting in China buying 40,000 tons of natural rubber from Malaysia. Following the normalisation of relations between both countries, bilateral trade increased. Shee (2004) observes that total trade between the two countries increased from US$27.8 million in 1971 to US$159 million in 1974; by 1980 it was worth US$424 million. The normalisation of relations in 1974 is an important benchmark in Malaysia–China relations, an event that continues to influence the nature of trade and investment for Malaysia.

In 1981, Mahathir Mohamed became Malaysia's fourth prime minister. Malaysia experienced an economic downturn between 1980 and 1985 and, following an economic recovery, Mahathir paid his first official visit to China in 1985. During Mahathir's first tenure as prime minister he undertook steps to encourage greater economic cooperation with China. Several measures were taken to encourage trade between both countries. First, the government abolished the pre-existing administrative charge on the import of Chinese goods. Earlier, permission was required from the government for these imports. Second, the government lifted restrictions on the travel of Malaysian businesspeople to China. They could travel to China with more ease and stay for longer periods. To that end, restrictive immigration practices were removed. Third, during Mahathir's tenure, several economic agreements were signed with the intention of promoting trade and investment, which included the Sino-Malaysian Trade Agreement, the Investment Guarantee Agreement and the Sino-Malaysian Economic and Trade Joint Committee. In his 1996 visit to China, Mahathir was instrumental in witnessing the conclusion of agreements between Malaysian and Chinese businessmen that included projects covering the construction of highways, mills and power plants as well as projects in the manufacturing sector, particularly vehicles and spare parts. Finally, the government encouraged students from China to study in Malaysia and tourists to visit Malaysia. Malaysia was successful in attracting both.

Shee (2004) credits these policies with an increase in two-way trade. In 1981, total trade between the two countries amounted to about US$289 million; this figure rose to US$877 million in 1988. Bilateral trade grew to US$1.3 billion in 1991 and rocketed to US$7.6 billion in 2001. The structure of trade reflected Malaysia's changing comparative advantage, shifting from commodities (tin, rubber and palm oil) in the 1970s, to goods from the manufacturing sector in the late 1980s. By 2001, Malaysia's major exports to China were not primary resources but mostly came from the electrical and electronics (E&E) sector, chemicals and their derivatives, and, to a lesser extent, machinery and appliances. Malaysia's imports from China increased in line with the increase in exports to China; this was necessary as the exports required imports for their production. Similarly, the sectoral distribution of Chinese investment in Malaysia reflected changes in Malaysia's industrial structure, moving from natural resources from the agriculture and mining sectors to the manufacturing sector, specifically in the metals, E&E and light manufacturing sub-sectors.

Since the mid-1970s Malaysia has demonstrated an interest in opening up to China. This is clear from the sequence of policies that have been introduced from the time of Razak's premiership, all of which work towards encouraging trade and investment with China. There have been shifts in the sectors and products that have been emphasised, and this has been consistent with changes in Malaysia's industrial structure. As I will outline shortly, Malaysia has consistently engaged with China in a manner that has been conducive to Malaysia's growth strategy. This is a strategy that has extended well beyond Mahathir's years as prime minister. Malaysia's economic policies have not been determined by adherence to economic ideology, neither have trade and investment relations been influenced by political ideology. Malaysia's accommodative stance towards China during Mahathir's tenure was not a new phenomenon. Although much has been made of Mahathir being partial to Japan, he was no less partial towards China, and was always keen to improve economic relations with both countries. Malaysia's economic policies, particularly its economic diplomacy, has generally been motivated by pragmatism rather than belief in any economic school of thought or philosophical position.

Malaysia under Najib Razak built upon previous policies that supported and encouraged trade and investment with China. Najib's pro-China economic policies were no different from those espoused by previous administrations. Najib had the further advantage of being Razak's son, which might have been viewed favourably by China's leadership. Alongside his attempts to cultivate friendly relations with the US, Najib was supportive of China's BRI. Najib's support for the BRI, and his keenness in strengthening China–Malaysia relations (Kong 2017) was epitomised by his attendance at the Beijing Belt and Road Summit in 2017.

Najib enthusiastically invited projects from China, signing no fewer than 16 memoranda of understanding with China in 2009 (Lee 2012)—a sure measure of his eagerness to cooperate. The extent of cooperation between the two countries can also be gauged by the large number of mega projects that involved China, either as part of private sector or government initiatives. These included the Malacca Gateway, Malaysia–China Kuantan Industrial Park, Digital Free Trade Zone and Forest City. A number of infrastructure projects were also undertaken such as Kuantan Port's expansion, Gemas Johor Bahru electrified double-tracking railway project and the East Coast Rail Link (ECRL). At least two pipeline projects were also included among others, including the Trans-Sabah Gas Pipeline and the Multi-Product Pipeline. Two other projects in which Najib had shown an interest in inviting Chinese involvement were the Kuala Lumpur–Singapore high-speed rail and the Bagan Datuk–Bachok gas pipeline projects. The negotiation of these projects was not completed because of intense criticism from Mahathir prior to the fourteenth Malaysian general elections (GE14) and due to the Barisan Nasional's subsequent election loss.

At a firm level, there has been increasing investment by Chinese companies in the Malaysian manufacturing sector. This has included investment in a wide range of areas spanning vehicles (locomotive and automobile), steel, solar energy and glass. Ngeow (2019a) commends Chinese participation in the Malaysian economy for 'creating jobs and transferring technology and knowledge', though it is perhaps too early to conclusively state that technology transfer has been successful. Although there has been a great deal of attention that has been directed towards Malaysia's participation in the BRI, non-BRI investment has received less attention.

Malaysia's participation in the BRI

The BRI has its origins in 2013, when China's president, Xi Jinping, decided to extend the original Silk Road with the 21st Century Maritime Silk Road. The latter included the countries lining the South China Sea, South Pacific Ocean and the Indian Ocean, running from China's coast to Jakarta, Singapore and Kuala Lumpur in the south through to Hanoi. The route would then flow through the Strait of Malacca to Colombo, towards Male, and from there to Mombasa, Djibouti and subsequently through the Red Sea to the Mediterranean via the Suez Canal. From the Mediterranean the maritime route would go to the Upper Adriatic region to Trieste in Italy before passing through Haifa, Istanbul and Athens. Thereafter the link would extend to the Baltic States and Northern and Central Europe. The original Silk Road, a land route, connects China, Southeast Asia, the Indian subcontinent, the Arabian Peninsula, Somalia, Egypt and Europe.

Malaysia is an important node in both the original Silk Road and the Maritime Silk Road. As part of the Silk Road Economic Belt, Malaysia lies along the Kunming–Singapore railway line. Malaysia is also a crucial hub along the maritime route since the Strait of Malacca connects China with Southeast, South and Western Asia. Besides, the Strait of Malacca is one of the busiest shipping lines in the world, with more than 25 per cent of the world's traded goods passing through the passage. This makes the Strait of Malacca a point of great importance for China since much of China's exports (manufacturing), palm oil and oil moves through the strait, connecting it with many of its export destinations.

As part of Malaysia's participation in the BRI, several infrastructure projects were planned. Aside from these mega projects, the government, then led by Najib, also arranged for a host of other agreements that were supposed to spearhead Malaysia's entry into the digital economy. The Malacca Gateway and Kuantan Port were two significant projects that were supposed to facilitate the maritime component of the BRI. Several projects were planned to facilitate land-based connectivity in the BRI, including the ECRL, Bandar Malaysia and Forest City. In addition, there were two planned pipeline projects, the Multi-Product Pipeline (MPP) and the Trans-Sabah Gas Pipeline (TSGP). The TSGP was supposed to connect Kimanis Gas Terminal with Sandakan and Tawau in Sabah, and the MPP was intended to run from Malacca to Jitra.

The Malacca Gateway project was supposed to be a cruise ship terminal and deep-sea port, budgeted at US$10 billion and located along the Strait of Malacca. It was supposed to be developed by KAJ Development Sdn Bhd (KAJD) and a consortium of Chinese companies. The latter was composed of Power China International, Shenzhen Yantian Port Group and Rizhao Port Group, while KAJD was a company with connections to the United Malays National Organisation, a political party. Malacca Gateway, as part of the Malaysia–China Port Alliance, is expected to enable cooperation between ports in Malaysia and China. As part of the Malacca Gateway, four artificial islands were to be built, two to encourage tourism, another for the refuelling of ships and the fourth for a container terminal and maritime industry park. These facilities would improve logistics and intensify trade between both countries. The Malacca Gateway would also be linked with the proposed Kuala Lumpur—Singapore high-speed rail.

The Kuantan Port is another cornerstone BRI project in Malaysia because it is the only port on the east coast, overlooks the South China Sea and has proximity to China and Vietnam. The Kuantan Port will negate the need for vessels to travel from Penang or Klang via the Strait of Malacca to Chinese ports such as Dalian, Ningbo, Hainan, Guangzhou and others in the region. This will make it easier for ships to move between Kuantan, Shanghai and Shenzhen, and will increase trade between the two countries. It will also help develop Malaysia's east coast, particularly Kelantan and Terengganu, which has lagged behind the other states in peninsular Malaysia. It will have the added advantage of expediting trade since containers could be unloaded in Klang, sent by train through the ECRL to Kuantan and then transported by ship to China and Vietnam.

The ECRL is a 640-km, high-speed rail that runs from the Malaysia–Thailand border, skirting the east coast of the Malaysian peninsular, detouring before Kuantan and connecting to Port Klang along the west of the peninsular. Najib was enthusiastic about the project, calling it a 'game-changer' because it provided the opportunity to link the Malaysian east and west coasts. Lesser developed states in the east would be connected with the most economically developed state in the country. This was a US$16 billion project connecting Kuantan, a port adjacent to the South China Sea, with Port Klang, which strategically overlooks the Strait of Malacca. The implications of this project are significant, as it gives China a vantage point over the South China Sea as well as the Strait of Malacca, both of strategic interest to China. Port Klang is of special interest since it counterbalances any advantage that Singapore might have over the Strait of Malacca. China also has fears that Singapore, viewed by Beijing as a US stronghold, could block the Strait of Malacca in the event of a conflict.

Despite the immense strategic significance of the project to Malaysia, the ECRL was awarded without any public tender. Malaysia has a long tradition of selecting investors and giving out contracts without open tenders. It was also agreed that the China Communications Construction Company was to be responsible for the operation and maintenance of the project. The main financier for the ECRL was supposed to be the Export-Import Bank of China.

Bandar Malaysia was another important project that was floated during Najib's tenure. It was planned as a transportation hub that was supposed to be built where the Sungai Besi Airport currently sits. Bandar Malaysia was to be the centre of the China Railway Group's Pan Asia Network, linking Southeast Asia with East, West and South Asia. The star feature was a high-speed railway connecting Kuala Lumpur to Singapore. A high-speed railway was also supposed to connect Bandar Malaysia to Bangkok. There were plans to extend the network to Kunming in China, Laos, Myanmar and Cambodia in the future. Bandar also had other links such as the KTM Komuter, Mass Rapid Transit, the Express Rail Link and 12 highways. Further, Bandar Malaysia was supposed to be the largest underground city in the world. This city was designed to have a subterranean shopping mall, canals, theme parks, cultural villages, gardens and a financial centre. Bandar Malaysia was expected to house China Railway Group's regional headquarters at a cost of CN¥8.3 billion. In 2015, 1Malaysia Development Berhad (1MDB) sold 60 per cent of its stake in Bandar Malaysia to IWH-CREC Sdn Bhd. The project ended up embroiled with the 1MDB financial theft scandal and came to a halt.

Forest City is yet another mega project that will involve heavy Chinese investment in Malaysia. This project, although not technically part of the BRI since it does not constitute an infrastructure project, is nevertheless described as being part of the BRI on Forest City's official website. Forest City is a real estate investment between Country Garden, a Chinese developer, and the Sultan of Johor. It is a futuristic town in the state of Johor, constructed on land that is presently jungle and that borders Singapore. Most of the major subcontractors for the project have been Chinese companies. Forest City's proposed population of 700,000 would likely have been made up of wealthy citizens from mainland China rather than Malaysians.

Debating the BRI

Malaysia's participation in the BRI was not passively accepted by Malaysian society when Razak announced the numerous investments he was inviting into the country. Based on the experience of Chinese investment in Africa, where Chinese labour followed Chinese capital with little local participation, caution was urged in accepting Chinese investment without thorough scrutiny. Concerns were expressed that Malaysia might not benefit from the investments if there was no labour participation and no technology transfer. The value-added that these projects would generate for the domestic economy would be low, as Malaysia would merely be a convenient location for Chinese investment without being an active participant.

Concern was also raised about the possibility that Malaysia might end up in a China-created debt trap much like Sri Lanka. The Sri Lankan Hambantota Port Development Project was cited as an example in which credit was obtained from China with inadequate income streams being generated to pay-off the loans. Others argued that Chinese investments should be viewed with caution and that efforts should be made to distinguish those directly involving China's government, bearing in mind that the private sector in China is intimately tied with politics and the Chinese Communist Party. There is a contrasting view that Chinese private investment in Malaysia should be seen purely as an initiative from the private sector, though the private sector in a capitalist democracy is not quite the same as one in a country in which the private sector owes allegiance to the government and its goals (Ngeow 2019b). In the Sri Lankan case, some scholars have raised the question of whether the country's 'debt trap' was a result more of poor macroeconomic policymaking within Sri Lanka rather than one set by Chinese predatory lending (Brautigam 2020)—a conclusion that some scholars have also drawn for the Malaysian case (Jones and Hameiri 2020).

There has been active national debate on the BRI in Malaysia. Some of the questions that have been raised—none of them unexpected—relate to financing, the construction and payment of the projects and their use (Gunasegaram 2017a). Projects in Africa and Sri Lanka have been financed by Chinese companies at very low interest rates and with facilities for delayed payment that have benefited corrupt leaders. These leaders have pushed the burden of repaying debts incurred during their terms of office to their successors.

The other question that has been raised relates to the participation of Malaysians in the projects. The Chinese model often involves Chinese companies undertaking projects and employing workers from China to build them. The most important question concerned the seriousness of undertaking feasibility and related environmental impact studies and making these outcomes available in the course of public and parliamentary debate.

With reference to the ECRL, both the viability and necessity of the project were questioned. The economic feasibility of the ECRL was thrown in doubt because it was thought that the project would not be able to generate enough income to produce a reasonable rate of return on investment (Gunasegaram 2017b). A comparison was drawn with the electrified double-tracking venture that was supposed to improve the railway network along the west coast of the Malaysian peninsular, but which failed to produce a sufficient boost in revenue. This led to losses and an operating cash flow that was in deficit.

The Forest City project was a frequent target of criticisms. Concern was raised over the manner of Chinese participation, with Malaysians being excluded from construction of the project and its ownership. A real estate project built by China that was destined to be occupied by Chinese nationals and paid for by China, but not on Chinese land, the outcome would be the creation of a foreign enclave.

There have been suspicions that investments from China are a cover for financial scams. It has been alleged that MPP and TSGP were related to the scandal-ridden 1MDB. It has also been suggested that loans from Chinese state-owned banks could have been used to repay 1MDB's debts, demonstrating that loan repayments were a front for money laundering arrangements. Aspersions of financial irregularity were made by members of the Democratic Action Party (DAP), who were in opposition when Najib was prime minister and subsequently supported Tun Mahathir when he returned as the prime minister in 2018 (*Star* 2018). The DAP was not alone in casting doubt on the propriety of the financial arrangements associated with Chinese investments in Malaysia. Parti Keadilan Rakyat's Nurul Izzah voiced her concern when she succinctly said that China's investments in Malaysia were 'too fast, too much, too soon' and were not prudently considered.

One should be cautious, however, in treating China's involvement in these projects as being the same. Some were completely private initiatives; some were initiated by governments on both sides, but with significant private sector participation; and some were government-to-government projects. Some projects were driven by local (state-level) governments. The financing also differed from project to project, and not all of them would result in an increase of debt. Some projects are not, strictly speaking, 'investments'; rather, Chinese companies won the construction contracts (although not always in the most transparent manner). The tendency of some foreign and domestic media outlets to lump all these projects together as if they are the same constitutive components of strategically designed 'debt trap' diplomacy by China is misleading.

Hedging and prevaricating

Kuik (2008) distinguishes between a variety of possible responses to China's emergence and describes a balancing-bandwagon spectrum. At one end of the spectrum is the acceptance of the power of a strong state, which results in bandwagoning; at the other end, a state can choose a balancing strategy, which rejects the need to blindly follow the dominant power. Between these two extremes lie other possibilities. Kuik argues that Malaysia has opted for a combination of strategies that include economic pragmatism and binding engagement. The mode of behaviour that Malaysia has displayed in its relationship with China is unusual, but symptomatic of its desire to hedge.

In view of the fact that China has displayed an aggressive stance towards Malaysia by making maritime incursions into Malaysia's exclusive economic zones since 2013, Kuik (2016, 156) finds Malaysia's response to China 'especially intriguing'. China's territorial claims over the Spratly Islands in the South China Sea are a matter that remains unresolved. Aside from recent incidents, Malaysia has experienced problems with China in the past. It is thus difficult to see why Malaysia has taken a passive attitude relative to other ASEAN member countries, Thailand excluded. Kuik points out that Malaysia's anxiety about China has been increasing, yet it has chosen to de-emphasise points of conflict with China. Instead, Malaysia has been strengthening its military cooperation with China, while understating its defence cooperation with the US. Yet, Malaysia's defence cooperation with the US is on solid ground and perhaps expanding, although this is being done quietly and without any reference to China. Obviously, Malaysia is keen to prevent any talk that its increased interest in cooperating with the US on security has anything to do with China. Malaysia's desire to play both sides of the street can be seen on social media: Najib tweeted on 14 May 2013 that he had had a 'very productive discussion with @BarackObama', quickly following this with the message that he had spoken with Premier Li Keqiang and was 'looking forward to expanding our relationship with China'.

This kind of behaviour is often pursued by weaker states to avoid the risks arising from the uncertainty associated with engaging with more powerful states. According to Mahathir, describing China as a threat could become a self-fulfilling prophecy. He said that 'if you identify a country as your future enemy, it becomes your present enemy' (*Asiaweek* 2000). That Mahathir took care to avoid being misperceived by China indicates that the relationship was not based on mutual trust and was not a sufficiently mature relationship that could allow dissatisfaction to be voiced.

Mahathir prevaricated between suggesting that China was practising a form of 'new colonialism' in its investment ventures in developing countries, and praising China for its BRI project, declaring 'the Belt and Road idea is great' (CNA 2019). This famous switch was made when Mahathir was returned as prime minister for a second time, indicating that his views were informed by pragmatism rather than any considered principle.

Within the domain of international relations, Malaysia has sought to pursue friendly relations with China since the premiership of Tun Abdul Razak. Mahathir took Razak's approach further and deepened economic cooperation with China. As we saw earlier, Mahathir greatly encouraged trade and investment from China, improved the ease of doing business with China (relaxing visa requirements) and promoted the inflow of students from China. The need to hedge was acute during the Najib years; it was at this time that a definite strategy became necessary, since China had emerged as a power to be reckoned with and was perceived to be at odds with US interests.

In the economic realm, Malaysia has a clear vision of its objectives. However, sometimes the articulation of these objectives veers towards simple-minded and contradictory assertions. These shifts became apparent during Najib's tenure and after. The economic objective is simple: Malaysia should seek to maximise the economic gains on offer from engagement with China. Of course, the pursuit of this objective is not necessarily risk free: associating too closely with one power or the other (or neither) could prove deleterious, while economic integration can lead to the erosion of sovereignty. Domestic influences on integration policy should also be emphasised. As has been stressed by Kuik (2013), two prominent domestic influences include the ruling elites' sense of what would best serve their interests and the management of local perceptions of foreign countries, including popular perceptions, ethnic sentiment, and the opinions of political oppositions and civil society. Attitudes towards the US are a prime example of this, as the country has drawn criticism for its handling of issues in the Middle East, its support of Israel and the purported discrimination of Muslims. Negative domestic sentiment towards the US played into the politics of the Trans-Pacific Partnership (TPP) agreement. While some objections centred on legal and economic issues, there was also a great deal of animosity that stemmed from domestic perception that the TPP furthered the US's imperialistic ambitions. These sentiments helped stoke protests from non-governmental organisations. A comparable sense of dissatisfaction was felt towards China and Najib's overtures towards Chinese investments prior to GE14.

It has been suggested that domestic elites play an important role in deciding how the trade-off between economic cooperation and security concerns is negotiated (Kuik 2013). But there is no clear explanation of the manner in which the elite influence policy nor the nature of their involvement. How the elite benefit and the determinants they take into account in their decision-making processes are unclear.

Managing the economic and security nexus

China's relations with the rest of the world are evolving and are likely to take a more complicated turn in the years to come. The US has had tense relations with China in the last few years, resulting in a trade war. It is unclear whether the US's economic relations with China will improve in the years to come. Indeed, based on tensions in the US and China, things may even worsen: for example, there is some evidence that prominent scientists in the US have been sponsored by Chinese agencies, China has been trying to exert its influence over US universities and the US has been unhappy with the turn of events in Hong Kong. These incidents will colour US–China relations regardless of domestic political developments in the US.

Elsewhere in the world, Japan, Australia and the United Kingdom seem to have rethought their views on China. India may be reconsidering its strategic approach to China. Germany, too, may be more cautious in its dealings with China. In the light of these trends, Malaysia's economic cooperation with China will take on a new flavour. This is not to suggest that Malaysia should allow itself to be forced into deciding on its trade and investment deals with China in a binary fashion, blocking Chinese investment solely to signal which side of the divide it is on. Malaysia should not be drawn into thinking it has to choose between the US or China. However, there is no doubt that more sensitivity will have to be exercised when dealing with economic engagement with China.

Huawei is an interesting case in point. The possibility has been raised that information could be compromised if it passes through the company's systems. Former US president Donald Trump's administration rallied a campaign against the company and several countries heeded his call. Tun Mahathir declared that Malaysia had nothing to lose by allowing Huawei's products and services to be used. He was right to criticise Trump by characterising the US's decision to ban Huawei as 'not the way to go' (Sukumaran 2019). But Mahathir trivialised the issue by asserting that Huawei could 'spy as much as it wants'. National security cannot be taken lightly and should be considered in conjunction with economic considerations where appropriate. Mahathir's statements ignored the strategic dimension; therefore, in a broader sense, they were unhelpful in addressing the dilemma of considering economic and strategic policy together.

The issues regarding Huawei are more difficult to manage than Mahathir would like to admit. While it is entirely Malaysia's prerogative to engage Huawei and award contracts to it, any such decisions should be weighed carefully. Other investors, particularly those from among the countries that were mentioned earlier, could feel that the privacy of their data are at stake. At its extreme, foreign investors could end up being reluctant to invest in Malaysia due to Huawei's presence on the presumption that their data are open to risk. Fears of intellectual property being stolen, computer systems being hacked and data being harvested, whether real or imagined, could be a serious dissuading factor for Western investors.

Malaysia plans to rollout 5G throughout the country. Huawei cannot be denied the opportunity to win the bid to rollout 5G, yet such a move runs the risk of repelling non-Chinese investment. Without investment from non-Chinese sources, a more objective approach will have to be taken.

This would require an evaluation of the risks involved by inviting Huawei, addressing the possible gaps in security, and ensuring that the accusations levelled against Huawei do not pose problems or are proved baseless. The Huawei case indicates how a security question, if not treated seriously, could morph into an economic problem.

Policymakers have differing views on how the security–economics question should be managed. Tun Mahathir, who did much to normalise relations with China, is of the view that economic gains should be prioritised over security considerations. His argument is based on the fact that Malaysia has had good relations with China for hundreds of years, and that China has never attempted to colonise Malaysia, although the Malacca Sultanate was, at one point, a vassal state to the Ming dynasty. According to Mahathir's thinking, unlike the West, China is not an imperialist power, and although Malaysia may not agree completely with China's views on all matters, there is no need to be suspicious of China. He points out that China is an economic superpower and that Malaysia should learn how to derive benefit from China's growth and development since 'Malaysia cannot fight with China' (*Malaysiakini* 2018).[1]

Mahathir's view is shared by other senior serving and retired diplomats and civil servants. A civil servant[2] who has had long experience with Malaysia's Ministry of International Trade and Industry (MITI) and has represented Malaysia in international negotiations opined that there are mechanisms to evaluate security considerations. Although the Malaysian Industrial Development Authority is the first point of reference for potential investments, it does not have the mandate to independently review and approve projects. Rather, proposals are jointly evaluated by relevant agencies; the decision-making process is an inter-ministerial process, which involves the ministries of Foreign Affairs, Defence and Home Affairs, as necessary. Based on this position, the government has the requisite mechanisms both to assess economic and strategic concerns as well as their interplay; security issues are taken into account, with the appropriate ministries giving their feedback on matters pertaining to both internal and external security, strategy and defence.

---

1   Interview with Tun Mahathir, 6 August 2020.
2   Personal communication with senior civil servant.

A serving ambassador[3] who has deep experience with China elaborated on the underpinnings of the mainstream opinions that have been described. He explained that 'the security-nexus dichotomy is a false dichotomy', adding that 'Malaysia knows that China does not think in terms of a security–economy nexus'.[4] The problem, as he sees it, arises from the West's profound misunderstanding of China, which it wrongly expected to evolve into a liberal democratic nation. Further, he stresses that 'there is nothing to suggest that China wants conflict and Malaysia knows that China does not think in terms of imposing a security–economic nexus'.[5]

The challenge, in his view, is not to fixate on the security–economics nexus—a misguided exercise—but to find a niche with China, as with any other country with which Malaysia has economic relations. In this ambassador's perspective, the long-term objective is to fit Malaysia into China's narrative of growth and development. In this respect, the ambassador's thinking resonates closely with Mahathir's, as Mahathir thinks Malaysia should capitalise on China's growth, without getting embroiled in the West's political decisions.

Other policymakers disagree. A retired civil servant thinks that, while there are processes and mechanisms to address security concerns when evaluating the advisability of investments, it is not clear if these processes are fully utilised.[6] Dennis Ignatius, a retired diplomat, has shown how Mahathir vociferously warned against the threat to the country's sovereignty and questioned the advisability of welcoming investments from China, the ECRL in particular, only to change his stance on becoming prime minister after GE14. Ignatius also finds the DAP guilty of policy inconsistency. He points out that 'the DAP which once hammered the MCA mercilessly over their support for ECRL and other [BRI] infrastructure projects is now a BRI supporter' (Ignatius 2019). The DAP did not support the ECRL project when it was in opposition; instead, it came around to it when it was in government. Ignatius (2019) adds:

> Despite the party blasting Najib for appointing politicians as special envoys, DAP national chairman Tan Kok Wai was more than happy to replace MCA's Ong Ka Ting as special envoy to China.

---

3   Interview with H. E. Raja Nushirwan Zainal Abidin, Malaysia's ambassador to China, 2 October 2020.
4   Personal communication with senior civil servant.
5   Ibid.
6   Ibid.

Ignatius's remarks reflect the view that, although there might be institutions for balanced decision-making processes, these might not be employed in practice. In this line of thinking, constant prevarication over Chinese investments, as in the ECRL, suggests that decision-making might not be based on objective facts and thorough analyses, but on questionable criteria. Ignatius (2019) argues that:

> There was hardly anything to celebrate given that we ended up with a RM[B]44 billion railway project we didn't need, couldn't afford and would have to subsidise for years to come. What is worse, we still don't know the full details about the renegotiated project and neither have we seen any feasibility studies to justify going ahead with it.

Najib's decision-making was possibly flawed because of weak institutions and/or the lack of political will to abide by the decisions taken through designated processes. Three requirements need to be fulfilled for collaborative mega projects to work. One, institutional processes need to be respected. Two, a proper assessment of the project is necessary and there has to be complete transparency. Three, given the risk of making decisions on the wrong side of the security–economy nexus, more effort has to be put into assessing the trade-off between these two variables. That will only be possible if there is the full participation of agencies other than MITI, such as the Ministry of Foreign Affairs and the Ministry of Defence. These ministries should work with think tanks and scholars in the field to better understand the complications regarding the interface between economics and security. The current process of investing absolute power in the hands of the prime minister to make these decisions must be re-evaluated. If there are avenues for transparency (to the extent permissible, given the sensitivity of security matters), then their proper implementation should be pursued. Otherwise, appropriate institutions will have to be devised to ensure that there are channels for the adequate consideration of relevant input (particularly security issues) and that there is ample discussion at various levels. There could be a hierarchy of levels starting with broad, open discussions involving scholars, think tanks and other stakeholders, rising up to discussions among officials from relevant ministries, culminating in the presentation of these findings to the Cabinet. Another possible format would be to have officials aware of multidisciplinary assessments and specially trained in evaluating projects from a strategic-economics perspective. This department could act as the link between civil society, relevant ministries and the Cabinet.

Conclusion

Malaysia's relations with China are constantly evolving. With the exception of the early period of the first prime minister, Malaysia has had warm relations with China and has attempted to encourage deeper trade and investment ties. Malaysia has prioritised its economic relations with China, which, owning to China's position and role in the global stage, was less of an issue until recently. However, with China's growing economy and its ambitious projects (best exemplified by the BRI), a different perspective is now required.

Policymakers face something of a policy quandary because they have to balance disparate factors. On the one hand, Malaysia would like to take advantage of China's economic growth as it is accustomed to doing. However, tensions may escalate between Malaysia and the US—and perhaps other countries in the West as well—placing Malaysia in a sensitive position. Malaysia cannot do without foreign trade and investment. China is too large and too important to be excluded, and the nature of its strategic actions cannot be ignored. These factors demand that Malaysian policymakers take a more careful view of their country's investments from China.

It would be naïve to suggest that investments should be rejected simply because they come from China. Careful and dispassionate evaluation of projects can enable Malaysia to benefit from economic integration with the Chinese economy while maintaining its strategic independence and national security objectives. While the mechanisms to undertake these kinds of evaluations exist, more work needs to be done to ensure that these mechanisms are made use of.

References

Asiaweek. 2000. '"I Am Still Here": Asiaweek's Complete Interview with Mahathir Mohamad'. Accessed 14 December 2021. edition.cnn.com/ASIANOW/asia week/97/0509/cs3.html.

Brautigam, D. 2020. 'A Critical Look at Chinese "Debt-Trap Diplomacy": The Rise of a Meme'. *Area Development and Policy* 5 (1): 1–14. doi.org/10.1080/23792949.2019.1689828.

CNA. 2019. '"The Belt and Road Initiative Is Great": Malaysia PM Mahathir'. 26 April 2019, www.channelnewsasia.com/asia/mahathir-endorse-belt-and-road-china-889066 (site discontinued).

Gunasegaram, P. 2017a. 'Do All Roads Have to Lead to China?' Hornbill Unleashed, 25 May 2017. hornbillunleashed.wordpress.com/2017/05/25/do-all-roads-have-to-lead-to-china/.

Gunasegaram, P. 2017b. '10 Reasons Why We Don't Need RM55 Billion East Coast Rail Link'. *Malaysiakini*, 8 August 2017, www.malaysiakini.com/columns/391163.

Ignatius, D. 2019. 'Rethinking ECRL'. Free Malaysia Today, 10 September 2019. www.freemalaysiatoday.com/category/opinion/2019/09/10/rethinking-ecrl/.

Jones, L. and S. Hameiri. 2020. 'Debunking the Myth of "Debt-Trap Diplomacy"'. Chatham House, 19 August. www.chathamhouse.org/2020/08/debunking-myth-debt-trap-diplomacy.

Kong, T. Y. 2017. 'Belt and Road Initiative: A New Impetus to Strengthen China–Malaysia Relations'. *East Asian Policy* 9 (2): 5–14. doi.org/10.1142/S1793930517000113.

Kuik, C-C. 2008. 'The Essence of Hedging: Malaysia and Singapore's Response to a Rising China'. *Contemporary Southeast Asia* 30 (2): 159–85. bookshop.iseas.edu.sg/publication/618.

Kuik, C-C. 2013. 'Making Sense of Malaysia's China Policy: Asymmetry, Proximity, and Elite's Domestic Authority'. *Chinese Journal of International Politics* 6(4): 429–67. doi.org/10.1080/14799855.2013.832211.

Kuik, C-C. 2016. 'Malaysia between the United States and China: What Do Weaker States Hedge Against?' *Asian Politics and Policy* 8 (1): 155–77. doi.org/10.1111/aspp.12240.

Lee, K. H. 2012. 'Malaysia–China Economic Relations'. In *China and East Asia: After the Wall Street Crisis,* edited by P. E. Lam, Y. Qin and M. Yang, 241–76. Singapore: World Scientific.

Malaysiakini. 2018. 'Malaysia Can't Go to War with China, Dr M Says'. 26 July 2018, www.malaysiakini.com/news/436062.

Ngeow, C. 2019a. 'Economic Cooperation and Infrastructure Linkage between Malaysia and China under the Belt and Road Initiative'. In *Regional Connection under the Belt and Road Initiative: The Prospects for Economic and Financial Cooperation*, edited by F. M. Cheung and Y-Y Hong, 115–33. London: Routledge.

Ngeow, C. 2019b. 'Malaysia–China Cooperation on the Belt and Road Initiative under the Pakatan Harapan Government: Changes, Continuities, and Prospects'. NIDS ASEAN Workshop 2019: China's BRI and ASEAN, NIDS Joint Research Series, no. 17, Tokyo: National Institute for Defense Studies. Accessed 14 December 2021. www.nids.mod.go.jp/english/publication/joint_research/series17/pdf/chapter02.pdf.

Shee, P. K. 2004. 'Political Economy of Mahathir's China Policy: Economic Cooperation, Political and Strategic Ambivalence'. *Ritsumeikan Annual Review of International Studies* 3: 59–79.

Star. 2018. '1MDB Scandal May Involve Money Laundering to China Companies, Tony Pua Tells BBC'. 17 July 2018. www.thestar.com.my/news/nation/2018/07/17/1mdb-scandal-may-involve-money-laundering-to-china-companies-tony-pua-tells-bbc/.

Sukumaran, T. 2019. 'Malaysia's Mahathir Backs Huawei, Snubbing US Blacklist of Chinese Telecoms Giant'. *South China Morning Post*, 30 May 2019, www.scmp.com/week-asia/geopolitics/article/3012469/malaysias-mahathir-backs-huawei-snubbing-us-blacklist-chinese.

Wong, J. 1984. *The Political Economy of China's Changing Relations with Southeast Asia*. London: MacMillan Press. doi.org/10.1007/978-1-349-27929-6.

Xia-Ming. 1990. 'Sino-Malaysian Trade Ties and Its Prospects'. *Economic Quarterly* (April): 21–22.

8

Economic integration and national security in a strategic policymaking environment: The case of Vietnam

Thanh Tri Vo and Duong Anh Nguyen

Introduction

Vietnam's approach to strategic and economic policymaking has consistently married a deep engagement with regional processes of economic integration with efforts to working with all major powers to ensure peace and stability.

Since Doi Moi, economic integration has been among the three key pillars of reforms in Vietnam, together with market-oriented reforms and macroeconomic stabilisation. A vast amount of literature (Dinh et al. 2009; CIEM 2013; Dinh et al. 2020) has shown that economic integration has been highly interactive with domestic economic reforms. Specifically, economic integration has broadened opportunities through access to foreign investment and foreign markets, adaptation to international trade rules and deeper participation in global value chains. Periods of progressive economic integration (i.e. 1989–96, 2000–07, 2014–19) also came with fundamental economic reforms, which led to significant socioeconomic development and thus nurtured greater consensus towards economic integration.

After numerous wars, including for national unification, Vietnam stresses the importance of protecting national security and, more broadly, a stable environment for socioeconomic development to take place. Over time, the country has gradually become more open to the international dimensions of national security. In 2020, the country was elected as a non-permanent member of the United Nations Security Council (UNSC). During its Association of Southeast Asian Nations (ASEAN) chairmanship in 2020, Vietnam was able to coordinate efforts to enhance UN–ASEAN collaboration. Within this context, the interaction between national security and economic integration in Vietnam is no longer unidirectional. Instead, economic integration helps to strengthen cooperation between Vietnam and its partners, which in turn leverages Vietnam's capacity to protect national security.

Looking forward, Vietnam will find the unfolding international environment challenging and highly uncertain. Trade tensions among major economies—namely the United States, China and those in the European Union—can induce shifts in global production and supply chain networks, creating both opportunities and challenges for Vietnamese enterprises. Non-traditional security issues, including the COVID-19 pandemic and threats to cyber security, are set to become more frequent. The COVID-19 pandemic necessitates a serious review of various dimensions of the development paradigm, including sustainable development, the role of the state and the emergence of the digital economy, all of which entail potentially increasing rivalry between superpowers. Even the initiation of new free trade agreements (FTA) may weigh further upon trade diversion driven by geopolitical competition. Still, new opportunities are emerging. The Fourth Industrial Revolution (IR 4.0) has brought on various achievements across many sectors. Some studies (e.g. PECC 2018) show that developing and low-income countries will not necessarily lag behind in accessing and taking advantage of IR 4.0.

Vietnam's overarching policy goal is economic development, which it has pursued through an outward-oriented approach that prioritises regional economic integration. More importantly, Vietnam consistently promoted regional economic diplomacy via a process that placed ASEAN at the central position. Its approach to security policy also heavily centres the role of ASEAN in creating a peaceful and stable regional security environment. Security policy is not separate from, but rather informs Vietnam's approach to economic integration.

This chapter aims to discuss, through three selected case studies, Vietnam's approach to economic integration and national security, and how ASEAN may complement and accommodate Vietnam's efforts to strengthen and uphold both. The remainder of the chapter is structured as follows. The next section elaborates some considerations of Vietnam's approach to economic integration and national security. This is followed by a discussion of three case studies that illustrate Vietnam's approach. The final section concludes the chapter.

Vietnam's approach to economic integration and national security: Some considerations

Economic integration efforts

Since Doi Moi, Vietnam has embarked on an open door policy and parallel economic reforms. The 6th National Congress of the Communist Party of Vietnam emphasised the importance of broadening opportunities and building capacity for all groups so as to promote economic development and improve living standards, among other objectives. Accordingly, Vietnam made early and progressive efforts towards trade and investment liberalisation. The 1987 Foreign Investment Law laid the first legal foundations for foreign direct investment (FDI) activities in Vietnam. Vietnam then established relations with multilateral financial institutions such as the International Monetary Fund and World Bank, and re-established ties with the Asian Development Bank in 1993. The US lifted its embargo on Vietnam in 1994 and the two countries normalised relations in 1995. That year, Vietnam also signed the EU Framework Cooperation Agreement and acquired full membership of ASEAN. Vietnam lodged its application for World Trade Organization (WTO) membership in 1995 and applied for membership of the Asia-Pacific Economic Cooperation (APEC) forum in 1996.

During 1997–99, Vietnam's trade reforms slowed due to the Asian financial crisis. The country imposed temporary import bans and restrictions on some consumer goods in 1997 to combat its sizeable current account deficit. In 1999, facing enormous risk of deflation, the Vietnamese Government implemented stimulus measures rather than accelerating structural reforms, to induce investment and growth.

From 2000 to 2020, Vietnam implemented various policies related to investment, trade liberalisation and integration into the world economy. Vietnam signed a bilateral trade agreement with the US in 2000, which took effect in 2001. Through the ASEAN community-building process, Vietnam was also a signatory to various FTAs of ASEAN and its partners (China, Korea, Japan, Australia, New Zealand and India). In January 2007, Vietnam became the 150th member of the WTO. Since then, Vietnam has deepened its international economic integration by internalising the rules and standards of the global economy and market. Vietnam has gradually opened its economy and market through establishing bilateral relations in trade, investment and finance, and by participating in multilateral mechanisms in those areas. By the end of 2020, Vietnam had become a member of all major international organisations, joining negotiations of various FTAs including the Comprehensive and Progressive Agreement for Trans-Pacific Partnership (CPTPP), the European Union–Vietnam Free Trade Agreement (EVFTA) and the Regional Comprehensive Economic Partnership Agreement (RCEP). Most notably, the CPTPP and RCEP overcame major hurdles at APEC in 2017 and ASEAN in 2020, both of which were hosted in Vietnam.

ASEAN integration remains highly important to Vietnam for several reasons (Vo 2012). First, ASEAN was Vietnam's first regional playing field for trade and investment liberalisation, which matches the relatively low level of development in Vietnam. The gradualism of ASEAN integration also permits capacity building and involves less regulatory and economic costs. Second, ASEAN integration has become more comprehensive, covering not only trade and investment but also socioeconomic cooperation, foreign affairs, security cooperation and non-traditional security issues. Third, ASEAN member states have been working together to reduce the intra-regional development gap, particularly between the CLMV (Cambodia, Laos, Myanmar, Vietnam) countries and other ASEAN member countries. Finally, ASEAN has been emerging in popularity in international and regional initiatives, such as the East Asia Summit and Asia–Europe Meeting. Thus, being a member of ASEAN has allowed Vietnam to contribute to the various regional activities and dialogues that have helped promote further economic integration and sustainable development in Southeast Asia.

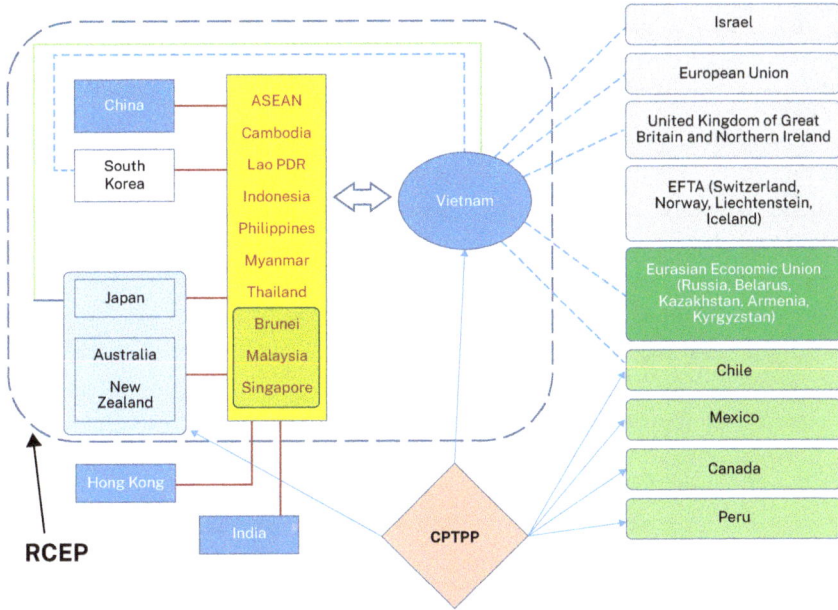

Figure 8.1: Vietnam's free trade agreements

ASEAN (Association of Southeast Asian Nations), CPTPP (Comprehensive and Progressive Agreement for Trans-Pacific Partnership), EFTA (European Free Trade Area), EU (European Union), Laos, RCEP (Regional Comprehensive Economic Partnership). Source: Tran et al. (2021).

Acknowledging that importance, Vietnam is keen on respecting ASEAN centrality in regional issues, including those related to non-traditional security. In the pioneering Hanoi Plan of Action in 1998, Vietnam and other ASEAN member countries recognised the need to facilitate regional economic recovery and regional economic integration after the Asian financial crisis. While engaging in strategic partnerships with other ASEAN members and other sub-ASEAN processes (such as Cambodia, Laos and Vietnam triangular development, or Mekong Subregion development), Vietnam duly supports the role of ASEAN in dialogues and in identifying measures to address common regional issues. As ASEAN chair in 2010, Vietnam undertook various initiatives to strengthen relations with ASEAN's dialogue partners, the most notable of which was the engagement of the US and the Russian Federation at the East Asia Summit. Vietnam also supported other ASEAN member countries and dialogue partners in coordinating the implementation of the Master Plan for ASEAN Connectivity, explicitly acknowledging the ownership of ASEAN in regional connectivity initiatives.[1] As a non-permanent member of the UNSC during 2020–21, Vietnam made efforts in 2020 to promote cooperation between the UN and ASEAN.

The second aspect of Vietnam's economic integration is its WTO-plus approach. With depth and comprehensive coverage,[2] WTO membership further consolidates Vietnam's approach to multilateralism. The FTAs Vietnam signed after 2007 reflect this approach, which aims to deepen trade and investment ties with key partners. Despite the events of 2020, Vietnam remains committed to multilateralism. Vietnam has cooperated with like-minded countries in efforts to revive international economic integration. Specifically, Vietnam worked with other CPTPP partners to revive the agreement in its host year of APEC in 2017, after the US withdrew from the Trans-Pacific Partnership in January that year. Likewise, Vietnam worked with ASEAN, China, Korea, Japan, Australia and New Zealand to conclude and sign RCEP in 2020 at the ASEAN Summit, after India withdrew from the agreement in 2019.

Vietnam's approach to security issues

One of Vietnam's top national interests is maintaining a peaceful and stable environment for socioeconomic development, while protecting national sovereignty. Vietnam has implemented a defence policy that is peaceful and focused on self-defence, as reflected in its unwillingness to use, or threaten the use of, force in international relations, resolving all disagreements and disputes with other countries by peaceful means. Vietnam advocates addressing flashpoints and potential conflicts in the region through dialogue and peaceful negotiation.

Vietnam advocates gradual modernisation of the military, increasing its defence capacity only to maintain military strength at the level necessary for self-defence. Vietnam opposes arms race activities. Having fought in various wars for its independence and freedom, Vietnam expresses its full respect for the independence, sovereignty, unity, territorial integrity and interests of other countries on the basis on international law and the principles of the UN Charter. In return, Vietnam demands other states to recognise its own independence, sovereignty, unity, territorial integrity and national interests.

---

1   Noticeable examples are the infrastructure projects financed by public–private partnerships in selected ASEAN countries, including Vietnam.
2   See CIEM (2013).

Vietnam also advocates for the settlement of territorial disputes on land or sea by peaceful means on the basis of international law. Regarding the South China Sea[3] territorial dispute, Vietnam firmly claims to have sufficient historical evidence and legal basis to prove undisputed sovereignty over the waters and islands, including Hoang Sa and Truong Sa archipelagos. Vietnam remains willing to resolve disputes through peaceful negotiation based on the provisions of the 1982 United Nations Convention on the Law of the Sea (UNCLOS). While continuing to seek a long-term solution to this issue, Vietnam advocates that all parties must exercise restraint and strictly implement the ASEAN–China Declaration on the Conduct of Parties in the South China Sea (DOC). Vietnam advocates for a move towards building a code of conduct (CoC), and for achieving a fair and long-term solution to this complex problem so that the South China Sea remains a sea of peace, friendship and development.

Actively preventing and repelling threats of war is one of Vietnam's key defence tasks in peacetime. Its optimal defence strategy is the safeguard of independence, sovereignty, unity, territorial integrity and other national interests without waging war. Vietnam advocates a defence strategy based on a range of political, economic, diplomatic, sociocultural and military activities aimed at eliminating the causes of armed conflicts and war. In addition, Vietnam's defence strategy uses integrated measures to maintain internal stability and prevent external interference threats.

Vietnam opposes acts of terror in all forms and opposes activities that take advantage of counterterrorism to interfere in the internal affairs of other countries. Vietnam works at home and abroad to prevent terrorist activities and activities that support terrorism in any form. Vietnam believes anti-terrorism measures and international cooperation against terrorism must be carried out within the framework of the UN, in accordance with the basic principles of the UN Charter and international law. Vietnam has signed eight out of 12 UN conventions on counterterrorism and is considering joining the remaining conventions (Luong 2020).

Finally, Vietnam is gradually adapting its approach to economic integration so as to make greater contributions to national security. Vietnam expanded its outward approach from international economic integration to international integration. The 2013 Resolution 22-NQ/TW on International Integration of the Politburo emphasises that economic integration is the centre of

---

3   Known in Vietnam as the East Sea.

international integration, and that integration in other areas contributes to enhancing economic integration. This is reiterated in the Resolution 06-NQ/TW of the Central Committee of the Communist Party of Vietnam on effective economic integration upon implementation of a new-generation of FTAs. In other words, international cooperation in security also contributes to effective economic integration.

In fact, national security is incorporated in all of Vietnam's strategies related to economic integration and international integration. For instance, the government's action plan towards effective and sustainable development after WTO accession (under Resolution 49/NQ-CP in 2014) identifies the need to combine economic development, national security and defence in marine, island and strategic locations. Vietnam has started several initiatives that combine national security and international integration. The country has also joined several international activities related to security. For example, Vietnam has deployed solders to international peacekeeping, most recently the second deployment of Military Level 2 Field Hospital to South Sudan in 2019. Vietnam was also involved in the first US–ASEAN military exercise in 2019.

Vietnam wants to become a reliable partner to all countries and territories. Thus, Vietnam needs to approach regional geopolitical developments with careful consideration. Balancing relationships with major powers is now almost unavoidable, especially when such powers engage in more direct strategic competition. Vietnam has consistently asserted the key principles of 'no military alliances', 'no siding with one country against another' and 'no foreign military bases on Vietnamese soil'. Since 2019, these key principles were elaborated, specifically:

> Vietnam consistently advocates neither joining any military alliances, siding with one country against another, giving any other countries permission to set up military bases or use its territory to carry out military activities against other countries nor using force or threatening to use force in international relations (Vietnamese Ministry of Defence 2019, 23–24).

There are several grounds for these principles. First, a history of complicated interactions with major powers has compelled Vietnam to adopt a balanced approach to international relations. Second, these principles are consistent with Vietnam's objective to diversify and multilateralise cooperative relations. Third, Vietnam perceives and supports the increasingly instrumental role of ASEAN in international issues (such as freedom of navigation and denuclearisation).

Finally, Vietnam must now navigate both trade and investment relations and maritime and land border conflicts. In the context of increasing information availability due to the internet, it is getting harder to ignore the impacts of maritime and land border conflicts on public sentiment, and in turn on trade and investment relations with the associated countries. In 2014, for example, Vietnam had to take measures to prevent and mitigate damages dealt by protestors to the production premises of foreign-invested enterprises.

In the face of increasingly complicated US–China rivalry that spans both economics and security, a naturally emerging question is whether Vietnam can continue its combined approach to economic integration and national security. We argue that US–China rivalry is further consolidating Vietnam's approach to economic integration and national security. More importantly, embracing the role of ASEAN in such an approach may help. This shall be the focus of the next section.

Selected cases

Case I: US–China trade war, 2018–19

During the months between June 2018 and 2019, trade tensions between the US and China became increasingly complicated and unpredictable. Both countries' behaviour had direct and indirect impacts on the world economy. The fallout of the trade war between the US and China indirectly impacted Vietnam, providing both opportunities and challenges for Vietnamese exporters.

Before analysing the evolution of Vietnam's response to the US–China trade dispute, it is worth briefly revisiting the timeline of events. During the presidential election in May 2016, Donald Trump emphasised the priority of addressing the US trade deficit with China. In April 2017, the United States Trade Representative started investigating the threat of imported steel and aluminium products to US national security. Its investigation into the regulations, policies and behaviour of the Chinese Government related to technology transfer, intellectual property and innovation was ongoing in August that year. In March 2018, the US imposed a 25 per cent tariff on all steel imports (except from Argentina, Australia, Brazil and South Korea) and 10 per cent tariff on all aluminium imports (except from Argentina and Australia). A week later, China imposed tariffs ranging from 15–25 per cent on 128 products from the US (worth about US$3 billion).

US–China tensions escalated in June 2018, and bilateral negotiations did not result in an agreement. The trade war officially began in July 2018 as the US imposed an additional import tariff of 25 per cent on US$34 billion of Chinese imports. China then imposed a retaliatory tariff of 25 per cent on US imports with the same estimated value. In August 2018, the US imposed an additional 25 per cent tariff on another US$16 billion of imports from China. China retaliated by imposing 25 per cent tariffs on US$16 billion worth of imports from the US. China also lodged an official complaint to the WTO against the US for imposing import tariffs on its solar panels. In September 2018, the US imposed an additional tariff of 10 per cent on Chinese imports worth US$200 billion (with a communicated plan to increase the rate to 25 per cent by 1 January 2019). China also imposed tariffs of 5–10 per cent on US$60 billion of US imports. At the G20 Summit on 2 December 2018, the US and China agreed to suspend the escalation of tariffs for the trade negotiation for 90 days. After some meetings, by the end of February 2019, President Donald Trump extended this suspension and continued negotiation in an effort to reach a trade agreement.

The truce did not last. In May 2019, the US–China trade war escalated after negotiations failed to reach agreement. The US increased additional tariffs from 10 per cent to 25 per cent on Chinese imports worth US$200 billion. Huawei, China's major technology company, was banned from purchasing products from US companies. In response, China announced that it would increase additional tariffs from 10 to 25 per cent on US imports worth US$60 billion by specific groups (officially implemented from 1 June 2019). China's Ministry of Commerce also published its 'Unreliable Entity' list. In early June 2019, China released a white paper on US trade talks. Just before the G20 Summit in June 2019 in Japan, China and the US made a truce and then restarted trade talks. Still, the talks progressed slowly until December 2019. Specifically, in August 2019, the US labelled China as a currency manipulator, while various threats to increase tariffs and products for tariff exemptions were made in parallel with bilateral trade talks during July–November 2019. It was only in December 2019, and just before a new round of tariff hikes, that the two countries agreed on the Phase One trade deal.

Impacts of the US–China trade war on Vietnam

The rise in tensions between the two powers had a range of impacts—positive and negative—on third parties in the region. By the end of 2019, Vietnam had managed to take advantage of the opportunities and deal with the challenges stemming from the trade war. Despite Vietnam's ex-ante assessment of the impact, economic and export growth rates were still relatively high, and implemented FDI was increasing steadily. These positive developments likely occurred due to the tit-for-tat tariff barriers imposed by the US and China increasing export opportunities for developing countries, including Vietnam. Increasing uncertainty surrounding the US–China trade war may also make major multinational companies consider shifting part or all of their existing manufacturing facilities in China to other countries like Vietnam. The exchange rate has been more or less stable, thereby contributing to mitigating adverse impacts from these external events on the domestic macroeconomic environment. Quantitative assessments (e.g. Malesky and Mosley 2021; Petri and Plummer 2020) have so far been restricted to the impact of tariff measures by the US and China. These assessments indicated benefits to Vietnam in the form of increasing national income, labour upgrading and so on.

Still, Vietnam has suffered impacts from the US–China trade war. Vietnamese exports to China only grew by 0.1 per cent in 2019, significantly below the figure of 16.6 per cent in 2018. This was partly due to Vietnam's participation in China-focused value chains: foreign investors decreased production in China, leading to weaker demand for imports from Vietnam. The depreciation of the yuan during the trade war made Vietnamese goods less competitive in the Chinese market. Additionally, by the end of 2019, both the US and China had already carried out actions and implemented policies that negatively affected Vietnam's exports to these countries. China increased the standards and regulations applied to imported goods, including those from Vietnam. For instance, China has applied additional technical barriers on Vietnamese agricultural imports. This may have been in retaliation to Vietnam enforcing stricter control over products imported from China to prevent origin circumvention. As for the US, the most remarkable action was in May 2019, when it included Vietnam on the monitoring list for currency manipulation.

Various assessments undertaken in 2018–19 (CIEM 2019; CIEM 2020; Nguyen and Dinh 2018) agreed on the possibility that Chinese goods would be exported to Vietnam before re-exporting to the US to circumvent

American duties on Chinese exports. By June 2020, some circumvention probes were launched by the US. Import and export data may also raise concerns about the impact of trade diversion. Although export growth to China decelerated significantly from 16.6 per cent in 2018 to 0.1 per cent in 2019, Vietnam saw its export growth to the US increase from 14.3 per cent to 29.1 per cent in the same period. Conversely, Vietnam's imports from China increased by more than 15.2 per cent in 2019, faster than in 2018 (11.7 per cent).

Investment data also indicate significant FDI inflows from China into Vietnam. In 2019, registered capital of FDI projects from China and Hong Kong amounted to US$2.4 billion and US$2.8 billion, respectively. China and Hong Kong were, respectively, the third- and second-largest sources of new FDI to Vietnam in 2019, only after South Korea. A potential concern is that investors just moved temporarily to Vietnam to shelter from the impacts of the trade war. Still, the implementation of the ASEAN—Hong Kong FTA in June 2019 may simply facilitate 'hot money' for capital contribution or purchasing shares from Hong Kong into Vietnam, in the absence of adequate measures and screening policies.

Vietnam's initial response to the trade war was closely aligned with its approach to economic integration—that is, working with all partners to improve trade management and facilitate trade without discrimination. Vietnam also provided regular justification and clarifications to the US on issues related to the bilateral trade deficit, product origins and the exchange rate. Vietnam engaged in frequent discussions with the US to address the issues related to the justification of Vietnam's share in value-added in exports, and its intention to buy more agricultural products from the US. Vietnam also enhanced its cooperation with the US in investigating the origin of Vietnamese exports. Apart from the bilateral working group meeting in June 2018, there has been no similar meeting for Vietnam to justify its market economy to the US, and Vietnam does not seem to be in a rush for more meetings. Regarding currency manipulation, even from early 2018, Vietnam explicitly stated that it had not sought and would not seek to devalue the national currency to support exports. Vietnam has continued to justify this approach even after the US included Vietnam in the monitoring list of currency manipulation in May 2019.

At the same time, Vietnam continues to improve trade with China. Vietnam made efforts to build capacity for domestic companies to comply with the stricter standards of the Chinese market. In doing so, the explicit statement was that China had applied stricter standards for several years already—even before the trade war. Vietnam continued to work with China, ASEAN and other partners to conclude the negotiation of RCEP in 2019 (and signed the agreement in 2020 even after the withdrawal of India). Vietnam was one of the first ASEAN member states to ratify the ASEAN—Hong Kong FTA, enabling the agreement to enter into force in June 2019.

Vietnam has also attempted to increase the quality of its trade and investment relations. For instance, the Ministry of Industry and Trade requested tighter control by relevant authorities over certificates of origin to minimise trade fraud. Vietnam also improved screening and selection of FDI projects via higher economic, social and environmental standards, under Resolution 50-NQ/TW of the Politburo on attracting FDI in August 2019. However, the country made it clear that these regulatory changes would be applied on a horizontal basis for its own development objectives, rather than trying to discriminate against any partners. More broadly, Vietnam continued to work with ASEAN to express support for the multilateral trading system,[4] including in specific areas like e-commerce.

Case II: COVID-19 pandemic in 2020

The COVID-19 disease was first reported in late 2019 and quickly became a worldwide pandemic. By the end of 2020, the pandemic had spread to 218 countries and territories, resulting in over 82.4 million cases and about 1.8 million deaths (Nguyen and Hoang 2020). The number of new cases skyrocketed, particularly in late June 2020. Throughout 2020, the risk of a 'second wave' or 'third wave' of COVID-19 became increasingly evident in various countries.[5]

Given the challenges facing the world economy before 2020,[6] the COVID-19 pandemic has only further intensified global economic, political and social uncertainty and instability. Unpredictability is reflected in the wide-ranging forecasts of global economic downturn and recession

---

4   Demonstrated in leaders' statements in October 2018 and June 2019.

5   For instance, in China, the US and Japan. From 11 to 17 June 2020, more than 130 new cases of community infection were recorded in Beijing, forcing China to reimplement drastic measures such as isolation, blockades, school closures and flights suspensions. Between 18 and 30 June 2020, 254 new infection cases were reported in China. Tokyo also reported new community infection cases, the number soaring to more than 40 cases daily.

6   Such challenges include economic downturn, geopolitical tensions and conflicts, protectionism and extremism, risks for global trade and investment, and competition among major countries regarding IR 4.0 and the digital economy.

in 2020 by international organisations and policy research institutions. Debates on recovery scenarios for the global economy (following a V-, W-, L-, U-shaped, or 'Swoosh' model) have become more frequent, indicating the complexity and uncertainty in the COVID-19 context.

In response to the COVID-19 pandemic, many countries implemented unprecedented measures, including movement restrictions, border shutdowns, temporary suspension of business activities and non-essential services, social distancing and large-scale expansionary monetary-fiscal stimuli (see CIEM 2020; World Bank 2020). As the number of new COVID-19 infected cases gradually decreased in the second quarter of 2020, some countries relaxed social distancing measures in an effort to restart production and business activities.[7]

Vietnam reported the first two cases of COVID-19 infection in late January 2020, and, by the end of 2020, had 1,465 cases (Ministry of Health 2020). The pattern of new cases was uneven across the year. Three major waves were recorded in the periods from early March to late April 2020, from late July to late August 2020 and in the second half of December 2020. Vietnam declared the pandemic situation nationwide and implemented stringent movement restrictions and social distancing on 1 April 2020. These measures were relaxed during the second half of April 2020. During the latter waves, Vietnam only implemented social distancing on a restricted basis (i.e. only in the areas with infected cases, rather than on a nationwide basis).

Economic policy responses of Vietnam

Throughout 2020, Vietnam focused on flexible and timely policy responses to the COVID-19 pandemic. Controlling the spread of the disease was the top priority to consolidate social stability and instil public confidence. Vietnam simultaneously paid close attention to businesses and communities facing economic hardship and undertook various measures to alleviate such difficulties. Specific measures included lowering interest rates,[8] debt

---

7   Most states in the US entered the first stage of relaxed COVID-19 measures during the second quarter of 2020. The stock exchange and Wall Street partially reopened on May 27. Japan relaxed social restrictions on 1 June 2020.

8   From September 2019 to the end of May 2020, the State Bank of Vietnam cut key interest rates three times, with a total downward adjustment of 1.75 percentage points (annualised), reduced the ceiling of deposit rates by 0.8–1.25 percentage points (annualised), and lowered lending rates for some prioritised areas. Compared to other countries in the region, the reduction in Vietnam was most significant (Thailand, Malaysia and Indonesia were down by 0.5 percentage points; the Philippines by 1.25 percentage points; China by 0.3 percentage points; and India by 0.75 percentage points).

restructuring, preferential programs, deferral and rescheduling of tax payment and land rental, and reducing the prices of electricity, services, and oil and petrol for prioritised groups. Apart from continuing previous priorities to promote exports and FDI, Vietnam made efforts to accelerate disbursement of public investment, and mobilise domestic investment and domestic consumption.[9]

The above policies allowed Vietnam to effectively control and prevent the spread of disease and implement the appropriate responses to mitigate the consequences of COVID-19. Policy measures were based on actual situations, regularly updated scenarios and related analysis forecasts—this approach stemmed from Vietnam's experience with previous difficult times such as the US–China trade war. According to the COVID-19 Government Response Stringency Index,[10] Vietnam's responses were implemented much earlier than those of other countries around the world (see Figure 8.2). From late April 2020, travel restrictions gradually relaxed, allowing business and production operations as well as normal daily life to resume, provided the necessary precautions were in place.

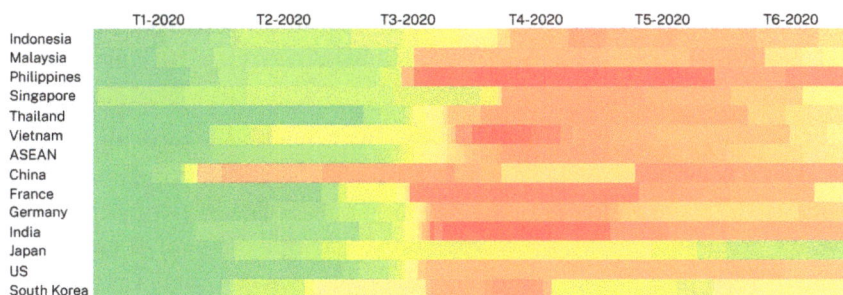

Figure 8.2: COVID-19 Government Response Stringency Index
Source: Hale et al. (2020, cited in CIEM 2020). Note: the closer to 100, the redder the colour. Graph displays data collected until 15 June 2020.

---

9   In a conference with the business community in May 2020, the prime minister pointed out five 'growth drivers', including mobilising domestic investment, boosting exports, fostering public investment, promoting domestic consumption and attracting FDI.
10   The COVID-19 Oxford Government Response Stringency Index is a composite measure that traces governments' responses to the COVID-19 pandemic. The index collects available information on 17 indicators of government responses, including 08 policy indicators of containment and closure policy such as school closures, movement restrictions and blockade; 04 indicators of economic policies such as income support to citizens or provision of foreign aid; 05 indicators of health system policies such as testing regime, emergency investments into healthcare services and tracing contacts. The index takes the value from 0 to 100, of which 0 is the least strict and 100 is the strictest.

Vietnam's fight against the pandemic instilled a high level of confidence across communities and in businesses, particularly in light of its 'dual target' of containing the pandemic and boosting economic recovery. Regular information on the COVID-19 pandemic and the various policy measures undertaken by government was conveyed in a transparent and diversified manner and was accompanied by wide policy consultation. Vietnam arguably turned the tide of public distrust, which had been somewhat eroded as a consequence of the Formosa disaster in 2016, enabling it to gain strong public support thanks to its 'ability to manage problems clearly and smoothly' (Clark 2020).

More importantly, Vietnam has retained macroeconomic policy space to respond to adverse developments (if any) in the future. According to the World Bank, Vietnam's balance of payments, budget deficit and the financial sector—major transmission channels of external shocks to the domestic economy—remained relatively positive. As a note, prudent fiscal management measures during the period 2016–19 improved policy space for the government in carrying out fiscal-monetary support in 2020 (CIEM 2020).

Opportunities and challenges for Vietnam in the context of COVID-19

Despite the consequences of COVID-19, the pandemic has arguably brought about important opportunities, even turning points, for the development of many countries, including Vietnam. One remarkable impact is that the COVID-19 pandemic has accelerated a partial shift in global supply chains, accompanied by the inflows of FDI. However, the CIEM (2020) contends that the shift of supply chains away from China (China Plus One) began prior to the COVID-19 pandemic due to economic downturn and increasing labour costs in China, the US–China trade war, and competition from ASEAN and India. However, in the context of the pandemic, the shift was reinforced not only by enterprises' own benefit calculations, but also by various countries' national policies that were aimed at reducing dependence on the Chinese market and lessening the adverse impacts of supply chain disruptions in the future.[11]

---

11   The US, EU and Japan initiated plans to encourage and provide financial support for enterprises to shift their production operations out of China. About 30–40 enterprises from the US and EU expressed their intention to move a portion of their business activities out of China. A survey by *Nikkei Asian Review* (end of May 2020) revealed that more than 70 per cent of respondents wanted to diversify supply chains to reduce dependence on China.

Vietnam had appealed to foreign investors long before the COVID-19 pandemic struck. This was thanks to drastic reforms of its domestic business environment (in particular, from 2014) and Vietnam's important FTAs (e.g. CPTPP, RCEP and EVFTA). The pandemic has not weakened or disrupted these factors. Instead, Vietnam's relatively effective response to COVID-19 has strengthened the confidence of its foreign investors. For instance, the implementation of EVFTA and expedited ratification of the EU–Vietnam Investment Protection Agreement by EU members may benefit EU investors who are considering moving investment out of China.

The COVID-19 pandemic did not shift Vietnam's focus away from the digital economy. Instead, the disruption of economic operations based on traditional platforms forced Vietnamese agencies and enterprises to be more active in utilising digital platforms for management, production and business operations. This includes implementing online delivery systems, introducing e-payments and online-learning. Both the Vietnamese Government and private enterprises have embraced these new economic models and methods. Applications of the digital economy and e-government development have accelerated since 2018–19.[12] The COVID-19 pandemic has also built greater consensus within Vietnam on the adoption of 5G technology, which is now seen as inevitable. Discussions of 5G adoption no longer refer to the risk of a 'digital divide', which was more commonplace during the time of US–China trade tensions in 2019. Vietnam has sought measures to improve access to 5G technology, including through the development of hardware by domestic firms.

COVID-19 has undermined strategic trust among the world's major economies. Confidence levels during the pandemic are influenced by a variety of factors: how well a country has managed to control the spread of infections, official statistics related to COVID-19, whether a country supports multilateral mechanisms in tackling COVID-19 and so on. As the 2020 ASEAN chair, Vietnam sought to promote regional cooperation and bilateral and multilateral relations in fighting COVID-19 (see Box 8.1). Vietnam's 'COVID diplomacy' was strengthened in both bilateral and multilateral frameworks with key partners, particularly through the Special ASEAN and ASEAN+3 summits on COVID-19, the Special ASEAN

---

12 According to the Ministry of Information and Communications (2020), before COVID-19, about 40 ministries and provinces had connected to national data integration and sharing platforms. About 27 per cent of ministries, line ministries and provinces developed data integration and sharing platforms at the ministerial and provincial level. By the end of October 2020, all ministries and line ministries had data integration and sharing platforms.

Foreign Ministers' Meeting on COVID-19, and the Special ASEAN Economic Ministers Virtual Conference Meeting on COVID-19, as well as through donating medical supplies to countries around the region.

Box 8.1: Some results of the Special ASEAN and ASEAN+3 summits on COVID-19 in April 2020

On April 14 2020, as ASEAN Chair, Vietnam held virtual Special ASEAN and ASEAN+3 Summits on COVID-19. The Joint Declaration of the Special ASEAN Summit emphasized ASEAN's solidarity in responding to COVID-19 in the spirit of a 'Cohesive and Responsive ASEAN'. ASEAN Leaders agreed: (i) to further strengthen public health cooperation to contain the pandemic and protect people; (ii) to promote the exchange of information and experience sharing, technical assistance and scientific and technological cooperation in containing and preventing the transmission of the disease; (iii) to discuss and develop a post-pandemic recovery plan, including liberalizing markets for trade and investment, recovery and development of regional supply chains, and strengthening food security; and (iv) to underscore the importance of a multi-stakeholder, multi-sectoral and comprehensive approach by ASEAN to effectively respond to COVID-19 and future health emergencies. The Summit led to numerous initiatives, including to encourage the development of regional reserves of medical supplies; to consider formulating a standard ASEAN response to public health emergencies; to develop ASEAN guidelines on the provision of emergency assistance by ASEAN missions in developing countries to nationals of ASEAN member countries in crisis situations; and to propose the establishment of the COVID-19 ASEAN response fund.

The Special ASEAN+3 Summit acknowledged the value of regional cooperation mechanisms in responding to disease emergencies. New mechanisms include national risk assessments, periodic reports on the Risk Assessment on the International Dissemination of COVID-19 in the ASEAN region, the virtual ASEAN+3 Senior Officials Meeting on Health Development, and the implementation of the International Health Regulations. Pre-existing regional cooperation mechanisms include the ASEAN Emergency Operations Center Network for public health emergencies, the ASEAN BioDiaspora Virtual Centre, and the ASEAN+3 Field Epidemiology Training Network.

The Special Summit Joint Statement reaffirms that ASEAN+3 is willing to share experience, policy responses, treatment methods, epidemiological research and clinical treatments; to provide medical supplies; and to promote cooperation on the production of COVID-19 vaccines. ASEAN+3 leaders also agreed on timely support for ASEAN+3 nationals (vulnerable groups in particular) in accessing healthcare services and returning to their home countries. In addition, ASEAN+3 leaders established an ASEAN+3 task force on responding to epidemics; requested China, the Republic of Korea and Japan to assist in building financial, technological and professional capacity of public health systems; proposed the establishment of an ASEAN+3 reserve of essential medical supplies; made a proposal on enhancing the role of the ASEAN+3 Macroeconomic Research Office (AMRO) in planning economic recovery and development post-COVID-19; utilised existing mechanisms that ensure economic and financial stability and food security such as the Chiang Mai Initiative Multilateralization (CMIM) and ASEAN+3 Emergency Rice Reserve.

Source: CIEM (2020).

Still, the COVID-19 pandemic poses challenges and obstacles for Vietnam. First, promoting exports of high-demand products like medical supplies is no easy task, because under-developed domestic industries may lead to potential input shortages. Second, without sufficient monitoring, the shift of global supply chains may force Vietnam to become the destination for the production of low-tech and environmentally unfriendly goods. Finally, the COVID-19 pandemic reinforces both traditional and non-traditional challenges to Vietnam's security. For instance, cybercrime and cyber attacks have increased drastically amid the unfolding pandemic and rising demand for online platforms.[13]

Strategic competition among major countries intensified after COVID-19, posing new challenges for Vietnam's foreign economic relations. Confrontation between the US and China and strategic gatherings around the world have become increasingly complicated and unpredictable. This can pressure countries like Vietnam to 'take a side' in certain key areas such as technology, medical supplies and supply chains. Therefore, rushed decision-making in this uncertain environment will only involve Vietnam in geopolitical competition with major countries, rather than improve its resilience (CIEM 2020).

Facing a mixture of both new and old opportunities and challenges, Vietnam's response to the COVID-19 pandemic in 2020 had some important implications. First, the conduct of policies should be associated with regular updates and assessments of growth scenarios. Such scenarios should not be narrowly defined with respect to the evolution of the COVID-19 pandemic alone but should instead cover aspects of strategic actions by major economies as trade investment partners of Vietnam. Second, the Vietnamese Government should retain policy space to respond to post-COVID-19 scenarios. Accordingly, macroeconomic stability remains fundamental to strengthen the confidence of enterprises and consumers as well as consensus on reforms and restructuring initiatives. Third, business environment reform should be promoted on the basis of the remarkable achievements during the period 2014–19. Thus, Vietnam should renew reforms to attract

---

13   In May 2020, the Vietnam National Cyber Security Center reported 439 attacks into the cyber networks of Vietnam (an increase of 16.3 per cent compared to April 2020). More instances of fraud and cheating in online applications were detected using sophisticated methods (e.g. pretending to be staff and officials of legal enforcement authorities or governmental bodies; sending messages of winning prizes; applying for jobs or working abroad; 'arranging' projects; applying for loans; calling for investment, aid and multi-level marketing; virtual money; establishing fake websites of banks to collect users' data; seeking support for pandemic containment; etc.), leading to great loss of assets and reputation for victims.

foreign investors, and, at the same time, improve the growth potential of the economy (which, in turn, will increase its appeal to foreign investors). These policies were identified before the COVID-19 pandemic and should be accelerated to adapt to the new context.

In Vietnam's view, the consequences of the COVID-19 pandemic have spread beyond the borders of individual countries. Thus, it is necessary to have a comprehensive, closely coordinated approach to recovery at regional and international levels. Effective international cooperation remains a pillar for development and economic restructuring. Concerns about the geopolitical implications of RCEP in the COVID-19 context are legitimate but must be addressed on the principles of supporting ASEAN centrality and adhering to Vietnam's long-term approach to economic integration. In this regard, Vietnam and ASEAN may work with external partners to set a good example of more friendly economic policies on some products—including medical supplies and rice—that may have a direct contribution to international cooperation after COVID-19.

Case III: South China Sea

The South China Sea (known in Vietnam as the East Sea) is a geopolitically important location. Sixty per cent of seaborne trade passes through Asia, and the South China Sea accounts for one-third of global shipping (China Power Team 2017). This maritime area is also rich in resources, with an abundance of islands, fisheries, oil and gas deposits. In 2013, the US Energy Information Administration estimated that the South China Sea had an oil reserve of 11 billion barrels and a natural gas reserve of 190 trillion cubic feet.

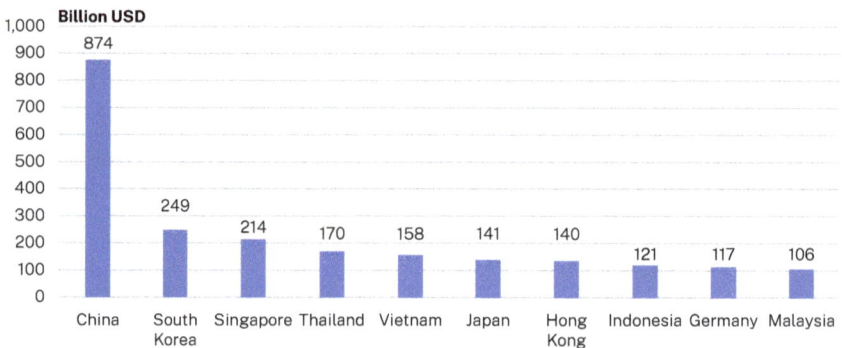

Figure 8.3: Exports through the South China Sea
Source: China Power Team (2021).

According to the EU-Asia Centre (2013), the South China Sea is arguably one the most disputed areas in Southeast Asia. Vietnam, China, Chinese Taipei, the Philippines, Indonesia, Malaysia and Brunei Darussalam have made overlapping territorial claims to the South China Sea waters, and to some islands and rocky outcrops in them. Meanwhile, disputes over the South China Sea involve a body of international laws that are both contested and difficult to interpret (Poling 2013). Incidents of small naval confrontations between official vessels and fishing boats of various countries in the South China Sea are not rare. While claims to natural resources like oil, natural gas, minerals and fish exacerbate these disputes (EU-Asia Centre 2013), protecting sovereignty over the territory and waters is also the highest priority for concerned countries, including Vietnam.

Vietnam has consistently emphasised that peace, stability, cooperation and development in the South China Sea are common desires and goals of all countries in the region and the broader international community. Vietnam underscores the importance of respect for international law, respect for legal order at sea and full and responsible enforcement of UNCLOS 1982. In line with this, Vietnam consistently welcomes efforts from all countries to maintain peace, stability and cooperation in the South China Sea, and encourages countries to settle disputes via dialogue and other peaceful measures in accordance with international laws.

Vietnam has firmly and consistently claimed to have sufficient historical evidence and legal basis to prove undisputed sovereignty over the waters and islands in the South China Sea, including the Hoang Sa and Truong Sa archipelagos. The Law of the Sea of Vietnam—passed during the third session of the 13th National Assembly on 21 June 2012 and effective since 1 January 2013—declared that Vietnam has sovereignty and jurisdiction over the Paracel and Spratly islands (National Assembly 2012). In addition, Vietnam has devised legal and propaganda strategies about its sovereignty and rights over its territories in the South China Sea. Vietnamese authorities frequently disseminate information about the historical evidence and legal basis for Vietnam's sovereignty. Vietnam actively engages in various workshops to present the historical evidence and legal basis for such claims.

Vietnam remains willing to use peaceful negotiation to resolve disputes based on the provisions of UNCLOS 1982. The country has engaged in both bilateral and multilateral negotiations to resolve the South China Sea dispute. Bilateral negotiations involve Vietnam and another party, while multilateral negotiations are reserved for issues concerning Vietnam and more than one other party. In official meetings between Vietnam and China, the issues and differences concerning the South China Sea were raised and discussed frankly. Vietnam supported putting the issue of the South China Sea on the agenda of an ASEAN-centred multilateral dialogue framework (Shoji 2012).

Vietnam attaches great importance to ASEAN's South China Sea policy. ASEAN and China signed the Declaration on the Conduct of Parties in the South China Seas (DOC) in November 2002 and adopted guidelines to implement it on 21 July 2011. The Joint Statement of the Foreign Ministers of ASEAN Member States and China on the Full and Effective Implementation of DOC was endorsed on 25 July 2016. At their meeting on 6 August 2017 in Manila, the foreign ministers of ASEAN member states and China adopted the framework of the CoC. At the twentieth ASEAN–China Summit in November 2017, ASEAN member states and China officially announced the launch of negotiation of the CoC, which was proposed by China to be complete by 2021 (ASEAN 2020). Throughout this process, while continuing to seek a long-term solution to the South China Sea issue, Vietnam has advocated that all parties must exercise restraint and strictly implement the DOC, towards building a CoC.

Finally, Vietnam actively participates in other mechanisms of ASEAN on security issues related to the South China Sea. ASEAN and China have been cooperating under the ASEAN Defence Ministers Meeting-Plus (ADMM-Plus) since it was established in 2010. Similarly, Vietnam also participated in the ASEAN Regional Forum, which reflects its ASEAN-derived approach to cooperative security, seeking to:

> Create a regional order based on: (i) transparency in strategic intent and threat perception; (ii) mutual trust and confidence with regard to the member states' military capabilities and deployment; and (iii) habit of cooperation which will facilitate the resolution of existing and future conflicts (Cruz de Castro 2017, 35).

While the ability to realise such a goal is open to question, the adoption of a gradual approach (i.e. the 'ASEAN Way') has been relevant to Vietnam.

Conclusions

Vietnam's strategy for pursuing economic integration in conjunction with other strategic goals since its accession to the WTO in 2007 yields several insights. First, notwithstanding efforts to diversify export markets and products, Vietnam continues to attach importance to trade with major partners. Times of global uncertainty and volatility have not reduced Vietnam's attention to these markets. Vietnam's increasing export competitiveness is reflected in growing trade and investment flows. Its approach to trade policy has evolved from unilateral and comprehensive liberalisation in the pre-WTO period to a more selective, partner-based and WTO-plus liberalisation arrangement, which has helped to improve and leverage export competitiveness. FDI inflows continue to have positive impacts on Vietnam's export growth, even in the context of the COVID-19 pandemic.

ASEAN played an important role, both as an entity undertaking ongoing community-building initiatives, and as a playground in which Vietnam could learn and adopt measures to enhance its economic integration. Given recent geopolitical developments, Vietnam views the need to balance relationships with major powers as unavoidable. Its approach to economic integration undergirds how Vietnam has adapted its approach to security, and this has contributed to ASEAN's mechanisms towards peace, stability and development of the region. This kind of approach is consistent with the association's gradualism: the 'ASEAN Way'. While outcomes may be path-dependent and the set of choices may vary at times, it is in Vietnam's long-term strategic interest to retain its commitment to economic integration and to address security policy within this context, notably by respecting ASEAN's centrality in regional issues.

Drastic contextual changes like geopolitical competition and non-traditional security issues are driving Vietnam's integration into the global and regional economy. While economic integration remains the focus, international cooperation in other areas has been promoted to support economic integration. Vietnam has also signed various agreements and strategic partnerships, most with key trade and/or investment partners. In return, expanded investment and trade relations contribute to improving Vietnam's economic and regulatory capacity, which in turn improves the country's contributions to international and regional institution-building processes. The three case studies in this chapter clearly portray such interactions between Vietnam's economic integration and security policies.

References

ASEAN (Association of Southeast Asian Nations). 2020. 'Overview of ASEAN–China Dialogue Relations'. April. asean.org/storage/2012/05/Overview-of-ASEAN-China-Relations-22-Apr-2020-00000002.pdf (site discontinued).

China Power Team. 2017. 'How Much Trade Transits the South China Sea?' 2 August 2017. Last modified 25 January 2021. chinapower.csis.org/much-trade-transits-south-china-sea/.

CIEM (Central Institute for Economic Management). 2013. *Comprehensive Evaluations of Vietnam's Socio-Economic Performance 5 Years after Accession to the WTO.* Hanoi: Finance Publishing House.

CIEM (Central Institute for Economic Management). 2019. *Vietnam's Economy in the First 6 Months of 2019.* Hanoi: Finance Publishing House.

CIEM (Central Institute for Economic Management). 2020. *Vietnam's Economy in the First 6 Months of 2020: Enabling Regulatory Approach for the New Normal.* Hanoi: Dan Tri Publishing House.

Clark, H. 2020. 'Vietnam Defies the Odds on COVID-19'. *The Interpreter,* 12 May 2020. www.lowyinstitute.org/the-interpreter/vietnam-defies-odds-covid-19.

Cruz De Castro, R. 2017. 'The ASEAN Regional Forum in the Face of Great-Power Competition in the South China Sea: The Limits of ASEAN's Approach in Addressing 21st-Century Maritime Security Issues?' 15 August 2020. www.kas.de/c/document_library/get_file?uuid=43dafd95-a5cc-e07e-6d14-73ac2 d12cda6&groupId=288143.

Dinh, H. M., Q. L. Trinh, A. D. Nguyen and T. T. Vo. 2009. 'Study 1: Trade, Growth, Employment and Wages in Vietnam'. In *Research Project: Globalization, Adjustment and the Challenge of Inclusive Growth: Furthering Inclusive Growth and Industrial Upgrading in Indonesia, the Philippines and Vietnam.* International Development Research Centre and CIEM.

Dinh, T. H., A. D. Nguyen, B. M. Tran, T. L. M. Do, T. H. Pham, T. N. T. Do, P. N. Le, M. A. Le and T. T. H. Dang. 2020. *Implementing CPTPP as a Part of Economic Integration Roadmap in Vietnam: Requirement for Structural Reforms and Firms' Preparedness.* Hanoi: Dan Tri Publishing House.

EU-Asia Centre. 2013. 'South China Sea: Background Note'. Accessed 17 December 2020.

Luong, C. 2020. 'Further Improving Regulations, Mechanisms and Policies of National Defense in the New Context' [Tiếp tục hoàn thiện hệ thống pháp luật, cơ chế, chính sách về quốc phòng đáp ứng yêu cầu, nhiệm vụ bảo vệ Tổ quốc trong tình hình mới]. www.tapchicongsan.org.vn/quoc-phong-an-ninh-oi-ngoai1/-/2018/815932/tiep-tuc-hoan-thien-he-thong-phap-luat%2C-co-che%2C-chinh-sach-ve-quoc-phong-dap-ung-yeu-cau%2C-nhiem-vu-bao-ve-to-quoc-trong-tinh-hinh-moi.aspx [in Vietnamese].

Malesky, E. and L. Mosley. 2021. 'Labor Upgrading and Export Market Opportunities: Evidence from Vietnam'. *Economics and Politics* 33 (3): 483–513. doi.org/10.1111/ecpo.12180.

Ministry of Health. 2020. 'Update on the Situation of COVID-19'. 31 December 2020. ehealth.gov.vn/Index.aspx?action=News&newsId=53558 [in Vietnamese].

Ministry of Information and Communications. 2020. 'All Ministries and Line Ministries Had Data Integration and Sharing Platforms' [100% Bộ ngành có nền tảng tích hợp, chia sẻ dữ liệu cấp Bộ LGSP]. Accessed 15 November 2020. www.mic.gov.vn/mic_2020/Pages/TinTuc/145371/100--Bo-nganh-co-nen-tang-tich-hop--chia-se-du-lieu-cap-Bo-LGSP.html [in Vietnamese].

National Assembly. 2012. *Law of the Sea of Vietnam* [Luật Biển]. Accessed 11 August 2021. thuvienphapluat.vn/van-ban/Giao-thong-Van-tai/Luat-bien-Viet-Nam-2012-143494.aspx [in Vietnamese].

Nguyen, A. D. and T. H. Dinh. 2018. 'New Trade Context: Outlook, Challenges and Policy Responses for Vietnam' [Bối cảnh thương mại mới: Triển vọng, thách thức và đối sách của Việt Nam]. Paper for the Forum on International Economic Integration, 4 December 2018 [in Vietnamese].

Nguyen, S. and H. Hoang. 2020. 'A Review of 2020 under COVID-19' [Nhìn lại năm 2020 qua biến cố COVID-19]. Accessed 2 January 2021. nhandan.vn/binh-luan-quoc-te/nhin-lai-nam-2020-qua-bien-co-covid-19-630086/ [in Vietnamese].

PECC (Pacific Economic Cooperation Council). 2018. 'State of the Region 2018–2019'. 12 November 2018. www.pecc.org/resources/regional-cooperation/2584-state-of-the-region-2018-2019.

Petri, P. A. and M. Plummer. 2020. 'East Asia Decouples from the United States: Trade War, COVID-19, and East Asia's New Trade Blocs'. *Working Paper,* no. 20–9 (June 2020). Peterson Institute for International Economics. doi.org/10.2139/ssrn.3630294.

Poling, G. B. 2013. 'The South China Sea in Focus: Clarifying the Limits of Maritime Dispute'. Centre for Strategic and International Studies, July. csis-website-prod.s3.amazonaws.com/s3fs-public/legacy_files/files/publication/130717_Poling_SouthChinaSea_Web.pdf.

Shoji, T. 2012. 'Vietnam, ASEAN, and the South China Sea: Unity or Diverseness?' *NIDS Journal of Defense and Security*, 13 December 2012. www.nids.mod. go.jp/english/publication/kiyo/pdf/2012/bulletin_e2012_2.pdf.

Tran, T. H. M., A. D. Nguyen, T. L. M. Do, T. P. L. Nguyen and T. H. Pham. 2021. *Making RCEP Work for Economic Well-Being and Autonomy in Vietnam: Required Reforms of Trade and Investment Institutions*. Hanoi: Dan Tri Publishing House.

Vietnamese Ministry of Defence. 2019. *2019 Vietnam National Defence*. Hanoi: National Political Publishing House.

Vo, T. T. 2012. 'Achieving an Efficient AEC by 2015: A Perspective from Vietnam'. In *Achieving ASEAN Economic Community 2015: Challenges for Member Countries and Businesses*, edited by S. B. Das, 161–77. Singapore: Institute of Southeast Asian Studies. doi.org/10.1355/9789814379656-017.

World Bank. 2020. *Global Economic Prospects*. Washington, DC: The World Bank Group.

9

ASEAN and the role of Asian regionalism in managing asymmetric power

Peter Drysdale, Dionisius Narjoko
and Rebecca St Maria

Introduction

Asia is host to some unique ideas and experiments in economic integration and international economic diplomacy. These are the product of thinking that emerged about increasing cooperation and integration at the end of the 1960s and developed through a range of regional projects. The consensus-building approach to economic cooperation and the idea of open regionalism, in particular, have been central in shaping the development of the Association of Southeast Asian Nations (ASEAN) as well as broader regional arrangements in East Asia and the Pacific.

These principles have also been successfully applied to international diplomatic initiatives, such as the formation of the Asia-Pacific Economic Cooperation (APEC) process and the G20. In the context of the varied experience with international economic cooperation around the world, the ASEAN model can be viewed as a significant and unique innovation and achievement in international economic diplomacy, and in managing the dealings of smaller countries with major powers. Other models of regionalism with expansive supranational characteristics, such as in Europe, are increasingly fractured.

The diversity of Southeast Asia, East Asia and the Pacific region—in terms of stages of economic development, political systems, ethnicity and religious and cultural background—required innovation in building cooperative mechanisms around the sensitivities of sovereignty (coloured as it was by the legacies of colonialism in the region), disparities in power and institutional differences. The coup in Myanmar in early 2021 tested these sensitivities in an extreme fashion.

The ASEAN model will be tested more broadly by increasingly confrontational and non-cooperative relations between the United States and China. Though the Biden administration will likely adopt a more measured tone than its predecessor, the basic assumption that China is more rival than partner now underpins much American strategic thinking, and ASEAN's preference for cordial relations with both will be put under severe pressure. The institutional response of ASEAN to America's Free and Open Indo-Pacific initiative, as well as to the Myanmar coup, is a promising sign that the historical focus of the association on acknowledging political and security disagreements within a broader framework that emphasises gains from economic cooperation and eschews zero-sum logic can be viable in dealing with the new challenges facing the model of open regionalism in Asia.

The design of ASEAN stands in stark contrast to the European Union's promotion of supranational institutions in a system of legally binding decisions. Instead, a key component of the ASEAN framework is still its adherence to the principle of noninterference and recognition of member state sovereignty. The ASEAN way of informal consensus in forging agreement and in decision-making has shaped the association's reputation as slow moving but has also, in many ways, contributed to its longevity and success.

ASEAN's outward orientation was economic as well as strategic. Unlike Europe's unification, Asia's economic integration was shaped by an openness and inclusiveness to countries outside its membership from the beginning, and by its global objectives. The inclusive approach of Asia's economic integration developed and was later enunciated using the dynamic term 'open regionalism'.

This chapter examines the success of this model in managing the region's economic relations with the industrial powers and the challenges it now faces with the intensification of strategic competition between the United States and China.

Evolution of Asian regionalism and its principles

The birth of ASEAN in 1967 gave strength to a historical shift in Southeast Asia's economies. The shift in thinking across the region and the domestic policy environment in member countries led to a move away from protectionism and import substitution towards a more outward-looking orientation, and acceptance of the role of expanding economic relations with the major industrial economies in their development. ASEAN became an endeavour for ensuring that national efforts resulted in more productive regional outcomes. It created a space where regional integration supported and promoted domestic growth on the one hand, while strengthening engagement with the global economic system on the other.

The rapid growth of Japan's economy in the late 1960s through to the 1970s created huge demand for Southeast Asian exports. In 1968, Japan absorbed 21 per cent of all Southeast Asian exports. Over half of Southeast Asia's export trade was with advanced Pacific countries, including the US. A large proportion of the remainder was with Europe.

Foreign direct investment (FDI), especially trade-oriented FDI from Japan, became an important element in Southeast Asia's trade and income growth. It soon became the key to early industrialisation through laying the foundations for the development of regional production networks.

The structure of ASEAN's engagement in the international economy thus recommended focusing on extra-regional markets such as Japan and industrialising Northeast Asia, and targets of growth opportunity in the industrial world. Intra-regional ASEAN trade in 1967 was only 9.5 per cent of total ASEAN trade. In the late 1960s, intra-ASEAN trade was dominated, as it is today, by Singapore's entrepôt trade with Indonesia and Malaysia. Today, intra-ASEAN trade is still less than one-quarter of total ASEAN trade (23 per cent in 2019), compared with 60 per cent in the EU and 49 per cent in North America.

The formation of ASEAN contrasted sharply with the earlier experience of Europe's integration in the 1958 European Economic Community, the early iteration of the EU. The two regional groupings developed for different reasons, according to different patterns and in response to their own set of circumstances. The differences between the two are evident in their different perceptions of sovereignty, formal institutions and leadership.

'Design choices [for ASEAN] have been framed as the choice between institutionalisation and flexibility or between closed and open regionalism' (Murray 2010, 603).

The differences between ASEAN and Europe are also evident in the logic and structure of political relations in each region. The European enterprise was an important part of the political defence against the Soviet Cold War threat. ASEAN was designed to mend fractious political relations between Indonesia and its neighbours as a bulwark against communism in Asia with a non-aligned posture.

The diversity of Southeast Asia and of the Asia-Pacific region required early innovation in building cooperative mechanisms around the sensitivities of sovereignty, disparities in power and institutional differences. The countries of Southeast Asia 'despite their heterogeneity had two key overriding common interests: strong economic growth and development and political and diplomatic interest in neighbourly cooperation' (Drysdale 1988, 18). Over the past half century, 'these common interests provide[d] the simple but substantial focus for economic policies directed towards closer ... economic cooperation' (Drysdale 1988, 18).

The EU's promotion of supranational institutions in a system of binding decisions with legal force contrasts with ASEAN's framework of adherence to the principle of noninterference and recognition of member state sovereignty (see ASEAN 2007, Article 2 [2][a]). The need to gain informal consensus in forging agreements and in decision-making have encumbered ASEAN with the reputation of being slow moving, but also have undoubtedly contributed to its continuing success.

Role of regional cooperation in alleviating conflict

ASEAN's economic focus has always been external, unlike the focus of the EU. Some see the difference as a matter of process: whereas the EU's integration is driven by policy, ASEAN's is driven by markets (Capannelli 2009). The markets in which ASEAN has had the largest stake have been large industrial powers and, increasingly, those within the neighbouring region.

Mahbubani warned in 1995 that Europe's exclusivism was a 'strategic error'. With the exclusion of Turkey, he argues, 'an opportunity was lost to demonstrate that an Islamic society could cross cultural boundaries and be like any other modern European state' (Mahbubani 1995, 109). ASEAN was able to integrate diversity, while the EU was not. Indeed, over 20 years later, with a domestic referendum in the United Kingdom driven, at least partially, along anti-Islamic lines, the people of Britain voted to leave the EU.[1]

While ASEAN has been warned against complacency and against not heeding the lessons of the EU losing one of its key players, the strength that its management of diversity brings to the ASEAN formula provides a measure of insurance.

ASEAN's outward orientation is both economic and strategic. Unlike Europe's unification, Asia's economic integration was shaped by an openness and inclusiveness to countries outside its membership from the beginning. Its outward strategic orientation is symbolised in the Treaty of Amity and Cooperation (TAC) of 1976 that encapsulates a non-aligned strategic posture (see Table 9.1). TAC saw ASEAN keep diplomatic lines open to the former Soviet Union (later Russia) and early normalisation of relations with China at the same time as some ASEAN members maintained deep military ties with the US.

The inclusive approach of Asia's economic integration evolved and was pursued under the rubric of 'open regionalism', which has the political connotation of non-alignment as well as the economic connotation of multilateralism. This posture has kept open the space for ASEAN's effective engagement with actively competing bigger powers.

Open regionalism 'seeks to promote economic integration among participants without discrimination against other economies' (Drysdale and Vines 1998, 103). While the idea of open regionalism and the term did not become commonplace until the beginning of the 1980s, the evolution of the thinking behind it has longer antecedents. It emerged when the ASEAN project was challenged by the idea of broader regional cooperation and became a central tenet on the way towards the establishment of APEC between the late 1970s and 1989 (Drysdale and Vines 1998). It found

---

1   It is notable that the EU has welcomed Serbia and Croatia into the union (both majority Christian states) while Bosnia has been put on the slow burner and France blocked further negotiations with Albania (majority Muslim) and North Macedonia (33 per cent Muslim).

support and intellectual development in the Pacific Trade and Development (PAFTAD) conferences that had run continuously since 1968 (Elek 1991). It was first articulated in the Canberra Pacific Community Seminar in 1980, later the Pacific Economic Cooperation Council (PECC), which was a precursor to APEC (Drysdale and Terada 2007). In ASEAN thinking it became entrenched in the notion of regional cooperation within a framework of concentric circles extending out around ASEAN centrality.

Open regionalism was largely based on the idea that, much like regional security cooperation, effective economic cooperation in Asia would have to conform to similar principles of openness, equality and evolution (Drysdale and Vines 1998). In this sense, ASEAN as an association for both security and economic cooperation was developed within the framework of similar conceptual parameters.

The ASEAN Free Trade Area, signed in 1992, is unique among such free trade arrangements in that it incorporates the purposeful multilateralisation of preferences initially exchanged between members (Hill and Menon 2014). In this sense, it is a model for any preferential agreement that claims to have the global liberalisation of trade as its core objective. There are no other such agreements that embed a sunset clause on discriminatory trade treatment in this way.

The principles of cooperation that came at the early stages of developing the concept of 'open regionalism' still dominate Asian economic regionalism and the philosophy of ASEAN, however challenged they are by contemporary big power tensions. ASEAN and Asia-Pacific economic integration has proceeded a long way under the aegis of these principles. Table 9.1 sets out the development of the key ideas and strategic commitments behind regional efforts that were ordered around the idea of an open regionalism in ASEAN and in Asia.

Foundations of ASEAN's centrality in Asia and its diplomatic success

There are two main elements in ASEAN's success in the management of its relations with the bigger powers. One, already noted implicitly, is widely understood. ASEAN's establishment saw a fundamental reshaping of its members' economic development priorities, led by the Suharto government in Jakarta, and the adoption of trade-oriented growth strategies—not every country all at once but step-by-step and irrevocably—rooted in the multilateral trading system and the protections it gave to smaller economic powers in their dealings with larger powers. Without the redirection of economic policies across the region, the innovation and success of ASEAN would hardly have become the lynchpin of East Asian political arrangements that it is today.

Table 9.1: Development of principles of Asian economic integration

	Inclusiveness and support for the global economic system	Support for multilateralism and non-discrimination
ASEAN Declaration 1967	'Open for participation to all States in the Southeast Asian Region subscribing to [ASEAN's] aims, principles and purposes' (Article 4).	'To maintain close and beneficial cooperation with existing international and regional organizations with similar aims and purposes, and explore all avenues for even closer cooperation among themselves' (Article 2 [7]).
Treaty of Amity and Cooperation in Southeast Asia 1976	Promoting 'close and beneficial cooperation with other States as well as international and regional organisations outside the region' (Article 6).	'Parties shall exert their maximum efforts multilaterally as well as bilaterally on the basis of equality, non-discrimination and mutual benefit' (Article 5).
The Canberra Seminar 1980	'The need to ensure that an outward-looking arrangement' would also be 'complementary' to existing arrangements.	'The need for an "organic approach" building upon private arrangements and exchanges which already existed in the Pacific' and in opposition to a discriminatory trading arrangement in the Pacific.
APEC Bogor Goals 1994	'To support an expanding world economy and an open multilateral trading system' (Leaders' Declaration, point 2 [2]) and to enhance regional and global growth.	'[Opposed] to the creation of an inward-looking trading bloc that would divert from the pursuit of global free trade' (Leaders' Declaration, point 6).
Cambodia, Lao, Myanmar and Vietnam join ASEAN, 1995–97	'The admission of Cambodia, Laos and Myanmar would serve the long-term interest of regional peace, stability and prosperity [and provide] … a firm foundation for common action to promote regional cooperation in Southeast Asia' (*1997 Joint Communique of the 30th ASEAN Ministerial Meeting*, Article 2).	'The Foreign Ministers welcomed Vietnam as the seventh member of ASEAN. They also welcomed the accession of Cambodia to the Treaty of Amity and Cooperation in Southeast Asia … these events marked a historic step towards building a Southeast Asian community' (*1995 Joint Communique of the 28th ASEAN Ministerial Meeting*, Article 2).

	Inclusiveness and support for the global economic system	Support for multilateralism and non-discrimination
ASEAN Charter 2007	To promote 'the centrality of ASEAN in external political, economic, social and cultural relations while remaining actively engaged, outward-looking, inclusive and non-discriminatory' (Article 2 [m]).	'Adherence to multilateral trade rules and ASEAN's rules-based regimes to move towards elimination of all barriers to regional economic integration, in a market-driven economy' (Article 2 [2][n]).
AEC 2015	'Furthering regional and global integration through bilateral and regional comprehensive economic partnerships' (Article 2E [79]).	'Continue strongly supporting the multilateral trading system and actively participating in regional fora' (Article 2E [80][v]).
AEC 2025	'ASEAN is continuing to make steady progress towards integrating the region into the global economy through FTAs and comprehensive economic partnership agreements (CEPs) with China, Japan, Republic of Korea, India, Australia and New Zealand' (Article 79).	'Reinforce ASEAN centrality in the emerging regional economic architecture by maintaining ASEAN's role as the centre and facilitator of economic integration in the East Asian region' (Article 6[ix]).
RCEP (negotiations concluded 2020)	'The completion of the RCEP negotiations will demonstrate our collective commitment to an open trade and investment environment across the region' (Joint Leaders' Statement, November 2019).	'RCEP will significantly boost the region's future growth prospects and contribute positively to the global economy, while serving as a supporting pillar to a strong multilateral trading system and promoting development in economies across the region' (Joint Leaders' Statement, November 2019).

Sources: Drysdale (2017), ASEAN (1967, 1976, 2007), Drysdale and Vines (1998), APEC (1994), ASEAN Secretariat (2015).

Economic cooperation and the growth of economic interdependence in East Asia occurred without preferential regional agreements, unlike in Europe through the EU or in North America through the North American Free Trade Agreement (NAFTA) and its successor. Yet economic integration in East Asia by many measures is already on par with that of these other regions. The main drivers were trade liberalisation (with successful commitments by the major East Asian players to liberalisation under the General Agreement on Tariffs and Trade [GATT] and World Trade Organization [WTO]), especially after and beyond the Uruguay Round of trade negotiations and competitive liberalisation of their investment regimes. The WTO International Technology Agreement gave a huge boost to the development of regional value chain production in the electronics sector (WTO 1999)—a regionally inspired initiative that was a product of work in the lead-up to the APEC Summit of 1996.

The second element is the space that ASEAN's complementary, non-aligned tinged and inclusive political strategy gave it in leveraging its weight and influence in dealing with pressure from bigger powers as they sought influence within the region. This realpolitik dimension of ASEAN's influence is under-appreciated. It is underpinned by, and has credibility because of, the variegated though constrained engagement of its members with the big powers. This derives from the foundational principles of openness on which ASEAN institutionalisation progressed.

There have been no major initiatives in the Asian region without due deference to ASEAN interests or absent of ASEAN consent. Take, for example, the Australian and Japanese initiative that led to the formation of APEC, to which ASEAN assent to its modus operandi and structure was essential. Or consider Chinese president Xi Jinping's socialisation of his Belt and Road Initiative (BRI) in Jakarta in 2013. Or, today, consider the ASEAN response to America's Free and Open Indo-Pacific initiative.

Economic development came to dominate other political objectives in countries across the region, including China, as they committed to opening up their economies to international markets. The understanding that opening up to trade and investment and political amity were necessary for growth, development and prosperity gained momentum in East Asia in the 1970s and 1980s. The growing weight of the East Asian economies in the international economy, combined with their proximity and the complementarity of their economies, is why intra–East Asian economic relationships have grown so large.

As the East Asian economies have climbed the income ladder—Japan, South Korea, Hong Kong and Singapore are already high-income economies—their international economic policy interests have shifted from trade in goods and direct investment to trade in services, investment in production networks and financial market integration through capital account liberalisation. The economic cooperation agenda in East Asia, including in ASEAN, now encompasses all these issues—not just border trade liberalisation but the economic and institutional reform behind the border that is essential to attaining the region's future economic growth potential.

However, the diversity of the regional economies and polities, and difficulties stemming from historical and political baggage among them, profoundly shaped the nature of economic cooperation in Asia. Building a framework of shared priorities and trust through non-binding economic cooperation arrangements allowed rapid catch up through the gains from trade and commerce for growth and development.

With multilateral trade liberalisation stalled and the Doha Round going nowhere, Asia turned to imitating the negotiation of preferential bilateral agreements. Bilateral 'free trade' agreements proliferated but brought neither the large gains proponents claimed they would nor the damage critics argued they might (Armstrong 2015). Limited coverage that excluded sensitive sectors, already low barriers to trade at the border and a lack of reform behind borders meant that these bilateral preferential agreements brought little significant benefit or large costs.

It is significant that the mega-regional arrangements, the Trans-Pacific Partnership (TPP) and the Regional Comprehensive Economic Partnership (RCEP), which had the potential to exclude others, have both been purposed in East Asia and ASEAN (Drysdale and Pangestu 2019) as instruments to defend the multilateral trading system in a period in which it is under substantial threat.

ASEAN and Asian cooperation arrangements continue to be important international diplomatic assets. They contribute significantly to shared prosperity and political security in the Asia-Pacific as pillars for trade liberalisation, investment, the movement of people and, most importantly, political certainty and trust. The political foundations of cooperation arrangements in East Asia and the Pacific were based on shared ambitions for regional economic development and appreciation of its different levels of development.

Regional cooperation arrangements, such as APEC, the ASEAN Plus frameworks or the emergent RCEP, are not fully hardwired institutionally into ASEAN. But they were born of the same parentage and are genetically inseparable from the principles and practices that sustain ASEAN's success economically and politically.

The diversity in stages of development, economic endowments, institutions, culture, religion and ethnicity may be an enduring source of regional political fragility. Yet it is also a fountain of strength economically, offering opportunity for specialisation that multiplies gains from trade for growth.

Growing economic security attenuated the politics of ASEAN and Asian diversity and ensured its reach and influence—though at times it surely appeared tenuous. It will be economic security and success that underpins Asia's political sway and effectiveness in the face of the greater political uncertainties that confront the world today.

The question today is whether the regional frameworks that ideas about Asian regional cooperation inspired remain resilient enough in dealings with two big powers that have increasingly begun to cast themselves as strategic competitors.

Where ASEAN's relations with China and the US have come from

Since the establishment of the ASEAN–China Dialogue Partnership in 1991, cooperation with China has expanded rapidly across all three ASEAN Community pillars: political security, economic and sociocultural exchanges. China may have been a latecomer to ASEAN, becoming a dialogue partner in 1996, but it moved fast to build on the relationship, and was the first dialogue partner to sign a free trade agreement (FTA) with ASEAN in 2002, acceding to the Treaty of Amity and Cooperation in 2003 and signing the Southeast Asia Nuclear Weapons-Free Zone Treaty without reservations.

In October 2013, President Xi Jinping, speaking to the Indonesian parliament, presented his vision for ASEAN–China relations: an ASEAN–China community 'of common destiny'. There is no doubt that ASEAN is integral to China's vision for an integrated region and that China has worked at initiatives to further that vision. ASEAN's response, on the other hand, has been more cautious, a posture calculated to maintain ASEAN centrality and balance its engagement with all its major dialogue partners.

In 2021, ASEAN and China will commemorate 30 years of formal relations. Both sides are likely to be working to design mechanisms and initiatives to advance the relationship on various fronts, perhaps significantly in maritime cooperation and in areas that would ease tensions and build trust and confidence in the region. After a time of escalating tensions between China and the US, the opportunity of this anniversary will be crucial to ASEAN's taking hold of that narrative and showing the leadership needed to manage the thorniest issue between ASEAN members and China—the issue of resolving territorial claims and interaction in the South China Sea.

The formalisation of ASEAN relations with the US goes back more than 50 years to 1977. Framed more by US foreign policy from the Cold War period than by commercial interests, the relationship was quiescent until the Vietnamese invasion of Cambodia brought the US together with ASEAN and China to pressure Vietnam's withdrawal. After the Cold War, ASEAN lost its importance as a US geopolitical asset and the relationship was on the wane.

Nonetheless, ASEAN's accelerated growth in the 1980s saw the economic relationship flourish. Trade between the US and ASEAN more than doubled between 1980 and 1990, rising from US$22.6 million in 1980 to US$47.7 billion in 1990. US investment in the region also grew, with major US multinational corporations establishing a strong presence in the region. Only after the 11 September 2001 attack did the US come to appreciate ASEAN's strategic value in the war on terror and ASEAN did not spurn US gestures to rebuild ties.

ASEAN and the US have shaped their economic relationship through various programs such as the Enterprise for ASEAN Initiative (EAI), ASEAN Cooperation Plan (ACP), ASEAN–US Technical Assistance and Training Facility and other USAID initiatives. In 2005, these programs were consolidated into an ASEAN–US Enhanced Partnership. The 2011–15 Plan of Action (POA) and, later, the 2016–20 POA were adopted to chart the implementation of the programs and activities under the ASEAN–US Enhanced Partnership.

The Obama administration brought a sharper focus on the region, driven not only by its need to balance the growing influence of China, but also by Obama's personal affinity with it. President Obama met ASEAN leaders eight times and visited the region more than any other US president.

Under Obama, the US worked to operationalise the relationship with ASEAN through the US–ASEAN Expanded Economic Engagement (EEE), a framework for cooperative activities to facilitate US–ASEAN trade and investment. Although this was welcomed, some ASEAN member states were wary of what they perceived as US hegemonic intentions, given that the EEE encompassed rules and disciplines for services trade and investment that were seen to be not just onerous but also intruding into domestic policy space.

Alongside its heightened engagement with ASEAN, the Obama administration employed the APEC forum as an umbrella under which to push the TPP arrangement. The TPP, among 12 key APEC member economies (including four ASEAN member states), was the harbinger of deeper US political reach into the Asia-Pacific (and pivot towards Asia) that aimed to reclaim leadership in setting new trade and investment rules.

While the Obama administration saw the US–ASEAN relationship as integral to the US pivot towards Asia, the Trump administration was less interested in deep engagement with the region. Although Trump attended an APEC and ASEAN Summit and Vice-President Pence visited Jakarta, the 'America First' rhetoric, the trade tensions with China, the abandonment of the TPP and the articulation of the Free and Open Indo-Pacific (FOIP) were all read in ASEAN capitals as signalling a lack of interest in the region— except through the prism of strategic rivalry with Beijing. Under the Trump administration, Southeast Asian policymakers sharply downgraded their assessment of American reliability (Anwar 2021).

The FOIP emerged, above all, as an attempt at balancing China's long-term strategy for the region, encapsulated in its BRI, and gathering partners to that cause. The Trump administration's focus on the FOIP and increasing tensions with China inevitably led to questions about the relevance and importance of ASEAN on the global stage that ultimately need an answer.

Challenge of the rise of China and 'America First'

The relationships between ASEAN, China and the US are evolving rapidly within a world in which the global order has changed dramatically in ways that threaten the shared prosperity and security promoted by Asia's economic cooperation arrangements. The change is a product of big shifts in the structure of global power facilitated by the success of those arrangements, with the rise of China (Mahbubani 2019) now a cause of deep disquiet within the US and elsewhere. These pressures have been intensified by the COVID-19 pandemic and its impact on big power tensions and the global economy.

There are five major theatres in which these gathering economic and political forces impact upon ASEAN and its dealings with the major powers: in the South China Sea over territorial and freedom of navigation issues, over the Chinese BRI, in the escalating trade and technology war between the US and China, in the response to the US's FOIP and in relation to the COVID-19 pandemic.

Challenge of China's rise

The rise of China as a world economic power has increased its confidence and influence in the region, including vis-a-vis ASEAN and ASEAN's member states. Two areas in which China's growing power directly impacts ASEAN members are on territorial and navigation issues in the South China Sea and in responding to the large-scale financial assistance that China has offered through its BRI.

China's growing power is matched with a geopolitical ambition that now encompasses a broader conception of its maritime security interests including over large areas of the South China Sea that border ASEAN member states. President Xi Jinping's vision of a 'Chinese Dream' presented before the 13th National People's Congress in March 2018 embraced China's territorial claims in the South China Sea (*China Daily* 2018) as part of a grander effort to rebrand China's image and polish its credentials as a global actor (Casarini 2018). These developments and calls to leave Asian affairs for Asians have fuelled concerns about China's embrace of its own Monroe Doctrine in the Asian region (Acharya 2011). Meanwhile, with China's military modernisation, the gap in military power between China and ASEAN countries has widened over the past few decades, elevating the threat perception in ASEAN member states, such as Vietnam and the Philippines, in dispute with China over territorial issues (Kosandi 2014). Elevation of the perception of China as a threat has lowered its standing among Southeast Asian policymakers in recent times (Anwar 2021).

There are three related challenges in ASEAN's diplomacy on the South China issue towards China. First, all touch upon the key question of ASEAN centrality as a credible paradigm for East Asian integration and the maintenance of regional peace and stability. Second is the question of unity among ASEAN members, and how to approach China over individual member state disputes. The disputed territories and areas directly affect some member states only, namely Vietnam, the Philippines, Malaysia and Brunei Darussalam. Efforts to reach solutions by ASEAN as a whole have always been fraught, as there are significant differences in national interest among member states on what is at stake. Third, the issue affects ASEAN's posture towards economic cooperation with China more broadly, especially within agreements with China under the ASEAN leadership.

The challenge to ASEAN unity was famously exposed when Cambodia was ASEAN chair. Cambodia moved first to exclude the South China Sea issue from the agenda of the ASEAN Summit in 2012 and, although forced to reverse this tactic under pressure from other member states, especially the Philippines and Vietnam, it failed to craft a joint communique that covered the matter. ASEAN unity on the issue was also tested when ASEAN's secretary general suggested that China be engaged in negotiating a code of conduct on the South China Sea, with the Philippines arguing for prior ASEAN consensus and Indonesia favouring China's involvement.

Negotiations between ASEAN and China on a code of conduct commenced in 2013 and are due to conclude in 2022. While the drawn-out negotiation has been cast as portraying ASEAN fragility and weakness in the face of Chinese pressure (Nguyen 2019), there is no evidence that it has thus far threatened ASEAN unity (Koh 2020). A crucial test would be third-power intervention, especially from the US through its unilateral freedom of navigation operations, its established relations with member states or through the ASEAN East Asian dialogues processes.

A second major challenge for ASEAN members is over investments under China's BRI. As the 'land bridge' connecting China with the rest of Asia and Europe, the BRI envisaged ASEAN member states as frontline targets for the expansion of China's international infrastructure investment. The infrastructure gap meant that there was a large appetite for commitment to infrastructure projects across ASEAN member states. Table 9.2 sets out commitments to projects across ASEAN valued at US$55.8 billion as at August 2018.

The promise of infrastructure investment on this scale, while seen as a positive and appreciated development, was not without potential complications for both recipients of the investment and its Chinese funders. Capital flows are inevitably accompanied by the scaling up imports of goods and services from China used directly or indirectly in these projects. Growing imports heightened perceptions of dependence on China, however well the projects were managed and executed. The interplay between the recipient countries political and official players in the delivery of projects raised political sensitivities about who benefited from this dependence. The context of expanding trade deficits with China highlighted these perceptions of economic dependence and domination (Jusoh 2018) even if uncertainties about project governance were the core problem, not the trade deficits themselves.

Table 9.2: BRI projects in ASEAN member states, August 2018

No.	Project	Type	Expected commencement	Expected completion	Country	Value (USD)
1	Bangkok–Nakon Ratchasima (Phase 1)	Railway	2017	2021	Thailand	539 mn
2	Vientiane–Boten	Railway	2015	2021	Lao PDR	5.8 bn
3	Cirebon–Kroya	Railway	2017	2019	Indonesia	105 mn
4	NR 55	Road	2015	n.a.	Cambodia	133 mn
5	East Coast Rail Link	Railway	2017	2024	Malaysia	13.47 bn
6	Gemas Johor Baru Double Tracking	Railway	2016	2020	Malaysia	2.18 bn
7	Melaka Gateway	Port	2014	2019	Malaysia	1.96 bn
8	Muara Terminal	Port	2014	2019	Brunei D	3.4 bn
9	National Nighways No. 5	Road	2013	2016	Cambodia	160 mn
10	Phnom Penh–Sihanoukville Expressway	Road	2017	2020	Cambodia	1.9 bn
11	Preah Vihear–Koh Kong Railway	Railway	2013	2017	Cambodia	9.6 bn
12	KA Purukcahu–Bangkuang Railway	Railway	2018	2023	Indonesia	5.3 bn
13	National Road 214	Road		Completed	Cambodia	117 mn
14	Sumsel 5 Power Plant	Power		Completed	Indonesia	318 mn
15	Jakarta–Bandung	Railway	2016	2019	Indonesia	5.5 bn
16	Morowali Industrial Park	Industrial	n.a.	n.a.	Indonesia	1.6 bn
17	Nam Ou Hydro	Power			Lao PDR	2.8 bn
18	Phongxaly–Yunnan	Road			Lao PDR	910 mn

Source: Jusoh (2018).

Project evaluation and implementation risks caused project failures, completion delays and, especially in the case of large-scale strategic projects, compromised development plans, with political and diplomatic consequences. The Jakarta–Bandung railway project in Indonesia typifies problems of inexperience in large-scale international project delivery and management (*Jakarta Post* 2018). The Indonesian Government's vision of installing a very fast train network across Java in a relatively short time in the end required wholesale reassessment because of failures in project preparation, consultation with local government and in creating a joint-venture entity to operationalise the project. These implementation problems are common, a consequence of the scale and the speed as well as the inadequate preparation of what is being put in place, and they contrast sharply with the success of China's multilateral Asia Infrastructure Investment Bank initiative.

US challenges

ASEAN member states are not alone in Asia as they confront the problems that result from the radical changes in the foreign and international economic policies of the US under Donald Trump's presidency. President Trump's 'America First' policy and his administration's rationalisation of trade protectionism in response to American job losses associated with offshoring production facilities to other countries, notably China, undermined commitment to the open multilateral trade regime. Trump's attack on the WTO's dispute settlement mechanism, his espousal of bilateralism and renegotiation of NAFTA in North America and KORUS with Korea, his withdrawal from the TPP and his effective launching of an all-out trade and technology war with China have rocked the foundations of the international economic system on which ASEAN relies. Trump's disrespect of its alliance relationships in the region added an additional level of uncertainty in Asia about US reliability (Anwar 2021).

In unveiling his 'Indo-Pacific Dream' at the twenty-first APEC Summit in Da Nang, Vietnam in 2017, Trump set American policy on a new course in Asia and the Pacific, declaring that he would 'make bilateral trade agreements with any Indo-Pacific nation that wants to be our partner and abide by the principles of fair and reciprocal trade'.

President Trump's 'Indo-Pacific Dream' is, deep down, about US strategic rivalry with China. It was crafted in response to American fears about the rise of Chinese power, putatively directed at revision of the American-led global order (Grossman 2018). Therefore, US–China rivalry is not so much about trade and commerce as it is about Washington's concern over China's potential to challenge US global technological supremacy and security dominance (Schneider-Petsinger et al. 2019). In this American conception of things, China, due to its state-driven technological advance, is cast as an unfair competitor that will overwhelm the competitiveness of US technology in the longer term if it is not stopped short now.

Although it is not clear that Trump himself had any coherent or consistent strategy of confrontation with China (despite the rapid ramp-up of his anti-China rhetoric in his bid for re-election), the forces in the US that advocate extreme economic decoupling (such as trade adviser, Peter Navarro) and strategic rivalry or containment (such as Secretary of State Mike Pompeo) coalesced within, and captured, the policy space surrounding him to forge a new direction in US foreign and security policy. These developments, whatever their ultimate consequences for the US itself or for China, leave ASEAN and most states in Asia, deeply enmeshed as they are in China–US interdependence, struggling to find a way through. Even now, with the new Biden presidency, Washington cannot soon or easily reverse course on the retreat from globalisation or China decoupling strategies, especially in the aftermath of the COVID-19 pandemic crisis, despite its return to multilateralism on climate change and health.

These developments present ASEAN and the heavily economically integrated states of East Asia, which have long relied on rules-based, step-by-step diplomacy and multilateralism, with stark choices. They are choices that will put heavy internal pressure on ASEAN with its members' variegated structure of political and security ties with the US. They are pressures that have the potential to drive big wedges among ASEAN members but also between ASEAN and its dialogue partners, in the ASEAN+6 group and the ASEAN+8 (East Asian Summit) processes and inflict irreparable damage on the ASEAN-led East Asia integration enterprise. The cement of Asia's intense economic ties with China is susceptible to corrosion by the conflicted political relations of some regional states with China and, more importantly, by being jack-hammered asunder by the US through bilateral heavying on forcing choices between the two big powers. Unless it is resisted and an alternative strategy is articulated, a US strategy that unravels economic interdependence with China could well take East Asian interdependence in its path.

ASEAN response to early play among the big powers

The Free and Open Indo-Pacific idea is the first essay by the US in pressuring ASEAN to choose sides and sign on to 'the new Cold War' in the gathering geopolitical tussle with China. Acceding to this framing of its diplomacy would present the prospect of an ASEAN divided and institutionally weakened, its centrality to regional diplomacy in tatters. ASEAN's response has been to take ownership of the idea and develop its own Outlook on the Indo-Pacific (AOIP). A stepchild of the Cold War itself, ASEAN had, in its over half century of existence, successfully straddled that ideological divide without so far being overwhelmed by it. ASEAN, and even those of its members who confront Chinese maritime power directly, have no inclination for the region to become the theatre of a 'new Cold War' great power conflict.

At its 34th Summit in Bangkok in 2019, ASEAN settled on a course for dealing with the possibility of being dragged into a period of prolonged US–China tensions. ASEAN's response was 18 months in the making, reflecting not a lack of will to tackle the issue but the intense backroom exchanges typical of ASEAN diplomacy in formulating it: that is, without openly acrimonious negotiations and with an outcome driven by the spirit of ASEAN consensus. The Outlook 'was cautious, muted and underwhelming … [but] displayed ASEAN's ability to come together to set the direction for a sub-regional institution in light of the rising uncertainty in the strategic environment' (Singh and Tsjeng 2020). Indonesia was very much back in the driver's seat in shaping this response.

ASEAN's Outlook on the Indo-Pacific ensured, above all, that the conversation about the Indo-Pacific idea was firmly embedded in the structure of ASEAN arrangements, specifically the East Asia Summit. Locating the AOIP in the East Asia Summit agenda cleverly obviated the need to create any other platform to prosecute these issues and captured ASEAN's veto power over its progression in the region. At the same time, it demonstrated ASEAN centrality in a matter of strategic importance to the region, served to dismiss perceptions that ASEAN was divided in the face of the rivalry between the US and China, effectively upgraded the ASEAN Regional Forum and reflected ASEAN's determination to shape the future narrative around Indo-Pacific diplomacy.

ASEAN's Outlook is built on ASEAN principles. Importantly, it is inclusive and adds economic and development dimensions—two key aspects that demonstrate a clear departure from the maritime security conception that looked to China like a containment strategy. For ASEAN, RCEP is an instrument that helps to institutionalise that strategy.

ASEAN needed such a strategy in the face of the competing US FOIP and Chinese BRI initiatives. It was a strategy not unlike the genesis of ASEAN's collective response to the then TPP that set in train the negotiation of RCEP. Indonesia, as the ASEAN coordinating country for RCEP, played a key role in ensuring that ASEAN became the driver of that process of regional economic integration embracing China.

The rhetoric is that RCEP is a forward-looking, inclusive agreement that can be a twenty-first-century model for integration among countries with different levels of economic development, political systems, ethnicity and cultural backgrounds. The reality, as with any free trade agreement, is that there are challenges, as evidenced in the missed deadlines that began in 2015 and the withdrawal of India from the final agreement. Despite this, what is important is that around the conception of RCEP there developed the political will to see it through.

ASEAN's success in the 16-party negotiations (and 15-party agreement) has been its ability to bring to the table China, Japan and Korea, countries that have not been able to find common ground for an FTA among themselves. Likewise, the engagement of India and China was crucial. While 15 of the parties agreed to sign the agreement in late 2020, India has not been able to make this commitment. The challenge for ASEAN, and Indonesia in particular, is to ensure that the agreement, which was eight years in the making, remains open to India to come on board at an appropriate time, and allows India to engage in its regional cooperation agenda. It is hoped, for example, that RCEP 'will provide a more stable and predictable economic environment to support the much-needed recovery of trade and investment in the region, which has been adversely affected by the COVID-19 pandemic' (ASEAN 2020).

Unlike the TPP (now the CPTPP), RCEP was envisaged as a trade and investment agreement that had a strong economic cooperation element. RCEP's economic cooperation agenda positions it as a valuable vehicle for building economic and political confidence in effecting the next big structural transformation in Asia, right across the region between East Asia and South Asia, with China and India drafted to play leading roles, and ASEAN central to that endeavour.

Unfinished contest

A peaceful balancing of power between Washington and Beijing suits ASEAN best, allowing it to retain its own space to serve the interests of its member states rather than those of any hegemonic power. Power politics in Asia no longer need to hang on hegemonic power (Acharya 2015). The focus in East Asia is on interdependence stemming from economic ties, regionalism and the equal role of smaller, weaker states. It is in this context that the centrality of ASEAN has been so important to regional cooperation more broadly in Asia. This thinking also underlines the importance of the RCEP as a process for furthering and broadening regional and global economic integration and the position of ASEAN in the global system.

The ASEAN story is one of success in openness to the global economy. This is partly because that is where the economic opportunities and benefits are largest and partly because open dealings with other major economic powers have built ASEAN its own quotient of political security. Open regionalism, it turns out, has been both a good economic and political strategy. There have been bumps along the way—in liberalising trade, dismantling protection, and maintaining an open and inclusive system that is able to cope with diversity—but the overarching ASEAN strategy has got it right and is key to continuing to secure the prosperity and security of Southeast Asia in the region and in the world.

The next several decades, especially the decade through to 2030, however, will see momentous change and challenges for ASEAN with the countries of East Asia caught in the middle of the looming contest between the US and China (Soeya 2020). The story of ASEAN's success over the past five decades offers guidance to managing the challenges ahead but, in a global economic policy environment that has changed profoundly, past appeal to the global framework in which its multilateral interests were secured will no longer be sufficient.

ASEAN brings to the task, as its legacy, a policy philosophy and an experiment that has succeeded. Shaped by its underlying commitment to open regionalism and to an outward-looking and inclusive economic strategy, ASEAN has delivered economic improvement and cooperation that has underpinned political security. Despite variegation in its memberships' diplomatic posture, inclusiveness and multilateralism are also reflected in its overall non-alignment politically. The big difference for ASEAN and for its partners in Asia in the decades ahead is that they can no longer simply be support players with the established industrial powers writing the script, as has largely been the case in decades past.

Success in achieving their economic potential and political security will now depend on their assuming a role that is much more centre-stage in the theatre of international economic diplomacy. The weight and importance that Asia now has in the global system suggests that leadership must come from the region to preserve and to strengthen the multilateral regime that has been at its core. This call for leadership is all the more needed as the region focuses on collective COVID-19 recovery measures, with the added challenge for ASEAN of managing political crisis and violence in Myanmar. On Myanmar, ASEAN must ensure that it will not be used in a power-play between Beijing and Washington.[2] 'Instead of scoring points on Myanmar, both countries should work quietly with ASEAN to slowly and steadily persuade the Myanmar generals to reverse course and go back to status quo ante' (Mahbubani 2021).

No one country can lead in Asia, which has several large powers and divergent interests. Asian collective leadership is now critical to global economic and political outcomes that are at the centre of the interests of ASEAN and the arrangements that surround it (ABER 2020).

---

2   In the face of the violence and fatalities, there are calls for ASEAN to take firm action against Myanmar. But Myanmar's membership of ASEAN needs to be kept in perspective. When Malaysian prime minister Mahathir Mohamad succeeded in getting ASEAN approval for Myanmar's admission into ASEAN in 1997, it was believed that its economic and political transformation would come from its economic integration in the region and the benefits it would accrue from outward-looking policies, increased foreign investment, and expanded trade and tourism. Indeed, ASEAN faced a similar crisis point on Myanmar in 2007, when there was a violent coup just as the ASEAN Charter was on the launching pad. ASEAN's way of dealing with that crisis then, as now, was to avoid public moralising while delivering strong messages in private. Significantly, in 2021, ASEAN foreign ministers have publicly urged the Myanmar military to desist from violence and respect the will of the people.

References

ABER (Asian Bureau of Economic Research). 2020. *An Asian Strategy for Recovery and Reconstruction after COVID-19*. Canberra: ABER.

Acharya, A. 2011. 'Beyond the Chinese Monroe Doctrine'. *East Asia Forum*, 11 July 2011. www.eastasiaforum.org/2011/07/11/beyond-the-chinese-monroe-doctrine/.

Acharya, A. 2015. 'ASEAN Can Survive Great-Power Rivalry in Asia'. *East Asia Forum*, 4 October 2015. www.eastasiaforum.org/2015/10/04/asean-can-survive-great-power-rivalry-in-asia/.

Anwar, D. F. 2021. 'What Southeast Asia Wants from the Biden Presidency'. *East Asia Forum Quarterly*, 13 (1): 36–37. press-files.anu.edu.au/downloads/press/n8204/pdf/book.pdf.

APEC (Asia-Pacific Economic Cooperation). 1994. 'Leaders' Declaration—Bogor'. 15 November 1994. www.apec.org/-/media/Files/LeadersDeclarations/1994/1994_LeadersDeclaration.pdf.

Armstrong, S. P. 2015. 'The Economic Impact of the Australia—United States Free Trade Agreement'. *Australian Journal of International Affairs*, 69 (5): 513–37. doi.org/10.1080/10357718.2015.1048777.

ASEAN (Association of Southeast Asian Nations). 1967. 'The ASEAN Declaration (Bangkok Declaration)'. 8 August 1967. agreement.asean.org/media/download/20140117154159.pdf.

ASEAN (Association of Southeast Asian Nations). 1976. 'Treaty of Amity and Cooperation in Southeast Asia'. 24 February 1976. asean-aipr.org/wp-content/uploads/2018/07/Treaty-of-Amity-and-Cooperation-in-Southeast-Asia-1976-TAC.pdf.

ASEAN (Association of Southeast Asian Nations). 2007. *The ASEAN Charter*. asean.org/wp-content/uploads/images/archive/publications/ASEAN-Charter.pdf.

ASEAN (Association of Southeast Asian Nations). 2020. *Joint Statement of the 29th Regional Comprehensive Economic Partnership Trade Negotiating Committee (RCEP TNC) Meeting*, ASEAN. Accessed 23 August 2021. asean.org/speechandstatement/joint-statement-of-the-29th-regional-comprehensive-economic-partnership-trade-negotiating-committee-rcep-tnc-meeting/.

ASEAN (Association of Southeast Asian Nations) Secretariat. 2015. *ASEAN Economic Community Blueprint 2025*. 31 December. asean.org/asean-economic-community-blueprint-2025/.

Capannelli, G. 2009. 'Asian Regionalism: How Does It Compare to Europe's?', *East Asia Forum*, 21 April 2009. www.eastasiaforum.org/2009/04/21/asian-regionalism-how-does-it-compare-to-europes/.

Casarini, N. 2018. 'Southeast Asia's Security Dilemma—How the West is Responding'. In *China's Belt and Road Initiative and Southeast Asia*, 26–30. Kuala Lumpur: CARI.

China Daily. 2018. 'Speech Delivered by President Xi at the NPC Closing Meeting'. 22 March 2018. www.chinadaily.com.cn/hkedition/2018-03/22/content_3589 4512.htm.

Drysdale, P. 1988. *International Economic Pluralism: Economic Policy in East Asia and the Pacific*. Sydney: Allen & Unwin.

Drysdale, P. 2017. 'The Experiment in Open Regionalism that Succeeded'. In *The ASEAN Economic Community Into 2025 and beyond*, edited by Rebecca Sta Maria, Shujiro Urata and Ponciano S. Intal, 64–86. Jakarta: ERIA.

Drysdale, P. and M. Pangestu. 2019 'Getting Asia's Act Together on Trade'. *East Asia Forum*, 5 August 2019. www.eastasiaforum.org/2019/08/05/getting-asias-act-together-on-trade/.

Drysdale, P. and T. Terada, eds. 2007. *Asia Pacific Cooperation*. Vol. I–V. London: Routledge.

Drysdale, P. and D. Vines, eds. 1998. *Europe, East Asia and APEC: A Shared Global Agenda?* Cambridge: Cambridge University Press.

Elek, A. 1991. 'Asia Pacific Economic Cooperation (APEC)'. In *Southeast Asian Affairs*, edited by Sharon Siddique and Chee Yuen Ng, 33–48. Singapore: ISEAS Publishing. doi.org/10.1355/9789812306814-005.

Grossman, M. 2018. 'Energizing Strategies for the Indo-Pacific'. YaleGlobal Online, 3 April 2018. yaleglobal.yale.edu/content/energizing-strategies-indo-pacific (site discontinued).

Hill, H. and J. Menon. 2014. 'ASEAN Commercial Policy: A Rare Case of Outward-Looking Regional Integration' ADB Working Paper Series on Regional Economic Integration, no. 144, November.

Jakarta Post. 2018. 'Jakarta–Bandung Railway Project Won't Meet Target: Minister'. 18 June 2018. www.thejakartapost.com/news/2018/02/19/jakarta-bandung-railway-project-wont-meet-target-minister.html.

Jusoh, S. 2018. 'The Impact of the BRI on Trade and Investment in ASEAN'. In *China's Belt and Road Initiative and Southeast Asia*, 10–18. Kuala Lumpur: CARI.

Koh, C. 2020. 'Standing Up for ASEAN in the South China Sea'. *East Asia Forum*, 23 July 2020. www.eastasiaforum.org/2020/07/23/standing-up-for-asean-in-the-south-china-sea/.

Kosandi, M. 2014. 'Conflicts in the South China Sea and China–ASEAN Economic Interdependence: A Challenge to Cooperation'. *ASEAN-Canada Research Partnership Working Paper Series*, no. 7. Singapore: ASEAN-Canada Research Partnership.

Mahbubani, K. 1995. 'The Pacific Impulse'. *Survival* 37 (1): 105–20. doi.org/10.1080/00396339508442779.

Mahbubani, K. 2019. 'What China Threat? How the United States and China Can Avoid War'. *Harpers Magazine* 338 (February): 38.

Mahbubani, K. 2021. 'The Oxygen of ASEAN Is Critical to Singapore's Existence'. *The Straits Times*, 6 March 2021. www.straitstimes.com/opinion/the-oxygen-of-asean-0.

Murray, P. 2010. 'East Asian Regionalism and EU Studies'. *Journal of European Integration* 32 (6): 597–616. doi.org/10.1080/07036337.2010.518718.

Nguyen, M. Quang. 2019. 'Negotiating an Effective China–ASEAN South China Sea Code of Conduct'. *East Asia Forum*, 31 July 2019. www.eastasiaforum.org/2019/07/31/negotiating-an-effective-china-asean-south-china-sea-code-of-conduct/.

Schneider-Petsinger, M., J. Wang, Y. Jie and J. Crabtree. 2019. 'US–China Strategic Competition: The Quest for Global Technological Leadership'. *Chatham House Research Paper*, 7 November.

Singh, B. and H. Z. Tsjeng. 2020. 'ASEAN Outlook on Indo-Pacific: Seizing the Narrative?'. *RSIS Commentaries*, no. 016–20, Singapore: Nanyang Technological University. hdl.handle.net/10356/136822.

Soeya, Y. 2020. 'Middle Powers Can Shape a New Security Framework'. *East Asia Forum*, 23 September 2020. www.eastasiaforum.org/2020/09/23/middle-powers-can-shape-a-new-security-framework/.

WTO (World Trade Organization). 1999. 'Trade in Information Technology Products and the WTO Agreements: Current Situation and Views of Exporters in Developing Countries'. Geneva: World Trade Organization. www.wto.org/english/tratop_e/inftec_e/infotech.pdf.

10

Asia's economic and political security in a shifting global order

Peter Drysdale, Amy King and Adam Triggs

The global order that has thus far shaped relationships between the United States and Asia, and underpinned Asia's prosperity and security, is under pressure in a world in which the structure of global power has changed dramatically. Significantly, the change has been driven by the success of that order, with the recovery of Europe after World War II and the economic transformation of Asia and China as major centres of global economic power. The rise of China, with its now considerable economic and political heft, is no longer seen within the US as a cause for celebration but of deepening disquiet. These pressures have been intensified sharply by the COVID-19 pandemic and its impact on great power tensions and the global economy.

This chapter traces the genesis and evolution of the present global order, how it managed the interplay between economics and security, and the importance of that order to the rise of Asia. It goes on to identify the weaknesses and fractures in the global order that undermine both economic prosperity and national security, highlighting the areas crying out for reform to deal with the claims of both the emerging and established powers. It shows how economic and security considerations, which were tightly enmeshed in the creation of the global order after WWII, are being recklessly traded off in a global order that has failed to keep pace with the global reality.

Asia is at the centre of these problems but no single Asian nation, not even one of China's size and geopolitical weight, is capable of unilaterally spearheading reform of the global order. The post-WWII global order was the product of *collective* ideas and effort, and a new collective authority is now needed to correct the current drift towards fragmentation of the multilateral global order. With the US stepping back, and actively undermining multilateralism while President Trump was in office, we ask how multilateral cooperation between Asian nations might be a starting point for achieving this collective authority. Because of the weight and potential they have in the world economy, Asian countries are now central both to the recovery from the COVID-19 crisis and the key to renovation of the global order that has so far served them well. We also ask how a new US administration under President Joe Biden might shape the outcome of any regional attempts at global order reform.

Understanding the origins of the present global order reveals how order has been constructed at past moments of crisis, helps to pinpoint fragilities in the present global order and allows us to identify what the priorities might be in trying to address them.

Genesis of the postwar global order

The origins of the contemporary global economic order lie in WWII, when the Allied powers came together in 1944 at the Mount Washington Hotel, Bretton Woods, New Hampshire. At Bretton Woods, their goal was to put in place a new system of internationally shared ideas, norms and practices—that is, an order—that could stem the trade protectionism, currency wars and economic deprivation that had characterised the world economy throughout the 1920s and 1930s. In practical terms, this meant the introduction of a new system of fixed exchange rates, tariff reductions, short-term financial assistance and aid to developing countries; the creation of two new multilateral institutions—the International Monetary Fund (IMF) and the International Bank for Reconstruction and Development (IBRD, later renamed the World Bank); and steps put in place for the development in 1947 of the General Agreement on Tariffs and Trade (out of which the World Trade Organization [WTO] was later formed).

It is no coincidence that this new global economic order was established in the middle of a global war. Indeed, economic and security challenges were tightly enmeshed in the creation of the order at Bretton Woods.

The Great Depression and unchecked economic competition of the 1920s and 1930s had helped to fuel national rivalries that propelled states into military conflict in WWII. Against this backdrop, economists and officials across the world laboured to first understand, and then develop ways to manage, the economic crises of the interwar period.[1] Central to this process was the emergence of three new ideas that would underpin the order established at Bretton Woods. The first was the idea of 'managed multilateralism'—or the notion that a liberal, open world economy would not simply emerge out of the laissez-faire behaviour of markets, but instead had to be managed through multilateral coordination of global monetary and trading arrangements (Ikenberry 1992, 292; Clavin 2013, 300). The second idea, often called 'embedded liberalism', was the notion that the state should play a more intrusive role in the domestic economy to protect domestic populations from the ravages of an open, but often unstable and unpredictable, international economic order (Ruggie 1982, 393; Gardiner 1969, 4). The third was the idea of development, which broadly encompassed new understandings of global wealth and income inequality, the need for international reconstruction aid to war-torn and poverty-stricken countries, and the ways in which the global trading system was structured so as to benefit industrialised rather than agrarian countries (Clavin 2013; Helleiner 2014).

While these ideas had evolved over the course of the 1920s and 1930s, it was the unprecedented military crisis of WWII that provided impetus for global cooperation to institutionalise them. In the US and Britain, in particular, leading officials and economists articulated clearly the relationship between the economic drivers of interstate conflict and their views that a liberal international economic system would provide the best foundations for a lasting postwar peace. Indeed, the roles of the US and Britain were crucial in catalysing the creation of this new global order: a combination of US material power and the ideas and wartime economic plans of US and British economists and officials provided the necessary convening power around which the Allied nations deliberated over the course of 1943–44.[2]

---

1   Much of this work took place via the auspices of the League of Nations and its Economic and Finance Organisation (Clavin 2013).
2   For leading accounts of the US and British role, see Ikenberry (1992, 289–321), Van Dormael (1978) and Gardiner (1969).

Yet this traditional view of the creation of the Bretton Woods order must be modified in two ways, both of which offer important lessons for our thinking about the creation, evolution and rebuilding of orders. First, creating the postwar global economic order was a highly contested process, exposing the conflicting ideas, interests and values of states who were traditionally allies and who shared similar political systems. The US and Britain, for example, clashed frequently over issues such as the desirability of a non-discriminatory trade system, the removal of protectionist measures such as tariffs and quotas, the degree of intrusiveness allowed by newly created multilateral institutions over a state's domestic economic affairs and the relative power of a hegemonic US within the newly created order. The order ultimately agreed upon at Bretton Woods represented a combination of compromise and, on certain key issues—such as the intrusiveness of new multilateral institutions—a failure to reach true consensus at all (Gardiner 1969; Van Dormael 1978). Second, creation of the Bretton Woods order involved not just ideas and contributions of powerful states such as the US and Great Britain, but also the ideas of other countries, including Australia and key developing countries in Latin America and East Asia. Australia tried to influence the outcomes on commodity trade and the issues affecting a small open economy. Developing countries helped to enhance the 'development mandate' of the IBRD by ensuring that it would provide long-term international finance for non-industrialised countries and succeeded in obtaining a resolution for the creation of a future international agreement on commodity prices (Helleiner 2014). The contested nature of global order creation and change, and the role of smaller and weaker states in shaping orders, remain crucial in understanding the unravelling, preservation and rebuilding of the contemporary global order.[3]

Evolution of the global order

The order established at Bretton Woods was intended to be a genuinely global order, led by the four leading Allied powers—the United States, the Soviet Union, Great Britain and the Republic of China—whom US president Franklin D. Roosevelt had described as the 'four policemen' that would govern the postwar world. The role of the 'four policemen' was embedded into the architecture of the emergent United Nations framework and its Security Council.

---

3   For similar arguments in relation to contemporary East Asian order, see Goh (2013).

However, growing tensions between the US and the Soviet Union in the late stages of WWII and the onset of the Cold War, first in Europe and then in East Asia, fundamentally disrupted the global character of the Bretton Woods economic order. With the onset of the Cold War, security tensions and the bipolar alliance framework that grew out of it skewed the practice of international economic relations well into the 1970s and 1980s.

Through much of the Cold War, the international economy was artificially divided into two separate orders: a US-led capitalist order centred around both the Bretton Woods institutions and the Coordinating Committee for Multilateral Export Controls in Western Europe, and a Soviet-led communist order organised around the Council for Mutual Economic Assistance in Eastern Europe and the wider Soviet bloc (see Zhang 2001). Parallel security orders were also established alongside these economic blocs, with the Soviet Union and US forging alliance relationships and military pacts with subordinate states in their respective orders. In the Asia-Pacific region, the US rehabilitated its wartime aggressor, Japan, as a Cold War ally and, in 1951–52, created security treaties with Japan, the Philippines, Australia and New Zealand—known colloquially as the 'San Francisco alliance system'. At the same time, the Soviet Union established alliances with, and provided extensive diplomatic and military support to, newly independent or divided states across Asia, including the People's Republic of China, the Democratic People's Republic of Korea, the Democratic Republic of Vietnam and Indonesia.

These Cold War economic and security orders worked in tandem, with trade, foreign aid and dual-use technology typically conceived as key elements in the superpowers' wider Cold War containment strategies. The US and the Soviet Union used the rival economic blocs to coordinate their trade, foreign aid and loans with member states and, particularly in the case of the US, required that allies maintain strict economic sanctions and controls over the export of technology and other 'war-producing materials' to China and the Soviet bloc. Thus, the Cold War economic blocs simultaneously preserved the 'special privileges' of each superpower, while providing economic and security benefits to bloc members (Mastanduno 2009, 122).

Of course, the Cold War order's bifurcated character was not absolute. In Asia, for example, trade, people and economic ideas eventually began to flow across Cold War lines and helped to create a distinct sphere of *regional* economic activity that burgeoned despite the divided global order. These economic flows often stemmed from older trade and investment links developed between an imperial Japan and its colonial Asian subjects, and laid the foundations for supply chains that would later underpin the emergence of an East Asian economic order following the dissolution of Cold War tensions (see e.g. King 2016). Significantly, with their more 'comprehensive' notions of security, East Asian states did not always adhere to the same economic security logic that was articulated by the superpowers leading their respective blocs. Japan was deeply frustrated by US-led controls on trade with China, seeing the loss of access to Chinese raw materials and export markets as a key source of insecurity for Japan. Similarly, China viewed trade with Japan as a way to strengthen its industrial and technological capacity, and, therefore, as critical to its overall national security, despite Japan's role as a wartime aggressor and Cold War opponent (King 2016). Outside East Asia, such trade with China only accelerated following the Sino-Soviet split of the 1960s; Australia and other US allies began trading with China despite the ongoing US embargo.

Moreover, the bifurcated Cold War economic orders were not static, but instead evolved over time as a result of the changing behaviour and ideas of the states participating in and shaping them. It was the Western bloc, with its economic foundations based on Bretton Woods multilateralism, that sped economic recovery in Europe and opened opportunity for the transformation of the East Asian economy. The Bretton Woods order then underwent significant change in the 1970s, as the US unilaterally floated its currency in response to the drain on US gold reserves stemming from the postwar growth of Germany and Japan, rising domestic inflation and a spike in public spending associated with the costly military campaign in Vietnam (Mastanduno 2009). Similarly, Japan's rapid postwar economic rise, and the perceived threat Japan posed to the US economy and the US's place atop the liberal international economic order, catalysed a series of partial adjustments to that order. These included the creation of a new multilateral lending institution, the Asian Development Bank, in 1966, in response to Japan's dissatisfaction with its lack of power within the IMF and IBRD; periodic renegotiations over the terms of US–Japan trade and monetary relations in the 1970s and 1980s; and a major redefinition of the US–Japan security treaty in the 1990s as a way to prevent the economic tensions in the US–Japan relationship from damaging the wider alliance relationship (Mastanduno 2009; Foot 2017).

This brief sketch of the creation of the Bretton Woods order and its Cold War evolution highlights three key lessons of importance for thinking about the contemporary global order and its preservation, evolution and transformation. First, the creation of a global order is naturally contested, and the shared ideas that underpin it are arrived at through contestation, negotiation and consensus building. Second, powerful and weaker states alike are involved in the shaping of a global order and have an effect on an order's evolution and endurance. Third, economic and security logics have long intersected in different ways to shape the patterns of the global economic order, coalescing to produce the Bretton Woods order during WWII, driving the bifurcation of rival economic blocs during the Cold War and catalysing a nascent regional economic order in East Asia that helped to undermine the earlier bifurcated global Cold War order.

Stresses in the contemporary global order

With the end of the Cold War and the collapse of the Soviet-led order, the Bretton Woods system saw the gradual incorporation of major powers that had previously sat outside the Western order, including China, India and Russia. In turn, and despite having failed to keep up with a changing world, the institutions within the Bretton Woods system were gradually reformed over time. The growing gap between the global system and the global reality of changing economic power and issue areas has been a key source of stress and tension. An early manifestation of stress in the system was the patchwork of bilateral, regional and global arrangements that substituted for comprehensive multilateral reform, undermining its efficiency and effectiveness.

In global finance, the rise of China and other emerging economies has not been reflected in the governance of the IMF. China represents 16 per cent of global GDP at market exchange rates but only 6 per cent of the IMF's voting power. Europe, on the other hand, represents 8 per cent of global GDP but more than 13 per cent of the IMF's voting power. IMF quota reforms, most recently in 2015, have helped reduce these gaps but progress has been slow and piecemeal (Goodman et al. 2019).

This slow and piecemeal process, combined with inadequate IMF resourcing and a perceived mishandling of financial crises by the IMF, has led to the creation of competing institutions and mechanisms. At the regional level, these include the Chiang Mai Initiative Multilateralization in Asia, the European Stability Mechanism in the European Union, and similar initiatives in Latin America and Africa. At the bilateral level, these inadequacies have seen the creation of a plethora of bilateral currency swap lines, increasing from around just a handful in 1980 to more than 70 today. This fragmentation has seen the share of the Bretton Woods institutions in the global financial safety net fall dramatically, from 80 per cent in 1980 to less than 35 per cent in 2020 (Triggs 2018).

The same thing has happened in trade. The global trading system's failure to keep up with a changing world has seen increased tensions and led to a more fragmented order. In the previous few decades, the digital economy has grown rapidly. But the WTO's rules are largely silent on the digital economy and data flows that are important to the efficiencies captured in the digital economy. In addition, state-owned enterprises, subsidies, technology transfer and a host of other issues have ignited tensions in recent years. These inadequacies, on top of the stalemate of the Doha Round of trade negotiations, have led to a plethora of regional and plurilateral trade agreements, including the Comprehensive and Progressive Agreement for Trans-Pacific Partnership and Regional Comprehensive Partnership (RCEP); a range of thematic initiatives around the WTO, including on digital trade and services; and hundreds of bilateral trade agreements seeking to fill the gap.

These regional, plurilateral and bilateral trade agreements are not substitutes for a global, WTO-led agreement. They are premised on the WTO at their core. The benefits from trade liberalisation are greatest when it happens globally and smallest (and more temporary) when it happens bilaterally. While some trade liberalisation is usually better than none, the worry is that a patchwork of inconsistent trade agreements is raising the cost of doing business across borders and may form a roadblock more than a stepping stone to a potential global agreement.

This pattern, in which an out-of-date global order produces a patchwork of regional, bilateral or unilateral alternatives, is not limited to finance and trade. We see the same thing in global investment flows (in which there are a myriad of different national foreign investment regulatory frameworks) and in international economic development (with the World Bank at the global level and a host of regional development bodies and bilateral arrangements). The consequence can be increased inefficiencies and a higher cost of doing businesses resulting in a higher cost of capital, lower growth and fewer jobs being created. More significant has been the corrosion of commitment to global goals and the global order.

President Trump, COVID-19 and global fragmentation

In the context of an already weak and fragmented global system, 2016 saw the election of Donald Trump and 2020 saw the spread of COVID-19, leading to the biggest global economic contraction since the Great Depression. The election of Donald Trump in the US meant that one of President Franklin D. Roosevelt's 'four policemen' of the global system was now actively undermining that system.

Under President Trump, the US withdrew from the Paris Climate Accord and the World Health Organization (WHO). It refused to reappoint judges to the WTO's dispute settlement body, causing the body to collapse and resulting in the creation of an interim substitute mechanism without US participation, and it threatened to withdraw from the WTO entirely. The US refused to sign multilateral communiques in the G7 and Asia-Pacific Economic Cooperation, walked out of multilateral meetings and turned on traditional US allies and alliances. President Trump launched a global trade war, imposing tariffs on China, Europe and others. These developments quickly spread beyond trade and into other areas of international engagement: the blocking of international investment; restrictions on technology firms and technology trade; the arrest of, and placing of restrictions on, corporate officials; travel bans; threats of currency wars; and threats to deny entry to international students, tourists and businesspeople. President Trump withdrew US leadership and support for the global order, substantially undermining that order in the process.

Then, in 2020, COVID-19 spread around the world, bringing with it the worst economic outlook since the Great Depression. In its February 2021 World Economic Outlook update, the IMF predicted a baseline fall of 3.5 per cent in global incomes in 2020. Growth, it said, could rebound to 5.5 per cent in 2021 but it also warned of more dire outcomes. China's GDP dropped 6.8 per cent in the first quarter of 2020 on the previous year, Japan's dropped 3.4 per cent and the US's fell 4.8 per cent. Europe's GDP is forecast to fall 7.8 per cent this year (IMF 2020). China was the only major economy to achieve positive growth through 2020.

The pandemic has seen countries become much more closed to the world. Some of this is unavoidable. Restrictions on the cross-border flows of businesspeople, tourists, students, diplomats and immigrants are necessary to contain the spread of the virus. These restrictions will have significant economic costs, but these costs can be managed by governments through fiscal and monetary policies, provided they are temporary. The virus and the closure of borders has had a similar impact on international trade and finance. Businesses have been unable to access their international supply chains, resulting in reduced production, higher prices and shortages of some goods and services, while an inability to access migrant workers has impeded production in some industries. The financial impacts of COVID-19 have seen restrictions imposed by some economies on foreign investment, capital flows and exchange rate movements in an attempt to manage financial volatility and address concerns that undervalued assets may be purchased on the cheap.

Seeing relatively closed economies in the face of a pandemic is not surprising, nor is it necessarily bad policy. But a major risk to the global system is that COVID-19, combined with US–China geopolitical and economic tensions, sees the implementation of policy changes that favour more closed economies on a permanent, long-term basis. As discussed elsewhere in this book (see Chapter 5 by Armstrong and Urata), there is a growing push in many countries to on shore supply chains and reduce dependency on international markets. In some instances, this is limited to products like medical equipment; however, in other instances, it has a much broader focus on manufacturing capability more generally. Countries have increased the stringency of their foreign investment rules while the closure of national and subnational borders have grown in popularity in some countries.

These developments will have two major impacts on the global order. First, they mean that countries will be less engaged in the order that remains vital for long-run prosperity and, as discussed below, national security. Second, they mean that countries will be less willing to undertake the necessary reforms to the global order to address the structural problems fuelling tensions and undermining the efficiency and effectiveness of the global system. Thus far, and compared to the cooperation displayed in the aftermath of the 2007–09 global financial crisis, cooperation between the world's major countries has been absent. Whether this will change under President Biden remains to be seen.

Implications for Asia

A weakening global economic order has implications for national security, particularly in Asia. Economic and security logics coalesced to produce the Bretton Woods order during WWII, when it was recognised that global economic integration and national security were intimately linked. The prosperity that comes from international trade, investment and commerce not only provides governments with the funding for social and military spending that bolsters national security, but also provides a peace dividend by making conflict more expensive and diplomacy more effective. The economic ties between businesses and households across countries forced governments to expand their cooperation with one another while these economic links increased people-to-people connections, improving understanding and awareness of different cultures and societies. But it took a global vision and global leadership to produce the economic order that enabled this prosperity and security after WWII. A weakening of the global system undermines each of these elements and the increased security they provide. The question now is where that vision and leadership will come from to reverse these trends.

Traditionally, the world has looked to the US to lead global governance reform and global economic recovery on account of the size of its economy, its freedom of policy action (given the international role of the US dollar) and its long-established tradition of leadership in global economic diplomacy. Despite the outcome of the 2020 presidential election, it will be difficult for the US's approach to foreign policy to change quickly. The new US president, Joe Biden, has committed to reinstating a more multilateral approach that includes re-entering the Paris Accord, re-joining the WHO and reform of the WTO. But Biden will struggle to deal with the deep, structural challenges that have fuelled the strong domestic constituency within the US that opposes its contributions to global order building and, in some cases, opposes globalisation itself. President Trump's 2016 political success was the product of growing inequality and fast-moving economic and social changes, including automation and rapid technological change. Trump blamed immigration and trade for America's woes. In reality, these problems are principally a consequence of flawed domestic policies. Future US presidents will struggle to fix these domestic problems quickly. For now, there is a deepening bipartisan consensus in the US on toughness towards China and growing suspicion of trade.

Leadership on global governance reform will benefit from President Biden's election and his commitment to US leadership; however, it will need support from elsewhere to succeed, and Asia has the greatest incentive to reverse the accelerating momentum to protectionism and the breakdown of global cooperation by rebuilding trust, strengthening governance and updating global rules. Because of their dense populations and limited resource endowments, the economies of East Asia are more dependent on the international economy and global supply chains than economies elsewhere in the world. The World Bank estimated that the average trade to GDP ratio for all East Asia and the Pacific was 57 per cent in 2017, double that of the US. East Asia's economic and political security crucially depends on open trade and commerce. Closed economies will face slower recoveries and stagnation of income growth in the longer term. International economic cooperation will be vital to managing the crisis and to supporting the recovery through trade, a faster reopening of business supply chains and lower investment costs. Economic integration is central to Asia's economic prosperity and national security—concepts that have always been tightly linked in the various Asian conceptions of 'comprehensive security'. Therefore, a shared strategic objective will be to preserve an open global economy and the global, multilateral cooperative institutions and arrangements that underpin it.

The global nature of the COVID-19 health and economic crisis calls for faster and better coordination among governments (rather than each economy trying to go it alone) and demonstrates the importance and the value of multilateral cooperation. Promoting international solidarity based on trust and sharing as a basis for collective action to deal with all dimensions of the crisis is central to success.

Asia's challenge in defending and renovating the global order

The rise of China as a world economic power has increased its confidence and influence in the region. Two areas in which China's growing power directly impacts its neighbours are in regards to territorial and navigation issues in the South China Sea and in responding to the large-scale financial assistance that China has offered through its Belt and Road Initiative. China's growing power is matched with a geopolitical ambition that now encompasses a broader conception of its maritime security interests, including over large areas of the South China Sea that border on Association of Southeast Asian Nations (ASEAN) member states.

East Asia also confronts the problems that result from the radical changes in the foreign and international economic policies of the US since Trump assumed the US presidency. President Trump's 'America First' policy and his effective launching of an all-out trade and technology war with China rocked the foundations of the international economic system on which East Asian economies rely. President Trump's disrespect of alliance relationships in the region has increased uncertainty in Asia about US reliability (Anwar 2021).

These developments present the heavily economically integrated and internationally exposed states of East Asia with stark choices. They are choices that will put significant internal pressure on the region because of the variegated structure of its political and security ties with the US. They are pressures that have the potential to drive large wedges, for example, among ASEAN members but also between ASEAN and its dialogue partners in the ASEAN+6 group and the ASEAN+8 (East Asia Summit) processes, and inflict unrecoverable damage upon the East Asia integration enterprise (see Chapter 9).

To this point, in addition to its multilateral system commitments, ASEAN has played a central role as a political fulcrum around which big power jostling in the region has been stabilised, and ASEAN's cooperation arrangements have served as an effective mechanism for engaging and managing big power interests in the region. But can ASEAN and its regional frameworks continue to be resilient in dealings with the two big global powers as they increasingly cast themselves as strategic competitors?

There is growing pressure on ASEAN and its individual members to choose sides in the 'new Cold War' around the US geopolitical tussle with China. Acceding to this framing of diplomacy presents the prospect of an ASEAN divided and institutionally weakened, its centrality to regional diplomacy in tatters. So ASEAN's response to Washington's Indo-Pacific idea has been to take ownership of it and develop its own ASEAN Outlook on the Indo-Pacific (Acharya 2019). ASEAN, and even its members who confront Chinese maritime power directly, have no inclination for the region to become the theatre of a hostile, new great power conflict (Drysdale 2020).

If it is to avoid this outcome, ASEAN will need to be an active player—not just a pawn in today's contest over the global order between the world's two biggest powers.

The fracture of trust in multilateral cooperation and Asia's role in rebuilding it, and in defending and renovating the global order, is a task much easier identified than done. A new collective authority will be needed to correct the current drift towards fragmentation of the multilateral global order. With the US stepping back under Trump, and actively undermining multilateralism, no one country is capable of delivering the leadership now required to defend and renovate the system. A compact for multilateral cooperation between Asian nations could be a starting point, particularly on the aftermath of the COVID-19 crisis. Asian economies can contribute through a compact to rebuild trust, strengthen governance and update global rules.

Asia, like the rest of the world, has to deal simultaneously with twin challenges: the big international health challenges and the economic policy challenges of exit from the crisis. Failure to navigate judiciously between the two will cause social disruption, more deaths and economic hardship. The task of defining the way forward on both fronts at the same time is urgent (ABER 2020). The foundations for gearing up regional policy action in Asia were laid at an ASEAN+3 Summit in June 2020 that included leaders from Southeast Asia, China, Japan and South Korea, and committed to health and economic policy coordination. Australia, New Zealand and India (given its record in managing the virus and its economic policy heft) have an important and influential contribution to make in working with their neighbours in ASEAN, Japan, South Korea and China in meeting the challenge posed by recovery from the pandemic.

International organisations need to play a central role in monitoring and assessing the impact of the COVID-19 crisis on trade, investment and global value chains. Joint commitments at the regional and multilateral level will ensure that national measures are transparent, proportionate and temporary, and are removed when no longer justified, based on the evidence and data—not economic exigencies or political pressure. Mutually agreed guiding principles will help constrain the actions of Asian nations to ensure that responses to the crisis do not reinforce or entrench existing inequalities. Asian nations can adopt the World Bank Group's COVID-19 response priorities of poverty alleviation, gender equality and environmental sustainability. A pressing issue for coordination is the treatment of migrant workers. Government-to-government collaboration is necessary to resolve cross-border issues like migration and the access of migrants to healthcare and social protection.

These are all foundations on which confidence could be restored in international cooperation. The bigger task, for which there is little preparation or precedence, is Asian initiative in for collective action on the global economic order.

The institutional arrangements on which economic certainty and political confidence in the US-led, postwar global order was built—the institutional framework that guaranteed economic openness and the prospect of economic and political security—are of central importance to Asia. The rules as they stand are far from adequate. They do not comprehensively cover important elements of contemporary commerce like digital commerce, and there are unsanctioned and sanctioned derogations. However, they have been critical to the robust growth of the international economy and trade for the seven decades they have been in place.

In a geopolitically fractured world, strategic competition between the US and China ultimately limits both countries' capacity to contribute constructively to global recovery and renovation of the global order. The US, the world's biggest power, lost its appetite for multilateral cooperation under its last president and is at odds strategically with China, the world's second-largest power. Constrained though he is by enormous domestic economic and political problems, President Biden has signalled his inclination to mobilise multilaterally on core international problems.

Small and middle powers now have to play an unfamiliar leadership role. A compact for multilateral cooperation between Asian nations could be a starting point. But how can Asia step up to their defence or their reform alongside the US and China at the same time?

While collective leadership from Asia will not be easy to coordinate, there are two assets that the region brings to the global initiative that are now needed (ABER 2020). First, it has the architecture in place. The East Asian Dialogue arrangements (ASEAN +3, ASEAN + 6 and ASEAN + 8) are ready, standing platforms from which to launch it. Second, the ASEAN+6 group is already actively engaged on the trade and economic cooperation agenda that can help the world to stand against the tide. The conclusion of RCEP in 2020 is a ready starting point for the global effort now required.

The growth of Asia's economic power, and the potential that allows for the projection of political and military power, has thrust the region onto the centre stage of changing, great power global politics. The huge change in the contours of Asian power has raised questions about the stability of the political order today. Are we doomed to an inevitable divide between the established powers, led by the US and China, as they jostle for political space? This is not a narrowly economic problem: it affects economic and security issues globally as well as in Asia and the Pacific. The big challenge will be to broker a geopolitical bargain that restores a measure of stability and the political confidence to repair an order that is now badly broken.

References

ABER (Asian Bureau of Economic Research). 2020. 'An Asian Strategy for Recovery and Reconstruction after COVID-19'. ABER, 3 June 2020. adamtriggs.files. wordpress.com/2020/08/aber_asian-covid-strategy-paper.pdf.

Acharya, A. 2019. 'Why ASEAN's Indo-Pacific Outlook Matters'. *East Asia Forum*, 11 August 2019. www.eastasiaforum.org/2019/08/11/why-aseans-indo-pacific-outlook-matters/.

Anwar, D. F. 2021. 'What Southeast Asia Wants from the Biden Presidency'. *East Asia Forum Quarterly*, 13 (1): 36–37. doi.org/10.22459/EAFQ.13.01.2021.

Clavin, P. 2013. *Securing the World Economy: The Reinvention of the League of Nations, 1920–1946*. Oxford: Oxford University Press. doi.org/10.1093/acprof:oso/9780199577934.001.0001.

Drysdale, P. 2020. 'ASEAN Feels Pinch of Big-Power Rivalry'. *Australian Financial Review*, 12 October 2020. www.afr.com/world/asia/asean-feels-pinch-of-big-power-rivalry-20201007-p562o7.

Foot, R. 2017. 'Power Transitions and Great Power Management: Three Decades of China–Japan–US Relations'. *Pacific Review* 30 (6): 830–34. doi.org/10.1080/09512748.2017.1303535.

Gardiner, R. N. 1969. *Sterling-Dollar Diplomacy: The Origins and Prospects of Our International Economic Order* (2nd edn). New York: McGraw-Hill Book Company.

Goh, E. 2013. *The Struggle for Order: Hegemony, Hierarchy, and Transition in Post-Cold War East Asia*. Oxford: Oxford University Press. doi.org/10.1093/acprof:oso/9780199599363.001.0001.

Goodman, M., G. de Brouwer, S. Armstrong and A. Triggs. 2019. 'Delivering Prosperity in the Indo-Pacific: An Agenda for Australia and the United States'. Centre for Strategic and International Studies, 18 April 2019. www.csis.org/analysis/delivering-prosperity-indo-pacific-agenda-australia-and-united-states.

Helleiner, E. 2014. *The Forgotten Foundations of Bretton Woods: International Development and the Making of the Postwar Order.* New York: Cornell University Press.

Ikenberry, G. J. 1992. 'A World Economy Restored: Expert Consensus and the Anglo-American Postwar Settlement'. *International Organization* 46 (1): 289–321. doi.org/10.1017/S002081830000151X.

IMF (International Monetary Fund). 2020. *World Economic Outlook Report October 2020.* Washington, DC: IMF.

King, A. 2016. *China-Japan Relations after World War Two: Empire, Industry and War, 1949–1971.* Cambridge: Cambridge University Press. doi.org/10.1017/CBO9781316443439.

Mastanduno, M. 2009. 'System Maker and Privilege Taker: US Power and the International Political Economy'. *World Politics* 61 (1): 122. doi.org/10.1017/S0043887109000057.

Ruggie, J. G. 1982. 'International Regimes, Transactions, and Change: Embedded Liberalism in the Postwar Economic Order'. *International Organization* 36 (2): 393. doi.org/10.1017/S0020818300018993.

Triggs, A. 2018. 'The Dangerous Inadequacies of the World's Crisis-Response Mechanisms'. Brookings, 4 May 2018. www.brookings.edu/research/the-dangerous-inadequacies-of-the-worlds-crisis-response-mechanisms/.

Van Dormael, A. 1978. *Bretton Woods: Birth of a Monetary System.* London: Macmillan Press. doi.org/10.1007/978-1-349-03628-8.

Zhang, S. G. 2001. *Economic Cold War: America's Embargo against China and the Sino-Soviet Alliance, 1949–1963.* Washington, DC: Woodrow Wilson Center Press.

www.ingramcontent.com/pod-product-compliance
Lightning Source LLC
Chambersburg PA
CBHW040142270326
41928CB00023B/3318